The Italian American Experience

PROTESTANT EVANGELISM
AMONG ITALIANS IN AMERICA

ARNO PRESS

A New York Times Company

New York — 1975

Reprint Edition 1975 by Arno Press Inc.

Copyright © 1975 by Arno Press Inc.

Italian Evangelical Pioneers by John B. Bisceglia,
  Copyright © 1948 by John B. Bisceglia was
  reprinted by permission of John B. Bisceglia.

Religious Work Among Italians in America,
  selections from The Assembly Herald and
  the Report of the Committee on Americanization ...
  were reprinted from copies in the Union
  Theological Seminary Library.

The Italian American Experience
ISBN for complete set: 0-405-06390-3
See last pages of this volume for titles.

Publisher's Note: The Evangelical Movement
Among Italians in New York City and the
Report of the Committee on Americanization...
were reprinted from the only available copies.

Manufactured in the United States of America

———◆———

Library of Congress Cataloging in Publication Data
Main entry under title:

Protestant evangelism among Italians in America.

   (The Italian American experience)
   CONTENTS: Mangano, A. Religious work among Italians
in America. 1918.--Selections from the Assembly herald,
v. 24, no. 3 (Mar. 1918)--Jones, H. D. The evangelical
movement among Italians in New York City. 1935. [etc.]
   1. Missions to Italians--United States--History--
Sources. 2. Protestant churches--Missions--History--
Sources. I. Series.
BV2788.I8P76 1975   266'.022'0973   74-17943
ISBN 0-405-06414-4

CONTENTS

Religious Work Among Italians in America

A SURVEY FOR THE HOME MISSIONS COUNCIL

BY

ANTONIO MANGANO

THE BOARD OF HOME MISSIONS AND CHURCH EXTEN-
SION OF THE METHODIST EPISCOPAL CHURCH,
PHILADELPHIA

Contents

Foreword

In the years 1916-17 the Immigrant Work Committee of the Home Missions Council, representing the interests of thirteen evangelical denominations, engaged in a survey of the Italian communities of this country, with particular reference to their religious needs and the work of the churches. A similar survey of "Religious Work among the Poles in America" has been made by Rev. Joel B. Hayden (Missionary Education Movement, New York, 15 cents, prepaid). A survey of conditions among the Bohemians in America is now being completed by Rev. Kenneth D. Miller. For the survey of the Italians, Rev. Antonio Mangano, of the Italian Department of Colgate Theological Seminary, Brooklyn, volunteered his services. His expense was met by the Home Missions Council. Mr. Mangano visited many city and industrial communities in the East, Middle West, and South. He was at the same time engaged in writing *Sons of Italy* for the Missionary Education Movement, a mission study book syndicated by the various denominational home mission societies. This pamphlet presents material collateral to this book and of particular interest to denominations and other agencies engaged in work with the Italians, and to leaders in home mission work. For the general point of view, the mode of presentation, and the recommendations, Mr. Mangano holds himself responsible. In the Appendix statements are furnished by denominational and other agencies.

In so broad a field with such rapid changes in population and in the work of the churches, a publication of this sort is soon out of date and subject to correction. The Immigrant Work Committee of the Home Missions Council, however, submits this study as the first effort at a comprehensive survey of religious work among the Italians of America from the standpoint of the Protestant church. It makes grateful acknowledgment of the painstaking service of Professor Mangano. Added information, corrections, criticism, and constructive suggestion will be heartily welcomed.

New York, July 1, 1917

RELIGIOUS WORK AMONG ITALIANS IN AMERICA

I. Population

It is impossible to state accurately the total number of Italians now resident in the United States, for these reasons: (1) No separate vital statistics are available to show the total number of Italian deaths. (2) It is impossible to tell how many have returned to Italy permanently. Many, especially single men, make the voyage back and forth several times. (3) The war has recalled thousands to fight under the banner of Savoy.

In 1914 a total of 294,689 Italians entered the country, and 97,073 departed, making a net gain of 197,616 in the Italian population; while in 1915 the Bureau of Immigration records show that a total of 51,655 were admitted and 116,985 departed, making a loss of 65,330.

We may perhaps get a fair idea of our Italian population by approximating it as follows:

A careful study of one of the Brooklyn colonies in 1910 showed the children born of Italian parents just about equal in number to the adult population of the colony. If then, as is indicated by the Bureau of Immigration statistics, 3,000,000 Italians have come here during the past thirty years, allowing 1,000,000 for deaths and permanent departures would leave us 2,000,000 of native-born Italians with 2,000,000 children born in this country. But it must be remembered that in many parts of the country there are construction and labor camps made up of men without families; also many thousands have departed for war service. To be wholly fair, we can take off 500,000 more, and then safely say that the Italian population in the United States is at least 3,500,000.

There is not a single state in the Union that does not have Italians within its borders, but they are most numerous in New York, Pennsylvania, New Jersey, Massachusetts, Connecticut, and Rhode Island. In recent years they have made their way westward, and large colonies are now found in West Virginia, Ohio, and Illinois. A large group of northern Italians have settled at Asti, California, and are engaged in vine culture. It is estimated that there are 91,000 in the state. The recent industrial development of the Southern states has drawn a large number to Alabama, Georgia, Florida, Louisiana, and North Carolina. It is estimated that no less than 100,000 Italians are employed on the sugar plantations in the Southern states.

The chief centers are New York City with its 600,000, the second largest Italian city in the world; Philadelphia, 200,000; Boston, 60,000; Chicago, 74,000; New Haven, 30,000; Providence, 40,000; San Francisco, 30,000; Newark, 36,000; and Bridgeport, 25,000. The state of New York has the largest Italian population of all the states of the Union, nearly 1,000,000, forming over one eighth of the population of the state.

II. Economic Conditions

a. Occupations

As Italians are to be found in every state in the Union, and even in Alaska, Hawaii, and the Philippine Islands, so it may justly be said that

5

they are engaged in all the occupations which are common to the life of the American people. The Department of Commerce and Labor Report for 1914 shows that out of a total of 294,689 Italians admitted to the United States in that year, there were 73,335 classed with no occupation, this number including women and children; 193,284 were classed as agents, bankers, teamsters, farm laborers, manufacturers, merchants, and servants; 28,679 were classed as skilled workmen, as barbers, carpenters, gardeners, jewelers, mechanics, painters, stone-workers, engineers, tailors, shoe-makers, etc.; while 1,116 were counted under the professions—actors, architects, clergymen, editors, professional engineers, lawyers, scientists, musicians, physicians, sculptors, and artists. While many of these do not secure employment in their own trade or profession, because of the handicap of language, still in our Northern states Italians are engaged in fifty-one different occupations and in twenty-four trades in the South. New York City alone has over 200 registered Italian physicians, 250 sculptors, and a goodly number of teachers in public schools and colleges. One Italian, Mr. Tanzola, has recently been appointed to teach mathematics at the Naval Academy at Annapolis.

b. Wages

The deft fingers of Italian women and children make $3,000,000 worth of artificial flowers annually. An expert colorist can make fifty dollars a week. By rapid and constant work, early and late, women can make from $4.00 to $5.00 a week in their homes. Glove-making is another home trade, practised especially in Gloversville, New York, and the surrounding towns. Also in New York City a woman by constant work can sew a dozen pairs a day, for which she receives $1.20.

Musical instruments, banners, and badges, *dolci* (sweet cakes), and caramels, wood-working, furniture, and decorating are industries employing hundreds of Italians, while silk-weaving and hat-making occupy thousands more. Fifty per cent. of the weavers in the factories at Astoria, New York; Paterson, New Jersey; and West Hoboken, New Jersey, are Italians from Piedmont and Lombardy. They average about $23 a week as do also the bookbinders and hat-makers of Orange, New Jersey. It may be worthy of note, in passing, that, contrary to public opinion, it is these northern Italian weavers in Paterson and stonecutters in Barre, Vermont, who are the most fiery and irreconcilable anarchists, and strikes are frequent among these justice-loving workers.

The great bulk of Italian immigrants fall into the ranks of unskilled laborers and are employed in the construction camps of railroads and subways, in putting in sewers, gas and water mains, and in road-making. In Barre, Vermont, the Italian stonecutters are indispensable in the granite sheds. In West Virginia they share with the Slav the task of mining soft coal. In Birmingham, Alabama, and Pittsburgh, Pennsylvania, they work in iron foundries; in Ohio the glass industry claims them. Massachusetts has thousands of Italians at work in her cotton mills and shoe factories. In New York and Brooklyn they throng the small tailor, cloak, cap, paper box, and candy factories, which are usually owned by Jews.

The Italians almost monopolize the barber trade. Hundreds are waiters at the large hotels. The Greeks are now rivaling the Italians as street venders of small fruits and are also crowding them up and out of the shoe-shining business. The wholesale fruit trade in our large cities is almost entirely in the hands of Italians, and they have their own chambers of commerce in such centers as New York, New Orleans, and San Francisco. There are 3,000 fruit stores owned by Italians in Greater New York. Their merchants import $3,000,000 worth of lemons and oranges besides $5,000,000 worth of oil and wine annually, not to mention macaroni, cheeses, and dried fruits.

It is greatly to the credit of Italian self-respect that, in spite of low wages, less than one-half of one per cent. of the Italian population seeks charitable help. The report from our public almshouses and charitable institutions made for 1910 shows:

Foreign-born White Paupers in Almshouses

1,048.5	per	100,000	Irish
410.9	"	"	Swiss
390.7	"	"	French
313.0	"	"	Scotch
304.7	"	"	English and Welsh
300.0	"	"	German
75.0	"	"	Austro-Hungarian
43.7	"	"	Russian
31.8	"	"	Italian

Taken as a whole, the Italians are distinguished not only as to their high quality of industry but in their love of saving and ambition to rise in the world. A well-known senator was having his shoes blacked late one afternoon and noticed an open book on the stool the bootblack had just left. "What are you reading?" he asked. "Livy," replied the youth. "Livy?" "Yes, I attend City College."

c. Housing

Unmarried men find the housing problem easier to solve than the men with their families. They either board with the family of some *paesano* (compatriot) in the cities, or live in the dilapidated box cars furnished by the railroads for the section gangs or in the patched tin and tar paper shacks of road construction groups. It is very unusual if in any of these places they find any privacy or comfort. If they board, they must share the room with several others. Miss Dunwiddie found during her investigation in Philadelphia that seven persons ate, cooked, washed, and slept in one room. Sometimes in the larger cities, in quarters where rents are exceedingly high, there are day and night shifts occupying the same beds, and even sweatshop work may be carried on at the windows during the day by women and children, while the beds are occupied by night workers. In the slums of our cities the small dark rooms are a serious menace to health as well as to morals, and tuberculosis, a disease formerly unknown among Italians in their native land, is claiming thousands yearly in such tenements.

d. Property Owners

It is the earlier Italian settlers who own most of the property within the limits of the Italian colonies, both dwellings and property used for business. In 1915, $100,000,000 worth of real estate in Greater New

York was listed under Italian ownership. Italians usually take up property that has little or no value and in the course of a few years improve it very greatly. In Rochester, New York, property in the Italian colony has increased 200 per cent. since the Italians became the owners of it. In Canastota, New York, they bought for a song large tracts of muck land and planted it with celery and onions. To-day that land is worth from $400 to $800 an acre. The Italians went to South Jersey and took up the sandy land about Vineland and Hammonton, and they have made it blossom like the rose. One man who ten years ago had nothing but strong arms and a stout heart sold his crop of peaches in 1916 for $15,000. He owns a fine farm and a comfortable home.

III. RELIGIOUS SITUATION

a. General Situation

It is a common belief among Americans that all Italians are Roman Catholics, and there seems to be good reason for this impression. Out of Italy's population of 36,000,000 there are not more than 60,000 Protestants, but there are unnumbered thousands, yes, tens of thousands of anti-clerics and even atheists. Ninety-nine per cent. of the Italians landing on our shores would give the Roman Catholic as their religious belief, but if questioned a large number would add that they were not faithful to its celebrations nor its services, except perhaps at times of births, deaths, and marriages. A questionnaire sent to all Baptist, Presbyterian, Methodist, and Congregational Italian pastors on the question, "What per cent. of Italians in your colony are loyal to the Roman Church?" evoked an amazingly unanimous reply, "About one third." One or two reported, one fourth; and one reported, one half.

In one city of Massachusetts, out of a population of 1,700 Italians, only sixty attend the Roman Church; and in another city there is a colony of 6,000 Italians of whom only 300 attend that church. There is a colony of 35,000 Italians in Brooklyn which has only one Italian church seating at the utmost 400 persons. It conducts three masses on Sunday, and granting it were filled to its capacity each time, it could only minister to 1,200 persons, less than four per cent. of the population. Out of the 600,000 Italian population of Greater New York, the Roman Church, by its own figures, so far as I could obtain them, lays claim to only 180,000, including children, as members of Roman Catholic Italian churches—less than one third of the total Italian population.

There is need for the widest publicity of these facts in order to refute the common charge of proselyting, which all evangelical mission work among the Italians meets, and also because officials of city departments, health, probation, juvenile court, and charity organizations and even school teachers commonly assume that all Italians, adults or children, are Catholics and insist on treating them as such.

Religiously then, Italians both in Italy and America may be divided into four general groups: (1) All who are loyal to the Roman Church; (2) a larger group who are indifferent to religion, because they are disgusted with the priests and have ceased to believe what they teach; (3) the atheistic, anarchistic, and socialistic group, which is actively hostile to religion of whatever name. To this latter class belong the great throng

8

of younger men who have lost faith in Roman Catholicism and who firmly believe that all religions are only worn-out superstitions, imposed upon ignorant people to keep them in subjection. They have rebelled against the soul tyranny of the Roman Church and, mistaking liberty for license, they acknowledge no authority except their own wish and individual advantage. They have an organized propaganda aided by public debates, street meetings, clubs, and socialist papers, all seeking to enlighten and free their fellow Italians from the yoke of superstition and their consequent condition of slavery for the benefit of the rich and the powerful. "You are taught," they say, "that it is wrong to steal and commit violence, so you will not injure the property of your oppressors, and they are flinging you a mere pittance, robbing you of a just share in the profit of your labor. You are taught that to limit your families is an awful sin, because industry must have a steady stream of workers, and if they are numerous your oppressors need pay them little. Men and women, control the size of your families. Do not raise up sons and daughters to be the slaves of the privileged classes." These newcomers, seeing for the most part only the under side of American life, and treated often, it must be admitted, unfairly and with discrimination, ought not to be allowed to blunder in their conceptions of liberty. If they continue to come, a million or more a year, they will soon rule America through the ballot-box. How will they rule? By what standards? According to what ideals? It is for us to determine, while yet there is time.

Among the better educated this revolt against the traditions and infallible authority of the Roman Church is called modernism, or perhaps it is better to say that modernism is an attempt to correct and modify the teaching and the practises of the ancient church and bring them into harmonious relations with modern thought and knowledge.

The fourth group is made up of what may be called "the faithful remnant"—men and women who have seen a new truth and have been willing to endure the bitterest criticism and unite themselves with the "insignificant" and "feeble" evangelical groups. As in the case of Israel, it was the few that held up true ideas about Jehovah, so it is only the few among the Italians who are holding up the vital and life-giving principles of Christianity before the eyes of their nationality.

b. Activities of the Roman Church

For a number of years the Roman Church paid little attention to the Italians in America. Consequently the work of Italian evangelization was much easier fifteen years ago than at the present time. The common report among Protestants throughout the length and breadth of our land is: "When we opened our mission the Catholics were doing nothing for Italians; now they have built a church, are building a parochial school, and are copying our various social activities." Realizing that the majority of the Italian priests were unable to hold the people, as early as ten or more years ago young American seminarians, mainly of Irish descent, were sent to Rome to learn the Italian language, and to become familiar with Italian thought and feeling. They are now taking part in this new aggressive campaign. In Lawrence, Massachusetts, where the evangelical work of the Rev. Ariel Bellondi has created considerable comment, a new Catholic church has just been reared and seven nuns

9

have been brought into town to visit the homes and so overcome the "devilish influence of the Protestants." In Providence, there is a large, prosperous, and influential Italian colony of 40,000. Two years ago in one section of the city there was built the beautiful church of Saint Anna. It is a copy of the church of St. John and St. Paul in Venice, and an Italian bell tower stands beside it. Padre Bove, who seems to be an energetic, wide-awake priest, is now completing an equally well-equipped parochial school building. The plant is estimated to cost $50,000. This school will contain an auditorium which will be used as a theatre and for concerts, rooms for an orchestra, and a day nursery with forty beds for babies. There are to be also eight good-sized classrooms where the religion of the fatherland will be taught and *l'Italianità*, which means "Italian feeling," and which can hardly be conducive to Americanization.

In other localities the Catholic Church conducts sewing schools, music classes, gymnasiums, athletic activities, classes for the study of English, kindergartens, day schools for the boys and girls, and boy scout troops. In a New York Catholic settlement, vocal, piano, and organ lessons are given free to the people. A large number of fresh air homes have been establishd, and there is a long list of homes and protectorates for foundlings, orphans, and wayward boys and girls. These children are committed through the courts, the city paying for their maintenance. These helpful ministries are the direct result of the example of Protestant work. Indeed the pope considered the apathy of the Italian clergy of such importance that he not long ago sent a special encyclical letter urging them to stop abuses in Italian parishes and do all in their power to hold the Italian people to the church. In August, 1915, an appeal was sent out to all the Catholic clergy to support and distribute a weekly Italian Catholic paper which it is proposed to publish. It will be ably edited and will make an up-to-date, valuable magazine for Italians in their own language.

Italian priests are both good and bad, but the doctrine the Church has taught her children for generations, and still teaches them, that the value of the priest's ministry, his authority, and power are independent of his character and private life, is the cause of much moral looseness in priestly life. "When the priest stands before the altar, he represents God, he stands in the place of God, and he is the only channel for the flow of divine grace."

Some priests take their office most seriously, and with the authority that such a doctrine confers, there is great opportunity for limitless good under wise leadership. Father Bandini is such a priest. He headed the little colony that founded Tontitown, Arkansas, in 1898. His courage and faith held them together in spite of a cyclone and frost which killed a first harvest. For more than twenty years he has been the veritable Moses of his flock. He has established good schools, taught his people to appreciate the best in American life, and has become the moral force of the community. I shall long remember my visit to the colony, to his home, to his church. He knew that I was of a different faith, yet we talked in a natural and friendly manner, even about things upon which we did not agree. It would be well for Italians, yes, and for America, if there were many more of his type. This splendid man has but recently **died.**

c. *Organizations Outside the Church Working for the Italians*

While the churches and religious bodies were the first to move in behalf of the social and general welfare of Italians in this country, there have been other organizations that have lent a helping hand. The public schools in many of the large cities have established night schools for the study of English, while New York, Pittsburgh, Chicago, and other large cities have a special lecture department of the public school system to give free illustrated lectures in the Italian language on subjects of interest, such as: "The Beauties of America"; "The Lives of Great Americans"; "The Value of the Public School System," etc. In Greater New York, the Board of Health has an Italian department which provides special lecturers to churches and social institutions who give in illustrated lectures information about how to avoid various diseases, especially tuberculosis, which is becoming a great menace among Italians here. In addition to this the organization known as the University Extension furnishes doctors, both men and women, to speak before mothers' meetings on such subjects as "The Home," "Ventilation," "The Care and Feeding of Children," and other important topics. The Y. M. C. A. has had a special branch for Italians in upper New York, the only institution of the kind in the United States, and the work which the Y. M. C. A. is doing for the foreigner in general has touched in a most helpful way the life of the Italian.

The one effort on a large scale to reach the foreigner with the English language and American influences is that which has been put forth in Detroit. The Board of Education and the Chamber of Commerce undertook jointly the task of getting the adult immigrant to study English as the first step in Americanization. The result was the organization of the entire industrial, educational, social, and religious force of the city into one whole, to carry on a campaign for the purpose of getting the foreigner under American influences. The public libraries, the City Recreation Committee, the Health Committee, all social agencies, the Y. M. C. A., Y. W. C. A., Babies' Milk Funds, Children's Home Society, the Salvation Army, Associated Charities, employment bureaus, Boy Scouts, women's clubs, and the great power of the foreign language press were all enlisted in the campaign. The campaign is only a year old and there was an increase in the registration at night schools of 153 per cent., a 25 per cent. increase of young mechanics in the high schools, and a greatly increased feeling of responsibility on the part of employers and community in general for their foreign population.

The National Americanization Committee is also occupying itself with the task of Americanizing the foreigner. It makes this fourfold suggestion to the American people:

1. Americanize one immigrant woman.
2. Get one immigrant to become a citizen.
3. Teach one foreign-born mother English.
4. Put one immigrant family on your calling list.

One of the most helpful signs in connection with the development of the life of the foreigner is the interest which the Americanized foreigner takes in his own people. A splendid example of this is the activity of the Italian Medical Association of New York City which publishes a biweekly magazine called "The Word of the Doctor," which furnishes information of a most valuable sort regarding all questions of hygiene and health. One of the chief objects of this propaganda is to eliminate the quack doctor, both American and Italian, who is so prone to become a parasite upon the life of the ignorant foreigner.

No right-minded person can fail to appreciate the value of the service which these different organizations are rendering in connection with the Americanization of the foreigner. And yet it must in all fairness be said that, with the single exception of Detroit, so far as the adult immigrant is concerned, the great Americanization influence throughout the entire country has not been the public school nor the social settlement, but the evangelical churches. Throughout the entire country our missionaries are everywhere teaching English, showing the people what is best in American life, in American history, and in our present political institutions. One of the finest examples of this kind of work is to be found in Fairmont, West Virginia, where a consecrated woman, with a real love in her heart for the foreigner, has reached through her English classes over 250 young Italians. But no one receives English lessons from this woman without receiving something that is infinitely better, the appreciation of the value of an upright, moral, and straightforward Christian life. In a word they learn English but also learn Christ. The biggest educational factor in the life of the adult is the evangelical church. Many a man who did not know how to read and write has been impelled to make every effort to learn how to read and write because he wanted to sing the hymns of the church. Even poor, peasant women have been inspired by the church atmosphere with the desire to read. Young men who knew nothing but a dialect have been led to study through the inspiration of the church to learn their native tongue as well as the English language.

Another factor in the educational process of the church is the Daily Vacation Bible School. Everywhere, especially in the South and the West, are to be found these schools in connection with our foreign churches and missions throughout the summer months. These provide a helpful influence for the thousands of children who would otherwise play in the hot streets, and bring to them the impressive Bible stories, the beautiful hymns of our Christian faith, and various lines of industrial activities, such as sewing, weaving, hammock-making, etc.

IV. Protestant Work among Italians

a. Early Stages

During the early years of Italian immigration, the evangelical churches of America assumed the same attitude toward Italians they had previously taken toward the Irish in the early fifties. The Italians were regarded as the natural property of the Roman Church. But, as we have already indicated, the Roman Church did not interest itself in attempting to reach this nationality, and this was due in part to a natural hostility on the part of the Irish toward the Italian. As they increased in numbers and Mulberry Bend grew famous for the violent crimes committed there, American people were roused to a sense of obligation toward these aliens. They believed that these people were in need of having the gospel preached to them since they were so largely outside of all religious influences.

The first mission for Italians in America was established thirty-seven years ago by that dean of Italian work in the United States, Rev. Antonio Arrighi, under the auspices of the New York City Mission Society. This church has had a wonderful history and at the present time it is keeping up its record by the aggressive work that it is doing. The work is housed in the old Broome Street Tabernacle, and according to its last report, it has a membership of 300, an average attendance in the Sunday-school for the past year of 453, while during the church's thirty-seven years of existence no less than thirty-two men have been sent out to preach the gospel to the Italians in the various parts of our country. The church has also sent out eight women workers. The bond of fellowship that is created within the church circle is so strong that no matter where the members live, in the Bronx, in Brooklyn, or even in the towns of New Jersey, they feel drawn back to their home church for communion service.

b. Denominational Survey and Comment*

A good deal of the work for the Italians during the first few years was necessarily in the nature of an experiment, feeling the way, as a good friend of mine used to say, "merely tentative," but as time went on and it became apparent that Italians are responsive to the gospel appeal, the various denominations began to plan for a permanent work and equipment.

(1) Presbyterian Church in the U. S. A.

The first to enter the field of Italian evangelization in this country were the Presbyterians, and as they were the leaders in the enterprise, so to-day, it must in fairness be stated, that they are setting the standards for all other denominations. They are doing a most thorough and aggressive work with the most far-reaching plans for future development. The immigrant work office of the Board of Home Missions is busy making thorough surveys of Italian colonies in many states. They aim to build up a system of parishes which shall lead and minister to the entire community life.

From the beginning the Presbyterians have been in close touch with the Waldensians, "The Israel of the Alps," the Protestant church of Italy which dates back to three centuries before the Reformation, and, surviving many cruel and bloody persecutions, has come down to the present day. Needless to say, the Presbyterians' work has gained much from its associations with these old Italian Protestants, and the Waldensian Church has furnished a goodly number of excellent ministers and missionaries for the Presbyterian work. Among this number none was more highly respected nor more valuable than the Rev. Alberto Clot, who has recently died. A cultured, Christian gentleman, born in the Waldensian valleys, speaking and writing French, Italian, and English with equal ease and polish, he had a remarkable grasp of all plans of Italian work

*See also the Appendix, A to E, for presentation of the work of denominations and other agencies for Italians as given in special statements of policy by denominational workers.

both here and in Italy. He left in manuscript a just completed history of the Waldensian colony in Valdese, North Carolina, which we may all hope to see in print. This Waldensian element has been a valuable asset to the work of this denomination in laying a broad and firmly reliable foundation for future work.

The Presbyterians have in a special manner caught a vision of the possibilities of the future, and are spending large sums of money in every department of their work, without putting too great emphasis upon immediate results. They are cultivating the community in a sensible and scientific manner. Twenty-five years from now they will reap an abundant harvest for the kingdom of God. They are endeavoring to minister to the foreigner not only through his spiritual nature, but to touch his life at as many points as possible; recreation, amusements, education, music, genuine friendship. The next generation of Italians in these centers will understand American ideals and will appreciate the significance of religion and the effect which it ought to have upon human life.

2. *Methodist Episcopal*

The beginning of religious work for the Italians by the Methodist Episcopal Church is well described in a report of their City Mission Society under the date of March 31, 1889. It contains the following statements: "There came to this country in May last, in company with Dr. Vernon and Dr. Gay a local preacher of our Italy Conference, by the name of Vito Calabrese. He offered himself for work among his country-men of whom there are more than 30,000 in New York. . . . The Rev. O. R. Bouton opened his chapel at the Five Points to us free of charge. [Then in the very heart of the Italian quarter.] . . . . In October Dr. Vernon, returning from fourteen years of work in Italy, visited this humble mission at the Five Points and told me that in the line of gathering a congregation willing to hear the gospel more had been accomplished there in four months than could be accomplished at any point in Italy in four years."

During the past thirty years the Methodists, under the inspiration of the splendid work which the denomination has been carrying on in Italy, have made great strides in the task of Italian evangelization. They depended almost entirely for missionaries on men trained in Italy, in their own Methodist Theological School. Some splendid work has been done by these men. Some of the leaders of the denomination, however, have felt for some time the need of workers who have been educated in this country under the influence of American Christianity. It has too often happened that a man who has received all his training in Italy, however excellent that may have been, has not been able to do effective work in America. The reason for this is that a man prepared in Italy under a social order where the priestly idea in religion is dominant can not very well adapt himself to the requirements of the work in this country. Usually the dominating idea of the ministry in Italy is that the only function of the minister is to preach the gospel, and they do not easily adapt themselves to the variety of social activities which we feel in this country are essential if we are to present to the foreigner the true meaning of religion and establish a point of contact with him, so that we may lead him to the knowledge of Jesus Christ.

For this reason arrangements were nearly completed for the establishment of an Italian department in connection with Drew Theological Seminary, where young men might be trained under the best American influences and ideals. But this idea has been dropped for the present.

For a number of years the Italian work of the Methodist Church has been under the direction of a Bishop and Superintendent, Rev. Dr. William Burt and Rev. Dr. Frederick H. Wright. The so-called "Italian Mission" of the Methodist Church has for the past seven years had an independent existence, meeting each year in an annual session, where the reports of the Superintendent and of the various committees of the mission were presented and discussed. At these annual sessions also each missionary gave a report of his own work and the examinations on studies pursued and books read were held.

During 1916 a change has taken place in the policy of the Methodist Church, regarding its Italian Mission. Indeed the "Mission" as an independent institution has been abolished. Hence there is no bishop or superintendent for Italian work as such. Each Italian mission and worker is now under the care of the respective local conference and the resident bishop. Other denominations will watch the experiment with interest.

The Home Mission Society of the Methodist Church during the past year has appropriated for the Italian work $50,000. This item, however, does not represent even one half of the sum that is spent in connection with the work that the Methodist Church is doing to reach the Italians of America.

3. *Protestant Episcopal*

The Episcopal Church was one of the early comers in the field of Italian evangelization, and during the time it has been at work, has made considerable progress, owing to its far-sighted policy of fine equipment in buildings and a large number of trained, characterful American women. Archdeacon Nelson of the Diocese of New York City is the source of the information concerning the beginnings of their denominational work. The Rev. Mr. Stouder undertook to minister to the Italians almost forty years ago. He began in a rented store, later transferring his activities to the old Grace chapel, opposite the Academy of Music. They had the use of the building for a service Sunday afternoon and a communion service in the early morning. Later, the old St. Philip's Church, Mulberry street, was bought by Mrs. Wolf and presented to the Italian Mission. Sixteen years ago the city preempted the property and the Mission was transferred to a rented store once again, till the new beautiful building on Broome street was erected at a cost of $100,000. This building is thoroughly Italian in its external as well as internal construction.

The largest work of the Episcopal Church is that housed in Grace Chapel, 14th Street and First Avenue, and Grace Neighborhood House, 98 Fourth Avenue, New York City, supported by the contributions of the historic Grace Church. The Neighborhood House serves as an effective point of contact with the people through its various activities, while the strictly religious services are held in the beautiful chapel on 14th Street.

This mission to Italians was begun in 1905 by the late William R.

Huntington, D.D., then rector of Grace Church, and was in charge of the Rev. Melville K. Bailey, who had loved and learned the Italian language so that he was able to preach to the newcomers.

Mr. Bailey was assisted from the beginning by a young Italian, the Rev. Francesco G. Urbano, at that time a candidate for orders, and since 1911 the minister in charge of this work. Mr. Urbano has a comprehensive grasp of the conditions under which his people live, and by his thorough American training is peculiarly fitted to be a leader in his community.

Today Grace Chapel numbers over 600 communicants and has an average attendance at its services of over 250 throughout the year. A confirmation class of 108 persons was received last April. There has been a steadily increasing growth from year to year. The broad, firm foundations of friendship and trust were laid by years of many-sided social ministry under the guidance of Deaconess Gardner. The various workers that cooperate in the several branches of the church activity unite in working together for a regular attendance upon the church services. The deaconesses are in constant touch with the different families of the church and are in a position to understand the problems of the people . There is such an attachment to this church that it is rare to lose any that have been received as members, and families that have moved to other quarters come back again and again to visit their loved church home.

The Episcopal Church has eight missions in New York City with fourteen paid workers. Other important missions of this church are in Philadelphia and Boston.

4. *Lutheran*

While the Lutheran Church is classed as one of the largest denominations in this country, it has done little mission work outside of the nationalities it would most naturally be interested in, as for example, Germans, Swedes, and Slavs of various nationalities. About ten years ago St. Peter's Church in Philadelphia found itself surrounded by Italians. Its own communicants were rapidly withdrawing to other parts of the city. The call of God to minister to these new neighbors came clearly one Sabbath day, when, drawn by the music, a black-eyed little child strolled wandering up the aisle, and the church was not disobedient to the heavenly vision. To-day an Italian congregation meets for worship in St. Peter's Church, while around the corner stands the Martin Luther House, equipped for various kinds of modern social and religious ministry to its needy neighbors. There is a daily kindergarten, a sewing school for girls, classes in English, industrial and recreational clubs for boys and girls, etc. This is the only mission work the Lutherans are conducting for Italians, and it largely owes its existence to the faith and courage of one woman, Mrs. Cassidy. "After five years of kindergarten and three years of church services, the results are a confirmed membership of thirty-three, a Sunday-school of sixty, a kindergarten attendance of eighty, and an evening class in English of fifteen." There is every reason to hope that the example set in Philadelphia may be imitated in other parts of our country where the Lutherans are strongly entrenched and where because of their financial ability they could render a worthy and effective service.

5. *Reformed Church in the U. S. A.*

The Dutch Reformed Church is not so widely distributed outside of New York City, hence one cannot expect to find a very extensive work for the foreigners under their auspices. What they are doing for the Italians is well done. Eight years ago they realized their responsibility toward the Italians of Newburg, New York, and commenced a work for them. It has grown so rapidly that they are now planning to build a church which, judging from the plans, will be the most churchly in appearance and the most artistic building used exclusively for Italian work in this country.

For the past three years the Knox Memorial Church of New York City has in its own building carried on a mission for Italians. Now the Waldensian Church of New York City meets in their auditorium every Sunday. During the past years there has also been opened a work for Italians in Hackensack, New Jersey.

It is to be hoped that this old historic church, in addition to its many noble activities in behalf of the kingdom of God, will take more strongly to heart this cause of evangelizing the Italians.

6. *Baptist*

The Baptist denomination was one of the pioneers in attempting to give the gospel to the Italians. The first Italian Baptist Church in the United States was established by Rev. Ariel B. Bellondi, in Buffalo, New York, in 1893, while he was still a student at Colgate Theological Seminary, and later at Rochester Theological Seminary. The history of the initiation and founding of this mission is unique in that it was the Baptist Young People's Union of Buffalo that made its existence possible. The Union not only studied the question of the necessity of Italian evangelization, but took an active and leading part in the actual work. It was this wide-awake organization, under the wise and efficient leadership of Dr. E. E. Chivers, of blessed memory, that raised the money, built the building, and induced Mr. Bellondi to do the preaching. This church has never become a strong organization numerically, as it was established in a small but select suburban colony on the outskirts of Buffalo; but it has always been a very effective institution. Some of its members are among the well-known business men of that community. Two years ago they contributed in money and work something like $2,000 for the improvement of their own property. But even prior to the establishment of the church in Buffalo, Baptists at different points had attempted to reach the Italian. English-speaking workers started Sunday-schools and meetings for Italian children in Newark, New Jersey; Stamford, Connecticut; Mount Vernon, New York, and Mariner's Temple, Chatham Square, New York City, as early as 1889. The early attempts at Italian evangelization were left for a number of years in the hands of the American Baptist Home Mission Society. This organization was greatly handicapped in the prosecution of the work because of the lack of properly trained and tried men. They had to employ such material as was available and in some cases with disastrous results. The need was realized by the Baptist Education Society of New York State, and in 1907, the Italian Department of Colgate Theological Seminary was opened in Brooklyn with two students selected from eight applicants. Of the sixty applicants during the nine years of the Department's existence, twenty-one have been graduated, while eleven are at present enrolled. The others were counseled to seek other lines of employment.

The course of three years prescribed by the faculty of Colgate Theological Seminary includes a systematic study of the whole Bible, courses in church history, English and Italian languages, New Testament Greek, theology, homiletics with weekly exercises in preaching, and a considerable experience on various mission fields. Provisions are also made for the most efficient students, after finishing the department's three years' course, to take a special course of two years in Colgate University at Hamilton, New York.

It is worthy of note that during the past seventeen years the Italian Baptist workers have met in their annual convention in connection with one of the Italian churches there to discuss problems affecting the development of the work entrusted to them. The last convention was held in Lawrence, Massachusetts, with forty-five missionaries and pastors present.

V. General Recommendations

1. *Attitude*

A change of attitude is necessary before we can Americanize the great mass of the Italian immigrants. Outside of pastors and settlement or lay workers, who come in close contact with Italians and both respect and love them, the ordinary American dislikes, distrusts, fears, and shuns Italians, noticing only their external dirt, the smell of garlic, and the picturesque violent crimes committed by their black sheep. Too often we study the Italian objectively and it is unfair for any one to pass unfavorable judgment upon a race group merely on hearsay. To deal fairly with any nationality we must enter into sympathetic and intimate relations with a number of these people at least, so that we may know them. Those who know the Italian at first hand all give testimony to the responsive attitude of the Italian and to his willingness to accept the best which America has to give. But with what Americans worthy of emulation does he come in contact? In his limited world he knows his boss, who in many cases lords it over him; he knows the political ward leader, who is usually an Irish-American; he comes into occasional contact with the police authority of the city; in a word, virtually everybody that has to do with him preys upon him. What conception can he have of America? He frankly says, "With money you can do anything in America." It remains with Christian Americans to give the Italian a different conception of American standards of life, but they must do it through the medium of personal contact.

2. *A More Comprehensive Attack*

In the course of our Italian work we have passed through two distinct stages. The first was the experimental stage; various denominations attempted something here and there; missions were opened in many places just to try out Italian evangelization. This stage, generally speaking, lasted from the beginning up to about fifteen years ago. Then came the stage of permanent work; buildings were erected and definite policies were adopted; workers commenced study and training for Italian work.

We are now entering upon the third stage, which we might call the intensive stage. There are still places where missions, as in the past, should be established, but the great work to be done during the next period of ten or fifteen years is to put upon more solid foundations the existing works. We must now select some of our greatest centers, and the most promising fields in these centers which are inadequately manned and equipped and bring them up to the highest state of efficiency. It is self-evident that, given a large community where we already have a work but which does not meet the needs of the colony, every extra thousand dollars which we put into such a field will place the entire work upon a more effective basis than if that sum were spread about at various points where there might be little or no support for the work beyond the meager salary of the missionary.

But there are certain strategic points which ought to have new and better equipments and more workers, in order to make the money now expended at those points tell for the most. In Providence, Rhode Island, for example, which has, outside of California, the finest and most highly developed Italian colony in the United States, the one colony known as Federal Hill has a population of over 30,000. They own millions of dollars worth of property, the houses they live in are modern, well built, and occupied by one or two families. There is no crowding, no dirty streets, no slums there. On Broadway, which up to within very recent years was considered one of the most select highways in the city, one third of that splendid boulevard property is owned by Italians. Everything about the entire community has a prosperous air; people are well dressed, stores are neatly and attractively kept, the streets are well lighted and scrupulously cleaned, and I am told that it is as well behaved a community as can well be found in any part of the city.

One of the striking features of the colony is that the Italians have succeeded in working together for common ends. This is rather unusual for an Italian colony. The impossible has happened in Providence. The Italians have elected by their own votes five members of the State Legislature, two aldermen, one councilman, a member of the Board of Education, and an assistant district attorney. One half of the male population is naturalized. They have twenty-two doctors, twelve lawyers, and many other men in the higher walks of life, especially prominent business men.

In this exceptional colony the Roman Catholics have reared a fine and imposing church building for those who are disposed to attend it, but as Protestants we have three tiny missions carried on by three different denominations, Baptists, Methodists, and United Presbyterians. The total property value is $18,500, while the sum of $5,140 is expended yearly upon these three fields, mainly for workers, and the total membership of these missions does not reach the 200 mark.

It is unreasonable, given the love of Italians for churchly buildings, to expect that these prosperous, intelligent Italians who are in no wise interested in religion are going to be drawn to these little, insignificant, unchurchly mission buildings. The wise thing to do in such a case is to face the situation squarely and determine to put up a church plant with facilities for social work in the very best spot obtainable on Federal Hill, a building which would command the attention and the respect of the people. Then place a group of trained and devoted men and women in this place and back them up in their efforts to possess the land for God. There should be no tentative spirit in the matter. We have passed the experimental stage, we know now what we must do and what we may logically expect. This, of course, would mean the expenditure of possibly $10,000 a year, a little less than twice the sum now spent upon the three fields, but it does not require a prophet to see that the fruits of such an enterprise would be more than double what they now are.

Now I realize that it might be impossible for any one of the denominations now engaged upon the field to undertake such a task single-handed. Then is it rash for me to hazard the suggestion that in order to obtain the end desired, one denomination should assume the responsibility for the work of that field, while the other denominations cooperate in the support and in the actual work with every means at their disposal? A splendid example of this principle has recently been furnished us in Middletown, New York, where the work was taken under the care of the Presbyterian denomination, while all the Protestant denominations of the town cooperate in gifts of money and helpers. Even in the matter of securing a building for the work, while the Presbyterian Church took the initiative, the Protestant people of every name contributed almost $5,000.

3. Concerning Self-Support

There are 326 Protestant churches and missions in the United States with something over 15,000 members who contributed during the past year a total of $50,000, at the rate of $3.25 per member toward their own support, while over $400,000 is annually spent by home and city mission boards and individual churches for the support of this work. The question is often raised as to how long it will be necessary to expend this large sum of money. When will Italian churches be able to care for their own work? In investigating causes for the present conditions certain facts appeared:

A. One of the main reasons for the alienation of Italians from the Roman Church is the fact that the priests have extorted money from the people in every way open to them. The people have felt the injustice of the system whereby those with plenty of money could get the services of the church while the poor must do without.

B. To offset the belief that religion can be bought and paid for, the missionaries have emphasized the fact that the gospel of Christ is free to all. In church and on the public streets the missionaries have done all in their power to make the people understand that everything is free to all alike, no special privilege, no paying for a dispensation. The people have accepted these statements and are acting upon them. It is a matter of concern to many of the leaders in Italian work to lead the people toward self-support. This must be done, but wisdom and tact must be used.

C. While the Roman Church manages to secure money from the people, she does not do it by the direct method of voluntary gifts. She receives it in indirect ways for which the people suppose they receive some valuable equivalent, such as masses for the dead, special feasts in honor of saints, the sale of objects of indulgence, as medals, scapulars, printed prayers, beads, and candles. Large sums of money are received also for the yearly masses, which societies pay for in honor of their favorite saints. The fee for baptisms, funerals, and weddings are taken as a matter

20

of course. It is difficult to train our church-members in direct, voluntary, regular giving, although it must be said that the converts to Jesus Christ who do give systematically through the envelope and pledge system give more than they ever gave to the Roman Church, in their regular collection.

D. The matter of regular contribution rests wholly with the Italian pastor. Some men secure a fine response from a small congregation. If he has taken special pains to educate his people as to the necessity and value of regular giving, he gets results.

According to a study made of the Italian churches in Greater New York, the following facts are brought out: One Italian Presbyterian church of 654 members raised in one year $1,360, while six other missions and churches of the same denomination with a total membership of 628 gave only $405. Eight Episcopal churches, with a total membership of 1,190, gave $1,037 during the same year. Forty-six Methodist churches and missions in various parts of the country, with a total membership of 3,952, contributed for all purposes $8,745, while a total of forty-five Presbyterian churches, with 4,290 members, gave $14,353. Forty-five Baptist churches, with a membership of 2,000, gave $7,000 during the same year.

A study of the detailed reports of each individual church shows that not always do churches upon which the most money is spent show the largest increase of membership. This is because considerable sums of money are spent in social and educational work, such as day kindergartens, clinics, Boy Scouts, gymnasiums, etc. This work is very expensive and does not bring immediate results in church-members, but if this work is adequately followed up by careful visiting in the homes and personal work with individuals, keeping in close, friendly contact with all that the various activities bring under the influence of the church, it is laying the foundation for large future ingathering.

4. *Workers*

It is one of the axioms of Christian work that the personal life of the worker is far more potent in the long run than what he or she may say. No man or woman should be entrusted with the important work of leadership in our Italian missions until they have given full proof of the necessary qualifications in character. There is too much at stake to run any risk in connection with this matter. Many a man has been alienated from the church and even from God because of the questionable and immoral life of religious workers. As I visited Italian missions in many cities from Massachusetts to Texas during the last summer, one of the expressions which I heard most often from Italians as well as from Americans was this: "We had a good work here some years ago, but then the Board sent us a man who ought never to have been authorized to preach. He destroyed not only what we had already accomplished, but he has made it impossible for us to continue our work with any success for a number of years to come. We must live down the bad example of that man." Such experiences not only turn the foreigner against the evangelical propaganda, but they are too effective in making our American friends who support the work lose their interest in our project.

One of the most essential things in a worker, aside from personal character, is a knowledge of the life, the customs, the views, the prejudices, the ideals, and the ordinary problems of life that the foreigner has to meet. There are too many people who have theories of their own regarding what should be done for the foreigner and how it should be done, but the theories are not based upon either knowledge or experience. All workers should study the national characteristics and dispositions of the people they are attempting to reach.

5. *Women Workers*

The part which the woman missionary can have in our great task of foreign evangelization is beyond our power to estimate. But it must be understood that it is not so much what she does in public meetings or in her departments in the Sunday-school and the sewing school that makes her work so important, but it is her personal influence with the young people, especially the girls of the mission church. These young folk are exceedingly anxious to acquire American ways, they are ready to imitate everything their leader does. What a great responsibility this lays upon the worker! We need the best educated, most refined, and truly cultured persons to advise and lead these responsive, loyal, idealistic young people. Too often we have had well-meaning, devotedly Christian, but light-weight women of scant education who were in culture and refinement little above the young people they were trying to lead. Their work for little children is in many cases excellent, but they cannot cope with the growing intelligence of the high school boys and girls. The worker must by her mere presence inspire to noble thinking, noble feeling, and noble acting. The worker must not feel above those she is seeking to reach, but she must be above them if they are to be drawn to a higher level.

The work of women missionaries should be planned in connection with the entire activity of the mission church. It is disastrous to separate the work too much into independent departments. All need the unified influence of regular conference to plan their work. Many little frictions that lead to serious disturbance between workers might be eliminated through this regular weekly or monthly conference.

6. *Associative Spirit*

The Italian minister has in the past held himself too much aloof from social, political, and other organizations composed of Italians. It is becoming more and more the conviction of those that have had considerable experience that it would be of great advantage if the Italian missionary would associate himself with various orders and would enter as fully as possible into the life of the community in which he works. One of the most powerful organizations recently formed among Italians is *I Figli d'Italia*, or "Sons of Italy." This is a strictly democratic organization where the Protestant missionary would be cordially welcomed. Already a number of our Italian pastors have seen their opportunity and thrown themselves into the task of giving direction and ideals to this rapidly growing order. This is one of the rare openings for the exertion of wholesome Christian influence upon an institution that is destined to mold to a great extent the spirit and attitude of the Italian people in the great centers of population.

7. *The Message*

Our Italian missionaries should be taught as far as possible to refrain from railing at the Roman Catholic Church. Preaching should be constructive and practical. It is necessary in many cases for the sermon to have an apologetic note. One of the common questions which even intelligent Italians ask is, "What is the difference between the Protestant religion and the Catholic religion?" It is very evident that to meet the state of the Italian mind with a religious message one must be familiar with Roman Catholic views, doctrines, and practises. In presenting the message to a non-Protestant audience, it is essential that a man shall draw comparisons between the two systems, but such comparison should be made in a conciliatory manner. Ex-priests who enter as workers in our missionary fields are usually the bitterest denunciators of the Roman Catholic Church and of its priests. I shall never forget an expression used by an ex-priest Protestant missionary in speaking about his antagonism toward the class from which he came, before a public audience: "If I had the hearts of all the priests in my hand, I would throw them to the dogs." It is unnecessary to say that this kind of preaching does not make indifferent Catholics favorable to the Protestant position. When the message of Christ is presented in all its simplicity and power and the moral side of religion is given emphasis and prominence, the Italian, whether a zealous Catholic or no, says: "Yes, you are right, that is true," and in many cases he is willing to confess, even though he is still attached to the Roman Church that Protestant teaching is better than Roman Catholic teaching and that Protestant ethics are better than Roman Catholic.

8. *Literature and Publications*

The four denominational Italian papers that are published weekly are of great value in the prosecution of our evangelical propaganda. But we need now, as we have needed in the past, tracts that may be freely distributed to the Italian people everywhere. The ready disposition on the part of the Italian to receive and read virtually anything that is placed in his hands gives us a rare opportunity. The old tract literature has served its purpose well, but we are now face to face with the problem of meeting certain well-defined and strongly entrenched views on the part of the people that we seek to reach. There is an imperative need for a new literature in order to present our fundamental ideas and conceptions of the religion of Jesus Christ to the Italian. This literature must be apologetic as well as evangelistic. Our motives as Christians and our methods of worship are now assailed, and so many false statements are spread broadcast by the Roman Church that we must prepare short tracts that in a clear and simple manner will state the Protestant point of view. This literature might very well be prepared in such a way as to be used by all the denominations, because the problems are the same for all. It would be an extravagance for each denomination to do its own work in the matter of preparing tracts to meet the same needs.

The importance of the press in all sorts of propaganda cannot be overestimated. The Christian church knows well its power. There are at the present time four denominational papers printed in the Italian language: *L'Era Nuova,* Presbyterian; *La Fiaccola,* Methodist; *Il Cristiano,* Baptist, and *L'Ape Evangelico,* United Presbyterian. While the denominational spirit is quite strong among Italians, it is a most interesting fact that, with only three exceptions, of the seventy-five or more missionaries whom I have interviewed, all approved of a plan to merge all the papers into one, having a board of editors drawn from the different denominations. This would have three great advantages: *First,* the financial burden, which now has to be borne for the conduct of four papers, would be greatly reduced; the conviction on the part of some is that such a paper could be made to pay for itself. *Second,* we Protestants should be able to present a united front before the bewildered Italians who are used to one church wherever they go. *Third,* we should without question be able to produce a much better paper than any one of the four can now be. Such a paper would include not only strictly religious articles, but a discussion of the leading topics of the day from the Christian point of view, an Italian "Outlook." It should also include a generous English department for young people and children.

9. *Work for Women and Young People*

Work for other women and girls is primarily woman's work. It is not enough to reach the fathers and develop them through the civic clubs and English classes nor yet enough to get the children into kindergartens or Sunday-schools. Unless the mother is reached, the children are invariably lost at confirmation age. This fact was soon discovered on our foreign fields, and specially trained Bible women are now sent into the homes to teach the heathen mothers the gospel.

All women who do missionary work among the Italians should learn the Italian language in order to converse directly with the mother about the care of her home, the health of her family, as well as about the religious training of her children. The life of the Italian mother in this country is very barren indeed. She slaves from morning till night and very seldom has she a moment's time for anything pleasurable and inspiring. A visit from the church missionary who knows her language and can speak to her about matters that are of vital concern to her can be very effective in influencing the mother along the lines of social and religious thinking. In some places classes in English for foreign mothers have been successfully conducted, but since unexpected duties or a sick child may make the mother's attendance irregular, it is better to have the woman teacher of English go regularly into the Italian homes, gathering in several of the neighbors who would be glad to listen to the lesson. The true missionary is able to give a religious message with every English lesson. But the mothers are in need every now and then of a little entertainment. A social gathering where there is singing and instrumental music, and light refreshments are served offers them some diversion in the midst of their life of drudgery and perplexities. The church must be to them not only a place where they shall come to hear sermons but where they shall receive a social ministry as well that may open up their lives to the legitimate pleasures of this world.

We need to do more effective work for our young people. In many mission churches we are facing a situation which will react very unfavorably upon our work in the future. All missionaries agree they have no great difficulty in getting plenty of little children into the Sunday-school, sewing school, play hour, and kindergarten. The difficulty comes when they leave school and go to work, to hold them until they establish Christian homes of their own. In our search for a solution of the problem, we have considered the activities for young people of many settlements and churches, camp fire groups, dress-making classes, gymnastics, Boy Scouts, athletic associations, and musical and dramatic societies. These serve to attract and hold large numbers, though in some places there are many comers and goers and often those who become prominent in an organization are quite alien to the ideals of the church. There are notable exceptions, but to my mind the reason for this is the inefficiency of workers entrusted with the young people's work in our missions. The emphasis has been placed on the value of the child for so long that women missionaries pay most of their attention to the children. They fail to realize that adolescence is the period when ideals are formed, personal problems arise, and the standards by which later life is ruled become fixed. Our duty by our young people is not done by having a few clubs or entertainments, excellent as they are, but by heart to heart talks about life's problems and ideals, by persons whom they cannot help respecting.

10. *Americanization*

The term Americanization is on the lips of many people in these days, and in many cases it is doubtful as to whether those who use it could give any definite idea about its meaning. To superficial people it means simply that a foreign-born individual must turn his back upon everything that has any association with the land of his birth, that he shall have no contact with people from his native land, that he shall even forget his language and take on external American customs. But surely a person may do this and still not be an American. We must be on our guard against zeal for quick Americanization of these people, by many of our well-meaning but short-sighted workers. They urge the young men and women to throw off their race customs and adopt the American ones. But this is exceedingly dangerous until moral character and the ideals of this country are understood. True Americanization comes from a culture of the heart and mind and when that is accomplished, external manners and customs will take care of themselves. Let those of us who are working with Italians value the best in everything connected with the land of their birth, their great men, their artists, their martyrs, their statesmen and writers, their wonderful history, and the present progressive state of their country. When we have made them see the best in their own land, we shall be in a far better position to make them see the best in American life.

11. *A Day and Boarding School*

So much of the work in our Sunday-schools, clubs, and classes is continuously counteracted by bad home influences and unwholesome effects of our city street life, that if we wish really to develop a strong leadership in an adequate fashion among the Italians, we should imitate the example of our foreign missionaries in India and China, where they have established missionary schools. The results of this work are discernible in the numbers of influential Christian men in the public life of China and India to-day. In a missionary school the best home influences and Christian ideals constantly surround the young people, systematic Bible study is a part of the regular curriculum, and home-making duties are carefully taught. I will venture to say that if we could have such boarding and day schools for Italians, in fifteen or twenty years their graduates would be leaders of thought in our Italian communities. The Roman Church realizes the value of environment and is busy establishing parochial schools to hold the Italian children to the church. One priest acknowledged to me that the leaders of the church "are crazy to get the Italian children; they are going to make a place for themselves in this country." We have our opportunity now. One hundred thousand dollars invested in a modern, well-equipped school along the lines that have proved so successful on the foreign field would yield rich returns in Christian Americanized Italian leaders for the next generation.

12. Local Supervision and Care

It is still too often the practise to appoint a missionary, provide him with a meager salary, and place him upon a field with a very inadequate equipment and with no backing of the English-speaking people of the community, and then tell him to go ahead and evangelize Italians. What has happened in so many cases will continue to happen unless we adopt a different policy, a policy which indeed has proved very successful in a score of places where it has been put to the test. My own impression would be that wherever it is impossible to secure the cordial and generous cooperation of the local church or churches for the Italian mission it would be better not to undertake the work at all. And a number of mission fields could be enumerated where after years of service, home missions and state organizations having put into the work many thousands of dollars, the missions had to be closed because they were accomplishing nothing. And this failure was due to the lack of hearty cooperation on the part of the local church.

On the other hand the most successful missions and churches are those which have the care and sympathetic and active cooperation of the local church, or at least of far-visioned individuals connected with the local church. For example, the success of the work in the Presbyterian mission in Newark, New Jersey; the Baptist mission in Orange, New Jersey; the Methodist church in Fall River, Massachusetts; the Congregational church in New Haven, Connecticut; and the Dutch Reformed church in Newburg, New York; the work of Grace chapel in New York City, and a host of others that might be mentioned have succeeded because of local whole-hearted cooperation.

13. Denominational Changes

There are certain men who have gone the rounds of the various denominations. In most cases, these men have not left a record which redounds to the glory of God or the success of the evangelical propaganda. Has the time not come, when for mutual protection, we should stiffen our attitude toward the men who have to change periodically their denominational affiliation? If they have not succeeded under the care of one church they will in all probability not succeed in any church.

My conviction is that the leaders in our foreign work should discourage this changing of denominations. If a man, already in the care of any denomination, desires to make a change to some other, the reasons should be carefully determined through counseling with those who have been responsible for his work. And here, perfect frankness and veracity cannot be too much insisted upon. There have been cases where an inefficient man or even one who did not enjoy the fullest confidence has been recommended to another body, to get rid of him. This is not fair, for it hurts the cause of Christ.

However much any denomination may be in need of workers, it is not just that it shall endeavor to meet its own needs by reaching out and taking that which belongs to another. We need in every way to create and sustain an attitude of loyalty toward one's denomination. While, on the other hand, we must endeavor to inculcate a spirit of fraternity and real cooperation among the workers of different names, we must at the same time see to it that nothing is done to loosen that bond of fidelity to the body to which a man is attached. Hence, every suggestion to leave one denomination and take up work with another because a little more remuneration may be offered, or because the man may be *persona non grata* where he is, should be strictly avoided. The only way to secure and maintain a stable corps of workers that can be depended upon, is for each denomination to create its own ministry. We must not attempt to fill our own ranks by depleting the ranks of others, because this method not only does harm to the worker in that it tears down in him the fine sense of loyalty, but such men as are not inspired with convictions of the value of their denominational ideals can never give themselves unreservedly to the ends and aims of the bodies under whose auspices they work.

14. *Types of Organization**

There are usually two types of churches and missions among Italians. The one is the branch church, where the converts are taken into the membership of some American church. In some cases the work of these branches is carried on in a room of the American church, while in others the Italian congregation meets in a separate building used exclusively for Italian work. The common experience is that the best results can be obtained in separate buildings, where the people feel free to come and go and the place is used every day in the week if need be; whereas, when the work is conducted in an American church, the mission can only have the use of the building for a couple of hours on Sunday, and once or twice during the week. Besides, the Italian is somewhat timid when he meets with Americans in the church building who are usually not overcordial to the foreigner.

The ideal is, wherever it is possible, to have a separate building and as soon as possible to effect a complete church organization having its regular officers and privileged to administer in their own place the rites of baptism and of the Lord's Supper.

A distinction should be made here, between a church that is organized for the conduct of its own work and an independent church, strictly so-called. When such a church is organized it should be made very clear to the members of it that no church can be actually independent until it is able to provide for its own expenses. There is no objection if the members of the organized church are considered members of some American church, if that serves the purpose of developing interest on

*See *Sons of Italy,* Chapter VI., for more detailed statement (Missionary Education Movement, New York, 60 cents, prepaid).

the part of the Americans in behalf of the Italian work. But the converts must be given a sense of responsibility for the conduct of their own work. If they are ever to reach the point of self-support, they must now be given considerable freedom of action, under wise direction, in order that they may feel their obligation for reaching the people of their community. The ideal that the work carried on for Italians is not an enterprise that devolves upon the Americans, but that the Italians themselves are to look upon it as their task and that they are to make every effort possible to maintain it financially, must be ever held before them. This can be done only when they feel that they are the masters of their work. Too often Americans have so completely dictated and controlled the work that the Italians have said, whenever an appeal was made to them for the maintenance of the work, "This is the Americans' business, let them do it," and unfortunately this has been the attitude even on the part of some of our missionaries. It is true that the Italians, unused to democracy in church life, if given large freedom, will doubtless make many mistakes. Every precaution should be taken to avoid serious blunders, but we must also recognize that by mistakes they will learn better to conduct their own affairs.

15. *Cooperation of American Christians*

In view of the many difficulties that have arisen in cases where the semi-independent mission churches have been left to govern themselves, an experiment has been attempted which has worked very satisfactorily. The following organization has been devised. The local church nearest to the mission or the one most vitally interested appoints a committee of three or four consecrated men from its own members, men who are sympathetic to the foreigner and who are willing to give some attention to study the people that they are going to try to assist, to meet at regular intervals and counsel with the official body of the Italian congregation. This group combined with the workers at the mission discuss together all problems that may arise and also all plans for any departures from the ordinary lines of activity. Reports of the work done by the staff are presented also to this body.

Two ends are effectively served by such an organization: First, it is a protection against ill-advised or rash actions on the part of the Italian congregation; and second, it enables the American people better to understand and sympathize with the Italian temperament and point of view. Both sides would learn to respect, love, and help each other more as they thus become acquainted.

16. *Large Opportunity to Reach the Foreigner*

When the real attitude of the Italian toward the faith of his fathers is understood, a great field is opened up before evangelical churches and consecrated individuals. It would be a splendid thing if every church all over this whole land in country or city, wherever there are foreigners, should have a standing missionary committee, not simply to arrange for a missionary meeting once a month, but which would act and go out and make a careful survey of the foreign peoples in the vicinity or community, gathering information about their economic, social, and religious conditions; and then seek through English classes, sewing schools, civic clubs, and friendly visitations, to establish a point of contact with the stranger. This would serve as the first step in the problem of leadership. If those undertaking the task cannot speak the tongue of the people, they can, with some effort, find some well-disposed man or woman who would willingly serve as interpreter for them.

VI. A Model Program of Work for Italians

Schedule—Good-will Center, Brooklyn

All meetings weekly unless otherwise stated.

Day	Hour	Activity
Monday	4-5	Girls
	5-7	Jolly Club (Polish Girls)
	7-9	Good Will Club (Girls)
Tuesday	4-5.30	Happy Girls' Club
	5.30-7	Bannerman Boys' Club
	7-9	Anita Garibaldi Club (Girls)
	7-9	Good Will Athletic Club
	8	Mothers' Meeting (Monthly)
Wednesday	4-5.30	Small Boys' Club
	6-8	Young Citizens
	8-9	Prayer Meeting
	9-10	Men's Citizenship Class
	3	Neighborhood Mothers' Meeting (Monthly)
Thursday	2-3	Mothers' Meeting
	2-3	Children in Gym
	4-5.30	Sunshine Club (Girls)
	8	Edmondo de Amicis Circolo
Friday	3.30-5	Sewing School
	5-7	Boys' Club
	8	Choir Practise
	8	Boy Scouts
Saturday	4	Children's Meeting and Motion Pictures
	8	Popular Entertainment and Lectures
	8	Boys' Neighborhood Club
Sunday	3-4	Sunday-school
	4.15	Italian Church Service
Others Unlisted		Girls' Protective League (Monthly)
		Kindergarten (Daily)
		Day Nursery (Daily)
		Italian and English Classes
		Cookery and Basketry
		Columbus Club (Monthly)

APPENDIX

A. THE POLICY OF THE BAPTIST CHURCHES AND MISSIONARY SOCIETIES IN THE EVANGELIZATION OF THE ITALIAN PEOPLE

By Rev. Charles A. Brooks

Superintendent City and Foreign-Speaking Work, American Baptist Home Mission Society

It is difficult to define our policy, because Baptists have no centralized ecclesiastical or missionary authority. Notwithstanding this there is a fairly uniform policy among our churches and societies.

First, a general word as to a fundamental principle which we recognize in all our missionary work among the various races in America.

1. Each race represents not only peculiar racial problems, but an important and distinctive contribution to the enrichment of the life of America and the kingdom of God.

2. While we expect and desire the Americanization of these groups, we do not desire the obliteration or destruction of their unique racial heritage, but invite them to share these gifts with us, as we seek to make our contribution to them.

It is important that we keep these two principles in even balance.

3. We believe that Christianity is a spirit of life with infinite variety of expression, and that our American conception of God and his kingdom needs enriching by the communion of all saints. Hence, we believe in the freedom of religious life according to racial type. An Italian Protestant church will have and should have distinctive characteristics, distinguishing it from an American Protestant church. This means the enrichment of the Protestant conception of God, and of social life.

There is no Italian gospel, but there is a gospel for the Italian, which is the secret of his highest and best development, and the rebirth of Italian character according to the mind of Christ. Italians will be won for the kingdom of God only as the gospel is interpreted to them in the terms of their own thinking. This is recognized as a fundamental truth on the foreign field, in China and India. It is no less true in America among the Italians, Poles, and Russians.

It is important that we keep this in mind, because some of our earnest people are alarmed if our foreign-speaking groups develop a distinctive and aggressive religious life of their own. Their idea and measure of success is the rapid merging and consequent loss of identity of the new converts in the life of the American church. But this means the loss of their distinctive influence in winning their fellow-countrymen for Christ. The use of the Italian language in worship and service is not primarily a matter of *privilege,* but of *responsibility* for winning the Italian people for Christ.

While no two of our missions have had the same history, the work has usually developed in one of two ways which have been determined by local conditions, such as the distribution of population and the location of the American church. Beginnings have been made more frequently through the local American church, as a part of its ministry to the community or "parish," which includes Italian families. This has usually been through clubs, classes, or the Sunday-school, which have included Italians but have not excluded others. The ministry of the church to some needy individual Italian or a family has demonstrated the friendliness of the American church and opened the door of access to the Italian heart.

Where a colony of Italians is segregated and separated by distance from an American church, a separate mission has often been established. The ministry of this mission at the first has been largely to the children through clubs, classes, kindergartens, or day nurseries, with Sunday-schools and classes in English. Workers have usually come from one fostering American church, or from various churches where a federated movement has promoted the work.

The conversion of one or more Italians has demonstrated the possibility of reaching these people in a larger way than through the English language, and has usually been the determining factor in the employment of an Italian missionary, who usually becomes a member of the staff of an English church. The same type of work, as we have already described, has been continued, but the Italian pastor or missionary supplements this with the preaching of the gospel and the proclamation of a distinctively evangelistic message.

The spiritual and disciplinary oversight of this work is usually in the hands of a local American church. But the general missionary policy is usually under the direction of a local city or state missionary organization, with the cooperation of the national societies, both general and woman's, who cooperate in the financial support of the work.

The Italian members of the mission usually become members of the American church and are received upon the recommendation of their Italian fellow Christians. We have been slow to encourage the organization of separate churches until mature Christian character and experience has been developed and a good deal of autonomy has been exercised for some time. We encourage such autonomy, and strive to develop a spirit of self-reliance and self-support.

We are developing a fine body of missionaries, trained in our American schools. The Italian department of Colgate Theological Seminary, of which Prof. Mangano is Dean, is training a splendid type of Americanized Italian missionary.

We are encouraging, and have succeeded in developing excellent material equipment, separate chapels and church edifices which are set apart for distinctively Italian work, and which the Italians may feel are their own. These are being built upon modern lines, making provision for social and educational work, as well as preaching and public worship.

We are emphasizing the fundamental importance and necessity of an adequately trained and trustworthy ministry, and an adequate interpretation of the gospel. Our disappointments and our failures have been due almost always to unwise and unworthy leadership. We have been constantly and firmly eliminating unfit men from our missionary staff, and are insisting upon as high a standard of Christian character for our Italian ministry as for our general ministry. By an adequate interpretation of the gospel we mean the warm, loving, intelligible presentation of the good news of God's saving grace, not in a controversial or polemic spirit, but in the characteristic spirit of Jesus; the training and development of Christian character by a thoroughgoing program of Christian education; and the interpretation of social relationships and responsibilities in the terms of human brotherhood and the kingdom of God.

B. ITALIAN CONGREGATIONALISTS

By Philip M. Rose

Supervisor of Italian Congregational Churches in Connecticut

Congregationalists have no country-wide or denomination-wide work for Italian immigrants. Without a doubt, the widest observation of their efforts would fail to discover any systematic policy with respect to Italian evangelization. Yet, just as Congregational influence has gone far beyond its own limited constituency to permeate the life of America, so its efforts in this particular line command a keen and intelligent interest out of proportion to their size and number.

The denomination is awake to its duty where this race enters its field. Where Congregational churches are springing up and growing strong in the miscellaneous life of the cities or suburban towns, they are taking note of the Italian in their midst. Witness the missions in South Brooklyn, in Grantwood, New Jersey; in Portland, Maine; in San Francisco. Occasionally a church in the mining regions has found Italians to whom to reach out the helping hand, as in Spring Valley, Illinois. In Maine, where Italians are invading various century-old Congregational parishes, a group of small missions is springing up. And in general in those portions of New England and New Jersey, adjacent to the great ports of entry, where Congregationalism is at all strongly entrenched, we find the most serious attempts to minister to the incoming Italian life. For instance, the fifteen Congregational churches of New Haven do not and cannot forget the fact of the 50,000 Italians in their midst, one third of the population of that city so historically Congregational.

31

The only policy discoverable that our churches have had toward the Italian work has been the policy of experiment. There have been some notable and varied experiments. According to the genius of the order, these have been on the account of the local church. At most, some state organization has been responsible. Moreover, Congregationalists have not been at all careful that all efforts should bear the Congregational name—enough for them that the work was being done. Denominational lines have bothered them but little more than they have bothered the rank and file of Italian pastors and communicants who grow impatient with the incomprehensible divisions with which their Catholic kinsmen reproach them. Congregationalists have therefore supported generously union missions in which often the missionary in charge was of another communion. They have been strong supporters of the Waldensian Aid Societies, casting their bread on the waters of over-sea Italian life whence in increasing frequency it comes back to them after many days. They have thrown their strength largely behind social settlements and independent boys' clubs. They have been slow to believe ill of the Italian Roman Catholic Church, and they still insist that all enlightened effort and sincere faith in that body be respected and be met halfway. Nevertheless they are saying to the Roman Church, "If you are feeding our Italian neighbors husks, if you refuse to give them real spiritual life, and thus fail to hold them, they are for us a legitimate field of effort." In a time when social effort has been popularly secularized, they are stoutly supporting Firman House in Chicago, Good-will Center in Brooklyn, Davenport House in New Haven, as religious settlements, with religious ideals, Christian workers, and church services held paramount. Withal the ideal is not proselytism but Christian character.

Many pastors of smaller towns are pondering on the "little Italys" of gardeners, quarrymen, or operatives in some neglected corner of their parish; a few have succeeded in drawing one or more Italian families into their church, and a larger number of Italian children into their Sunday-schools; one or two have had the joy of sending away a bright boy or girl to the American International College at Springfield, Massachusetts, or to the Bible Teachers' Training School. For oh, how great is the need for more and superior leaders for the race till now in ideals and faith so indifferently led.

The variety in the actual mission work is striking. Here is a mission in a New Jersey town with an isolated Italian colony to which the American pastor has deeply devoted and greatly endeared himself. His sympathy, the employment of an Italian worker at the right time, and the introduction of religious social effort has done wonders to evangelize and assimilate the strangers. Another mission, developed by its Italian pastor, who was a prince alike among Americans and Italians for his friendly qualities, contentedly shares the building, and joins in the Sunday-school and Lord's Supper of the American church. Still another becomes increasingly attached to its American woman missionary, although she speaks but little Italian. A member of this mission recently sent his personal check for $50 to the missionary society in recognition of his debt to it. The church at Waterbury, largest of all Congregational Italian churches, has been built up around and through music. Its pastor, unique as a music master, has sung and played the gospel into Italian hearts during many years, until his choir and orchestra are the pride of the city, and he can produce Italian young women Sunday-school teachers, trained by his own hand. The Hartford church makes a specialty of outdoor preaching during the summer. The Bridgeport church, housed in its own building, has a flourishing mutual aid society. The New Haven church, integral part of Davenport Settlement and ministered to by the residents as well as by its pastor and missionary, has, to serve it, perhaps the most beautiful church building, finest organ and plant of any Italian work in the country—a real cathedral. By all of which it may be seen that variety is prized in Connecticut.

But the boldest experiment of Connecticut Italian Congregationalism is yet to be told. It is almost unique of its kind in Italian work, and entirely unique in its thoroughness. Believing that the Italian churches and missions could be more efficiently directed, and their leaders inspired through his interpretation of Italians to Americans and of Americans to Italians, the proper authorities took a young man of thorough collegiate and theological training, and sent him to Italy for two years' training in the Italian language and character. He returned with this equipment, and assumed the full pastorate of the church at New Haven. He was received by his Italian colleagues with great satisfaction, and is gradually assuming his intended work of interpretation and superintendence.

To conclude: briefly, Congregational experience suggests the following lines of attack in Italian evangelization.

1. While showing all tolerance for and willingness to cooperate with the Italian Roman Catholic Church, we must recognize that the majority of our Italian-Americans are, spiritually, unchurched, and hence our legitimate field.

2. The first move in establishing an Italian Protestant mission or nucleus is *personal* sympathy and service on the part of American church-members toward the Italians, and especially of friendship between American and Italian women.

3. There is a loud cry for an itinerant missionary or colporteur, who can do the work of pastor for scattered and small Italian colonies.

4. Afterwards there should be employed in the larger colonies a man or woman missionary, better both.

5. Social and musical work and house-visiting are fundamental.

6. The careful, sympathetic superintendence by an American of a group of Italian missions is highly desirable.

7. We must urge our best Italian youth to prepare themselves to be the intellectual and spiritual leaders of their own race.

C. ITALIAN METHODISM IN AMERICA

By FREDERICK H. WRIGHT, D.D.

Formerly Superintendent of the Italian Mission

The Methodist Episcopal Church was perhaps the first Protestant church to do any specific work for Italians in America. This, as a matter of record, is interesting, and for historical purposes is worthy of note. In 1858 a young Italian vender of plaster models, Antonio Arrighi by name, was converted in a Methodist church in Des Moines, Iowa. After his conversion he attended the Iowa Wesleyan College, and while there delivered his first speech in Italian, on the invitation of President Charles Elliott, who was afterwards mainly instrumental in inaugurating Methodist missionary work in the Eternal City. This young man aided the pastor of the Mount Pleasant Church in the camp-meeting just outside the city. In 1860 he met Abraham Lincoln in Bloomington, Illinois, who told him that "Italy will never be great again unless united and one, but united upon the terms of Mazzini, 'a free church in a free state.'" About this time young Arrighi met Peter Cartwright, who later on furnished him with a letter of recommendation as follows:

"JACKSONVILLE, ILL., July 23, 1860.

"I very cordially and earnestly would recommend to all the friends of humanity the bearer, Antonio Arrighi, a poor young Italian lately converted from popery, who is striving for an education to qualify himself to return and preach the gospel to his benighted nation.

"*Signed,* PETER CARTWRIGHT."

When the war broke out, he volunteered and served during the whole of the war. Then he studied at Ohio Wesleyan University and Dickinson College, and in 1865 went to Boston Theological Seminary. In 1871 he started for Rome and labored with the Methodists and the Free Italian Church until 1880, being ordained to the gospel ministry by Bishop Matthew Simpson, probably the first Protestant minister ordained in the city of Rome. He then returned to America, and on June 21, 1881, preached his first sermon at the Five Points Mission in New York City. Still living, the erstwhile galley slave of Italy, a victim of papal intolerance, and a veteran missionary of the cross, has seen Protestant missions among Italians established by all churches throughout the land. It was a small beginning, but it meant great things for Italy and America, and at the time of the last report in 1916 of the organized Italian Mission of the Methodist Episcopal Church, which covered a territory extending from the

Atlantic Ocean to the Mississippi River, there were fifty-two preaching places with forty-six ministers. From the Mississippi River westward other missions were established at New Orleans and San Francisco and at Des Moines, Iowa; Denver, and Pueblo, Colorado; and Butte, Montana.

In the first years of the organized work very little was done toward self-support but the report of 1916 shows that the amount of $8,749 was raised for self-support and the benevolent enterprises of the church.

Methodism has shown its faith in the future of this work by investing in church edifices and other buildings a sum approximating $480,000. While the Board of Home Missions and Church Extension expends in round figures $50,000 a year, if the sums raised locally by the city missionary societies were added, it would be revealed that close to twice that amount is invested for Italian evangelization, though there are no exact figures available on this point.

The effort is made to emphasize the church as a social center, in direct opposition to the Roman idea, which places the stress upon the church edifice being simply and solely a place of devotion. Care is taken, however, to eliminate as far as possible any criticism, by keeping the church proper sacred for public and private worship, but in the other parts of the building every attempt is made to attract the people, so as to make it a community center, thus accentuating the social power of Christianity. This is an entirely new idea to the Italians, and as they enter into it, they soon appreciate its value. This social life is encouraged by (1) The organization of evening classes for the purpose of teaching the Italian the English language. A large percentage of the Italian immigrants are illiterates, and they must be taught their own language first before they can be interested in the English language; at least, that is the experience of our Italian missionaries. These Italian workers use these schools as feeders to our church services. There is no attempt to hide our identity. They know that we are Protestants, and by means of the disinterested spirit manifested by our Italian and American workers, confidence is won, and unreasoning prejudice is overcome.

(2) The classes for instruction in American citizenship are another powerful means of developing the social life of the Italian church. Hundreds of Italians have been aided in securing their citizen's papers. Our missionaries are continually in demand for services which are purely social in their character, and yet have a tremendous impact for evangelical faith.

(3) The organization of kindergarten schools, together with classes for instruction in cooking and domestic economy. In some centers, such as Five Points Mission and the Church of All Nations in New York City, day schools have been opened for the community, where ninety per cent. and even more of the pupils are Italians. Then on Sunday large Sunday-schools, averaging an attendance of from 500 to 800, composed chiefly of Italians, flourish, and the lessons of the Bible, in the English language, are taught. There is no reason for segregating the Italian children from other American children, for they are Americans in fact.

(4) Classes for physical exercises for both girls and boys, with baths and reading rooms, have done much to make the church a social center, and are being encouraged.

Added to all this, of course, is the preaching of the gospel in the Italian tongue. There is no wish to perpetuate this feature of the work, but only two things will lead to its discontinuance: (1) Cessation of immigration, and (2) Absorption of the young and rising generation into our American Sunday-schools and churches. As to the first, it is absolutely essential to have Italian services for the adult immigrant. He must go where he can understand and be understood, and as to the latter, this absorption will be gauged by the friendly attitude of Protestant Christians. It ought not to be necessary to have Italian Sunday-schools for children; they sit side by side with American boys and girls in the public schools; they prefer to speak English, and if we are to save them from being hyphenated Americans, we must give them the glad hand to our churches and Sunday-schools. This is the ideal of Methodism, despite all difficulties, and we shall win out only as we strive after this ideal.

The Methodist Episcopal Church is doing constructive work for Italian evangelization, and the future will witness great growth in interest and results.

Under the reorganization of the Board of Home Missions and Church Extension last year, the Italian Mission as a separate organization was discontinued, and each mission is placed under the direction of the local district superintendent, in the hope that greater efficiency and interest will be developed. This Board, through its Bureau of Foreign Work, at a conference of District and City Society Superintendents having oversight of Italian work has outlined its present policy as follows:

I. Program of work for the local Italian church.

    1. Approach to the family as a whole.

        (a) Home visitor, a woman speaking Italian, with the American training and American spirit. Such a one, bilingual, could work with little children in English, and conduct older classes possibly in Italian. The problem is one of young women as well as mothers. The future objective is to be young Italian women thoroughly trained.

        (b) Family gathering for everybody in the church parlors or church house. Music, games, pictures, etc. Recognize the family unit.

        (c) Meetings in the home. The coming of the stranger draws all the neighbors in so that a program may be used. Special attention to home meetings for girls.

    2. Approach in Italian for adult Italian groups.

        (a) Religious services of worship in Italian, (b) Bilingual staff members, a lawyer, physician, employment agent, and a printer, whose services may be used for help among the Italians in the community. (c) Mothers' club in Italian, (d) Men's clubs for learning English and citizenship (civic questions, citizenship papers, etc.). (e) Use of Italian literature. (f) Religious instruction in Italian. (g) Illustrated lectures. (h) Italian patriotism as point of contact (Italian days, the 20th of September, etc.). (i) Make use of musical interest.

    3. Approach in English to children and young people.

        (a) Attendance at English church services. (b) Religious instruction (Sunday-school). (c) Related week-day club activities, emphasis on expressional work, such as recreational clubs, gymnasium clubs, choral societies, dramatic clubs, Boy Scouts, Knights of King Arthur, Camp Fire Girls, Girl Scouts, sewing, painting, drawing, and sculpture. (d) Illustrated lectures and moving pictures. (e) Daily Vacation Bible School. (f) Flower mission. (g) Fresh air work. (h) Camps.

II. Program of training for non-English-speaking leadership by the Board of Home Missions and Church Extension of the Methodist Episcopal Church.

    1. The Board of Home Missions and Church Extension of the Methodist Episcopal Church, in cooperation with the Board of Education of the Methodist Episcopal Church is to begin immediately the task of (a) training American ministers for work among Italians in this country, these men to have a college and theological seminary training and, in addition, while studying at the theological seminary, to be in attendance upon a training center in connection with some Italian church where they may receive lectures in Italian and Italian culture, and be guided in clinic work in different Italian parishes; (b) training Italian ministers for work among Italians in this country, these men to have college and theological training and, in addition, while studying at the theological seminary, to be in attendance upon a training center in connection with some Italian church where they may receive lectures in Italian and Italian culture, and be guided in clinic work in different Italian parishes.

    2. Training institutes for Italian ministers in service are to be held in different parts of the country as the Board of Home Missions and Church Extension may be able to plan.

    3. The Board of Home Missions and Church Extension of the Meth-

odist Episcopal Church is to be made a clearing-house for information concerning Italian parishes and Italian workers; district and city society superintendents and pastors to report to the Board concerning their work twice a year.

D. AT WORK WITH THE ITALIANS:
THE PRESBYTERIAN CHURCH IN THE U. S. A.

By WILLIAM P. SHRIVER

Director of City and Immigrant Work, Board of Home Missions

In the spring of 1916 the Presbyterian Church in the U. S. A. had 107 churches and missions using the Italian language, with 4,800 members and more than 8,000 enrolled in the Sunday-schools. In the last year over 1,100 were received upon confession of their faith in sixty-one churches and missions alone. Sixty Italian-speaking pastors are employed; twenty-three lay workers, thirty-two visitors, and over 350 American volunteers are regularly engaged in the work of sixty-seven churches and missions reporting. Large funds have been invested in the permanent equipment of this work ($350,000 in twenty-eight churches and missions). The progress of these Presbyterian Italian churches and missions in the matter of self-support is highly encouraging; forty-seven churches and missions reported over $14,000 contributed for all purposes in the last year. Over $75,000 annually is being contributed toward this work by Presbyterian churches and home mission agencies, not including funds made available by the Presbyterian Board of Education, funds contributed by the Presbyterian Board of Publication and Sabbath School Work for colportage and publication, nor funds contributed for the maintenance of the Italian Department in the Bloomfield Theological Seminary, New Jersey, and for schools and seminaries in other parts of the country. At least $100,000 annually is being contributed by the Presbyterian Church in the U. S. A. for this work of evangelization among Italians, over and above the amounts contributed by its Italian-speaking constituency.

AUSPICES AND ADMINISTRATION

The Presbyterian Church in the U. S. A. has at this time no unified approach to this field of evangelization nor central administrative agency. Work among Italians is largely carried out under the auspices of the presbyteries or local churches, and in two cases is directly administered by synods (state-wide organizations). Over twenty Presbyterian Italian churches and missions are directly under the auspices of a local church, and this type of work is increasing in favor.

The Board of Home Missions, through its Immigrant Work Office, with headquarters in New York, endeavors to survey the whole field and to keep in touch with all Presbyterian work among Italians. It maintains in this office a card catalog of all such enterprises in which are collated the annual statistics of churches and missions. The Board, however, has no administrative responsibility, excepting as hereafter mentioned under its industrial parish plan, and employs no field representative whose time is exclusively devoted to Italian evangelization. In the fiscal year ending March 31, 1916, the Board of Home Missions disbursed approximately $32,000 for Italian evangelization, or 38.5 per cent. of its total appropriation for immigrant work.

PERMANENT CONFERENCE ON ITALIAN EVANGELIZATION

In the spring of 1916, at a Conference on Italian Evangelization held at Princeton, New Jersey, which included both Italian-speaking pastors and workers, and representatives from presbyteries and home mission agencies concerned, steps were taken looking to the setting up of a Permanent Conference on Italian Evangelization. It was proposed that delegates to this Conference include all pastors and missionaries of the Presbyterian Church in the U. S. A. who are regularly and definitely engaged in work with Italians, together with representatives of presbyteries and synods concerned, the boards of the church, and other agencies. For the present, biennial conferences will be held. Standing committees will be elected as follows:

1. Survey of the field.
2. Literature and publications.
3. Education.
4. Fraternal relations.
5. Community service and evangelism.
6. Program and arrangements.

The General Assembly of the Presbyterian Church in the U. S. A. has given its approval to this plan, which will bring about a greater unity in Presbyterian work among Italians. The method is original in that it proposes a conference not of Italian-speaking pastors and workers alone, but of all those who are definitely interested in Presbyterian work with Italians. By this method, it is felt, the various points of view will be harmonized and a better understanding brought about.

TYPES AND CONDUCT OF WORK

Among seventy-four churches and missions for which data is available, it is of interest to note that seventeen are conducted as organized churches, thirty-six as missions, and twenty-one as departments of established American churches. This latter, or departmental work, in many cases is most encouraging in its efficiency. Where Italian communities have grown up about well-established American churches, an Italian-speaking pastor has been added to the staff and departmental work has been begun. Frequently, as in the case of John Hall Memorial Chapel, the Church of the Sea and Land, and Spring Street Church in New York, and Olivet Institute in Chicago, the facilities of well-equipped institutional churches have been placed at the service of the Italian community. Presbyterian work among Italians has now happily outgrown the primitive mission stage. Among seventy-six churches and missions, only ten are housed in a hall or store. Thirty-four have separate church buildings or chapels, and thirty-two share the equipment of older American churches. In a number of city and suburban communities, new and beautiful buildings have been erected for Italian communities. The First Italian Church, Philadelphia, the Italian churches in Germantown, the Presbyterian Italian Mission at Bernardsville, several churches in Newark, Holy Trinity Church and the Church of the Ascension in New York are all illustrative of excellent new buildings erected for Italian evangelization.

The Board of Church Erection has shared in the building of a number of churches and chapels employed for Italian evangelization. While new buildings are seeking to provide facilities for educational and social work, full recognition is being made of the Italian's interest in a reverent place for worship. Nearly all Presbyterian Italian churches and missions engage in educational or social work. Forty-two report English classes for men. Twenty have English classes for women. Twenty-two have civic clubs. English in nearly all cases is used in the Sunday-school.

PARISH METHODS

While Presbyterian work among immigrants recognizes the importance of a sympathetic approach to the various racial groups, and that Presbyterian churches and missions employing a foreign language are indispensable, it also recognizes the increasing implications of community life and interests. Its objective is not only a work of evangelization projected from such churches and missions and in a foreign language, but the establishing of a Christian community life. This latter aim necessarily calls for the coordination of many forces and a larger and more comprehensive undertaking. Under the leadership of the Immigrant Work Office of the Board of Home Missions, industrial communities are being ministered to through the so-called parish plan, which federates all Presbyterian churches or agencies in a given community and supplies additional leadership and increased facilities which may be used in common by the churches or missions at work in the field. Thus in the Range Parish, in an iron ore producing region in Minnesota, where there is a population of from 6,000 to 10,000 Italians, a staff of five parish workers is employed in addition to the regular pastors of Presbyterian churches on the Range. This staff includes two Italian-

37

speaking pastors whose work is sustained and strengthened in this larger fellowship. The American Parish in New York, under the direction of Rev. Norman M. Thomas, includes two Italian communities with a population exceeding 100,-000, with four centers of Presbyterian Italian work, two being fully organized Presbyterian Italian churches, the third an Italian department, and the fourth a settlement or neighborhood work with an Italian constituency.

TRAINING SCHOOLS

The Bloomfield Theological Seminary at Bloomfield, New Jersey, with an academic and collegiate department, has a department especially for the training of an Italian-speaking ministry. Italian-speaking students, however, are enrolled in Dubuque, Princeton, Auburn, and McCormick Theological Seminaries and other schools. The Home Missions Committee of the Presbytery of New York has established a graduate training course for lay workers and is offering to a group of college women courses in "Immigrant Backgrounds," including the Italians, with instruction in the Italian language. In 1917 this training course will be carried on under the auspices of Teachers' College, Columbia University, and will be open to all who fulfil the conditions of matriculation.

PUBLICATIONS

The Board of Publication and Sabbath School Work of the Presbyterian Church in the U. S. A., Philadelphia, publishes an Italian religious weekly, *L'Era Nuova*, Rev. Francis J. Panetta, Editor, 114 East 116th Street, New York City. The Board also issues Sunday-school cards and has other religious literature in the Italian language.

E. MISSION WORK AMONG ITALIANS IN CANADA

By Rev. F. C. Stephenson

Secretary Young People's Forward Movement, Missionary Society, Methodist Church, Canada

The Methodist and Presbyterian Churches are the only Protestant denominations which have organized mission work among the Italians in Canada. The Presbyterians have missions among this race in Montreal, Sault Ste. Marie, and Winnipeg. The Methodists carry on work among them in Sidney, B. C.; Montreal, Toronto, Hamilton, Niagara Falls, Welland, Thorold, North Bay, and Copper Cliff. In all of these places, regularly appointed and, for the most part, ordained Italian missionaries are in charge of the work. In other places throughout the Dominion mission work is being conducted among European foreigners, among whom are many Italians.

In Toronto the work is carried on in three centers and may be classified under three heads, namely, educational, institutional, and evangelistic, and is typical of what is being done in a modified form in other places. The educational work includes kindergarten classes in each center, a primary class at Elm Street Church, and night classes for adults in all branches. The institutional work consists of clubs for boys and girls, sewing classes, athletic and gymnastic exercises, mothers' meetings, also citizen and musical associations for the young men. The evangelistic effort consists of regular Sunday preaching services, Sunday-schools, private conferences, tract distribution, and open air services.

The Italians in Toronto, and for the most part throughout Canada, came from Sicily and Calabria, though there are quite a number who claim northern Italy as their birthplace. They are an industrious people and most of them engage in heavy labor, or work in fruit or small grocery stores. Others pursue the same varieties of occupation as our own English people. The majority are illiterate, but very bright and ambitious. They have artistic temperaments, are naturally very religious, and, though born Roman Catholics, have little love for the Church of Rome, and are in danger of becoming atheists unless early brought under the influence of some church that will inspire their confidence.

Housing conditions among them are not satisfactory. They live in the most congested areas in the city and in the poorest houses, which are usually over-crowded with the children of the family and men boarders. One result of our work among the Italians in Toronto has been the movement from the separate Catholic schools to the public schools. Many scores of families are sending their children to the public schools, to which they now pay their taxes. There is no assimilator like the public school, and we hope this movement will continue. In many other respects our work among the Italians is producing most gratifying results.

There is no class of European immigrants among whom missionary work is so successful as among the Italians. A larger number have been converted and are leading upright Christian lives. Their migratory habits disorganize our work somewhat at certain seasons of the year, but wherever the Christian Italians go they carry the leaven of the gospel with them. From the construction camps of the north, from the cities of the far west, from the trenches in Flanders, and from the army in the homeland, come cheering words testifying to the permanent blessings received by thousands who have come under the influence of the gospel in Canada.

F. WORK AMONG THE ITALIANS BY THE AMERICAN BIBLE SOCIETY

By Rev. W. I. Haven, D.D., *Secretary*

In 1834 the Board of Managers of the American Bible Society became perplexed with the problem of immigration from Europe into the United States, and decided that these strangers could not be left without the Bible, of which many of them knew nothing whatever.

Accordingly the secretaries were ordered to obtain from the British and Foreign Bible Society Scriptures in Polish, Swedish, Dutch, Portuguese, and Italian. The report of 1837 shows that thirty-one Italian Bibles and Testaments were put in circulation in the United States. The growth of this work can be more quickly understood by noting the number of Italian Scriptures issued in each tenth year since that date. In 1837 it was 31; 1847, 289; 1857, 753; 1867, 1,494; 1877, 4,499; 1887, 6,786. This seems to have been the real commencement of a large influx of Italians, for in 1897 the number of Italian Scriptures put in circulation was 20,427. In 1907 the number was 38,282. There has been steady increase until the beginning of the war. The last year before the war broke out the number was 101,779 volumes. The figures for the report of 1917, eighty years since the work began, are not yet available, but the report of 1916 shows issues in Italian in the United States of 95,581 volumes. The falling off is probably due to the fact that a considerable number of Italians returned to their native land to go into the army.

These figures show one thing which is repeated again and again by the agents of the Society. Rev. Dr. Eckard, secretary of the Atlantic Agency, writes from Philadelphia: "In general there has been more success with Italians than with any other nationality of Europeans who come to the United States." The same sentiment is expressed in other words by Rev. Dr. Kirkbride, secretary of the Northwestern Agency, who says, "No class of foreigners are more accessible to the gospel and give quicker and fuller response to the gospel teachings, than the Italians."

Our reports of the work among Italians for the year 1916 have come from the secretaries of the nine agencies of the American Bible Society, and the fields from which they report work among Italians are as follows: Rev. Dr. Eckard at Philadelphia: Pennsylvania and New Jersey. Rev. Mr. Porter, Richmond, Va.: Virginia, West Virginia, Georgia, and Florida, the most important work for Italians in this field being in Florida. Rev. Dr. Broome, secretary at Cincinnati, Ohio, reports work for Italians in Ohio and at Birmingham, Ala. Rev. Dr. Kirkbride, the secretary at Chicago, has carried on work among Italians, especially in Illinois, in Minnesota, in Wisconsin, and adjacent regions. Dr. Ragatz, secretary of the Agency at Denver, Col., reports good work in St. Louis, Kansas City, Denver, and some of the mining regions of Colorado, besides the states of Montana, Idaho, and Utah. The Rev. J. J. Morgan, secretary at Dallas, Texas, reports several correspondents and a number of voluntary workers in Louisiana, Texas, Arkansas, and Oklahoma. The number of Italians in these four last-named states is estimated at 95,000. Rev. Mr. Mell, secretary of the Agency at San Francisco, reports that there were no Italian colporteurs at work this year, but the coast cities have been carefully canvassed in the three years previous. The work among the Italians this year has been conducted by two colporteurs and eight other workers who were engaged in general Bible distribution. These sold about 3,000 volumes in Italian. Mr. Mell adds that 100,000 Italians scattered along the Pacific Coast have been carefully served to the extent of the ability of the Agency during five years past. Rev. H. J. Scudder, secretary of the Eastern Agency, having headquarters in Brooklyn, has the assistance of several Italian ministers who make a point of giving a certain amount of time to Bible distribution among their compatriots. In this way Scriptures were circulated in Harlem, in different parts of Westchester County, and on Long Island, during 1916, amounting to 673 Bibles, 2,770 Testaments, and 13,121 Gospels, a total of 16,564 volumes.

As we said above, full returns for the year 1916 are not yet available, so that a general view of the circulation in the whole of the United States is not possible. The work of these agencies among Italians is carried on by Italians so far as Italian colporteurs can be found to do the work. It has been increasingly difficult to find men suited for this work in recent years because of the number of missions and evangelical churches which need the assistance of every thoroughly converted Italian they can find for their local work. It is the experience of the secretaries, however, that to attempt to circulate Scriptures among Italians through people of another race is very disappointing. Where a thoroughly converted Italian could persuade and convince a number of men and women in every place and induce them to buy Testaments or at least portions or Gospels, requests from a man of another race, even speaking a little Italian, would be immediately rejected. In many parts of the United States the Bible Society agencies have partly avoided this difficulty by making arrangements with wide-awake Italian pastors to give a certain amount of their time to Bible distribution. The Bible Society supplies them with Scriptures without charge and gives them a liberal discount on Bibles which they buy for their people, and they make it a point to take the books to the outlying districts and let them go for less than cost, if necessary, provided there is a serious willingness to read them. In this way the pastors increase their circle of acquaintance, and the people gradually become accustomed to reading the Words of Life.

Work among the Italians is not without obstruction, and sometimes violent opposition. During the past year Mr. Morgan reports that at Bryan, Texas, some priests came in, gathered up all the Bibles and Testaments in town, and made a grand bonfire. The spirit of the Italian pastor at this place, as well as of the people who lost their Scriptures, is seen from the fact that he immediately sent to Mr. Morgan, ordering a second shipment of Scriptures to take the place of those which had been burned.

At Denver, Colorado, one Sunday morning a mob of Italians surrounded the evangelical church with the purpose of killing the pastor. It seemed for a time that he could not escape. A dozen policemen, however, made a valiant fight and succeeded in saving his life. Such disturbances are not frequent.

It is pleasant to know that the work of Bible distribution has rapidly sown the seed of permanent growth. In Denver the evangelical Italian church is said to be the largest such church connected with the Methodist Episcopal denomination throughout the world, and this church was built up by the cooperation of home missionaries with the Bible Society's colporteurs. Mr. Sibilio, now the pastor of the Spring Street Church in New York City, was a colporteur of the American Bible Society in Denver. As little by little a group of Bible readers collected about him, his work was followed up by mission workers, with the result which has been mentioned. In Cincinnati and in Cleveland, Ohio, there are strong and influential Italian churches which have grown in the same way from the small groups of Bible readers brought together by the colporteurs of the Bible Society. Dr. Kirkbride of Chicago, writing about his work in 1916 among the Italians, mentions Mr. Frank Malta, who was working at Kensington,

Illinois, as a colporteur of the American Bible Society. The Reformed Church asked the Bible Society agent to allow Mr. Malta to give part of his time to work in their mission. From this labor sprang the Italian church at Kensington, Illinois, connected with the Reformed Church in the U. S. A., and making rapid growth.

Another case of the same character is the Italian Presbyterian Church at Hibbing, Minn., which grew out of the work of a colporteur of the American Bible Society, the Presbyterian Home Mission Board undertaking the work and following it up energetically. Another of the Bible Society's Italian colporteurs, Mr. Lizzi, is working at Virginia, Minn., with the prospect of a church of Italians being organized there very soon.

This hasty glance at the work of the American Bible Society for Italians in the United States suggests that the field is most comprehensive and encouraging, that a certain amount of progress has already been made in evangelizing these interesting people, and finally, that the greater the cooperation between home missionaries and the Bible Society laborers, the more thorough and permanent are the results of sowing the seed.

G. THE AMERICAN TRACT SOCIETY AND THE ITALIANS

By Judson Swift, D.D.

General Secretary

The American Tract Society is carrying in stock about 250 titles in the Italian language. The Italian hymnal, both word and music editions, has had a large circulation, totaling 48,000 copies. *Pilgrim's Progress* in Italian has had a circulation of 5,000 copies in the past few years. The total circulation of books, tracts, and hymnals in the Italian language reaches a grand total of 1,250,000 copies. During the past four years seven colporteurs have been working among our Italian population, and over 30,000 copies of books and tracts have been distributed.

From our records, going back as far as twenty years, we learn that upwards of 350,000 volumes have been circulated in Italian, and the colporteurs working among the Italians during the past four years have made in round numbers 75,000 family visits, and held about 500 meetings. It is understood, of course, that the holding of meetings is the most limited part of their work, as their principal and almost sole duty is to go from house to house, and also address themselves to individuals wherever they meet them. The Tract Society has no colporteur missions or churches.

H. THE Y. M. C. A. AND IMMIGRANTS

By Peter Roberts, Ph.D.

The Y. M. C. A. will next summer complete a decade of special service to immigrants coming to North America. It owes an answer to the Christian church and to the nation of what service it has rendered immigrants during this time. This article aims to do this.

In the fall of 1907 a special secretary was put in charge of work for immigrants. By conferences with European and Canadian representatives of the Y. M. C. A., secretaries were stationed at twelve European ports, six Atlantic, and two Pacific ports. The work of these men was so coordinated that a man leaving Liverpool, or Naples, or Libau, met representatives of the Y. M. C. A. at many points en route, and found himself at destination with a card of introduction to the secretary of the local branch or a corresponding member. A Pole who knew not a word of English remembered the letters, Y. M. C. A., and meeting them at Fiume, New York, and Chicago, placed confidence in the men who wore caps with the letters on them, and found guidance, help, and direction when in difficulty. The three men on Ellis Island serving the Y. M. C. A. have command of twenty-three different tongues or dialects. The organization has conducted twelve experiments on board ships crossing the Atlantic by placing men to work among immigrants. The service is worth while, and we hope a way to finance such a work will be found when the tide of immigration becomes normal. One of the many by-products of the present war is the complete disorganization of the port work in Europe and Canada conducted by the Y. M. C. A.

The second step in the program of service is the manning of points of distribution, such as Philadelphia, Pittsburgh, Buffalo, St. Louis, Detroit, Chicago, San Francisco, etc. Immigrants coming to these centers by main railroad routes from ports of landing are dumped by the government and left to their own wits. At these points vultures watch for prey. The depot secretaries protect the newcomer, they cooperate with the police, in some instances are clothed with police power, and are in alliance with trustworthy car conductors and expressmen, and in every way try to defeat the cunning devices of men who rob and cheat the immigrant. When immigration is normal, fifty such men could well be stationed and render valuable service to immigrants at points of distribution.

The third and greatest part of the program is the intensive work done in immigrant colonies in North America. This part of the program has four distinct aims:

1. To teach the foreign-speaking men the English language. A special course of instruction has been prepared for this work, issued by the Association Press. Thousands of men have learned to talk, read, and write our language in these classes, and at present no fewer than 30,000 people of forty-two different nationalities or dialects, are being taught. Students in colleges, clerks, and foremen—men of all classes—are enlisted to teach, most of whom give their services free of charge. It is missionary work of the first importance.

2. The advanced course in English comprises civics, by which the alien is prepared to take out his naturalization papers. Thousands have been and are still being helped to pass the examination conducted by the court, and on several occasions, both east and west, the judges on the bench have spoken most enthusiastically of the effort, not only as help to aliens, but also as reacting upon their work, making it more agreeable and pleasing.

3. The alien should know something about the history of America, the men and women who have made the nation, the form of government, the customs and institutions of the country, the standards which obtain on the continent, and the opportunities awaiting them and their children in the "land of opportunity." This information is imparted to the newcomers by slide and reel, in halls and parks, in schools and on highways. Last year the work was done by 110 associations, and an estimate of the people reached in these gatherings was 500,000.

4. The foreign-speaking people bring with them to North America much that deserves conservation. The Association tries to open an avenue of self-expression to these people. Hence branches of the Y. M. C. A. all over the land plan and carry out concerts, entertainments, and socials, to which come representatives of as many as twenty-five distinct peoples, most of whom witness friends taking part in the entertainment. Peoples of various groups are given the chance to meet each other and meet native-born men who believe in democracy and the kingdom of God. These cosmopolitan meetings have brought together representatives of nations now at war, and they have broken bread together, joined their voices in singing our songs, and joined hands and hearts in pledging allegiance to the Stars and Stripes.

From these services, meeting the needs of immigrants, as well as rendering service to the state and nation, many spiritual experiences have come. The centers established in foreign-speaking colonies have been rallying places for the best among the group to come together; many of them have sought higher spiritual realities; many have been led to closer affiliation with the church of their fathers; some Bible classes have grown out of them; and in a hundred ways the secretaries in charge of the work have had, through personal interviews, opportunities to render the highest possible service man can give his brother.

I. DISTRIBUTION OF ITALIANS (FOREIGN-BORN AND NATIVE-BORN OF FOREIGN OR MIXED PARENTAGE) BY STATES, ACCORDING TO CENSUS OF 1910

Maine	4,588	Missouri	21,118	Nevada	4,012
New Hampshire	2,942	North Dakota	1,365	Washington	16,576
Vermont	6,617	South Dakota	1,603	Oregon	6,819
Massachusetts	130,577	Nebraska	4,840	California	102,618
Rhode Island	42,864	Kansas	5,630	Tennessee	3,758
Connecticut	89,773	Delaware	4,529	Alabama	4,676
New York	739,059	Maryland	11,169	Mississippi	3,859
New Jersey	191,849	Virginia	4,069	Arkansas	2,652
Pennsylvania	298,554	West Virgina	21,183	Louisiana	42,911
Ohio	62,332	North Carolina	770	Oklahoma	4,069
Indiana	9,140	South Carolina	548	Texas	14,013
Illinois	116,685	Georgia	972	Montana	8,001
Michigan	24,753	Florida	7,413	Idaho	2,627
Wisconsin	13,240	Kentucky	2,545	Wyoming	2,489
Minnesota	13,007	Arizona	2,189	Colorado	14,190
Iowa	7,560	Utah	4,228	New Mexico	22,826

J. ITALIAN POPULATION OF LEADING CITIES AND THE PERCENTAGE OF THE TOTAL POPULATION ACCORDING TO CENSUS OF 1910

City	Italian Population	Percentage	City	Italian Population	Percentage
Albany	3,278	3	Milwaukee	4,788	1
Baltimore	8,473	2	Newark	35,861	10
Boston	49,753	7	New Haven	*30,000	22
Buffalo	19,123	5	New Orleans	18,581	5
Bridgeport	*25,000	24	New York	544,449	11
Chicago	74,943	3	Philadelphia	76,734	5
Cincinnati	3,924	1	Pittsburgh	22,258	4
Cleveland	16,989	3	Providence	*30,000	13
Detroit	8,092	2	St. Louis	12,002	2
Jersey City	20,691	7	San Francisco	29,081	7
Los Angeles	6,461	2	Washington	4,553	1

K. LOCATION OF ITALIAN AGRICULTURAL COLONIES IN THE UNITED STATES

ASTI, CALIFORNIA. A colony of northern Italians, engaged in vine culture, produces 13,240,000 gallons of table wine a year. Six small towns in the vicinity are inhabited mainly by Italians, owning 5,000 acres of land and working 10,000 more. These Italians are from Tuscany and Piedmont. They acquired land at $50 an acre and it is now worth $200.

ALEXANDRIA, TENNESSEE, is in the cotton belt. Fifty families from northern Italy are working plantations there.

BRYAN, TEXAS. There are from 300 to 350 Italian families, 25,000 souls. This colony was founded twenty-five years ago by railroad laborers who sent for their families and friends as they earned the passage money. More than one half of the families own their own farms of from 30 to 160 acres on which they raise corn and some cotton. The entire colony owns a district covering eighteen square miles.

BOOMER, WEST VIRGINIA, contains over 500 Italian families, mostly Calabrians and Sicilians. The people live in cheap company houses almost entirely isolated from outside influences. A quick workman earns $5.00 a day in the

* Estimated. 1917.

soft coal mines, but the work is dangerous. Twenty-four men were recently killed by an explosion. The Italians here feel keenly the lack of proper school advantages for their children. It is estimated that there are between 8,000 and 10,000 Italians in the soft coal regions of West Virginia, lacking all Americanizing influences.

CANASTOTA, NEW YORK. About 15,000 southern Italians are raising onions and celery on what was previously waste land and are making it pay very well.

AUSTIN GULFPORT, NATCHEZ AND VICKSBURG, MISSISSIPPI. There are several groups of families from Bologna anl vicinity that are successfully raising cotton.

DAPHNE AND LAMBERT, ALABAMA. There are small colonies in which every family possesses from ten to twenty-five acres of land and raises sugar and cotton.

DICKINSON, TEXAS. This is a community of 500 Sicilians who are doing market gardening. Their prosperity is swelling the numbers in the colony.

HAMMONTON, NEW JERSEY, has a population of nearly 4,000 Italians profitably engaged in raising berries, peaches, and vegetables. One Italian made $15,000 from his peach crop the past year.

INDEPENDENCE, LOUISIANA. The Italian colony here has a good location on an island in the Mississippi River, sixty-five miles north of New Orleans. There are about 200 Sicilian families from the province of Palermo, who raise strawberries. Eighty own their farms of from 20 to 80 acres. They cleared the land themselves and it now yields them incomes of $75 to $100 an acre.

Of the success of Italian immigration in Louisiana, some idea may be gained by the following letter from C. L. Bush of Independence (Lord, Trenor, and Barrows, *The Italian in America*, page 72): "Twenty years ago land could be bought in and around the town for $1.00 to $5.00 per acre that is now selling readily at $25 to $100 per acre. One tract here of 1,500 acres sold twenty-five years ago for $1,600. Two hundred acres of it was sold a few weeks ago for $10,400. One will ask what was the principal cause of the development. The answer must be the Italian immigration, which has come here and improved the conditions in respect to production. The majority of farmers have done away with negro labor. Why? Because the negroes are generally shiftless, whereas the Italian laborer is a success. The question of his desirability as a citizen is often asked. I can say that thus far, in our twelve or fifteen years' experience with them, they have given no trouble to any one. They are prompt to pay their debts at the stores, meet their paper at the banks when due and often before. I do not think there is a case on record in this parish where the state has had to prosecute them for a crime or misdemeanor, and that is saying a good deal, when we consider that there are 150 to 200 families living here and every berry season probably 500 more come to assist in harvesting the crop."

KNOBVIEW, MISSOURI. Contains fifty families who left Sunnyside, Arkansas, after malaria broke out there. Twenty of the Italian families have joined them. All have good homes and have paid for their land, which is worth $50 an acre. The men divide their time between working their fields and on the railroad. This colony was founded under the auspices of the Roman Catholic Church.

MARSHFIELD, MISSOURI. Contains another agricultural Italian colony composed of Tyrolese, men accustomed to mountain life, who find this region of the Ozark Mountains particularly congenial to them. They raise cereals and live stock.

SOUTHEASTERN TEXAS. There is a number of small colony groups of Italians working in the rice fields and lumber camps. Round about the cities of Galveston, Houston, Austin, San Antonio, and others are to be found settlements of Italians who devote themselves to market gardening.

SUNNYSIDE, ARKANSAS. This colony was founded by Austin Corbin and Prince Ruspoli, but great misfortunes due to climate and location, where strict sanitary precautions should be observed, have driven large numbers of Italians from the locality. There are still one hundred families, tenants of the estate, who remain because of the large profits in growing cotton. One man, after working a number of years, returned to Italy with $8,000 in his pocket. Many others are not so fortunate but spend a large part of their profits in trying to keep in good health. The company that runs the colony has charged the Italians exorbitant prices for land, tools, and farm animals, even as high at the very beginning as $160 per acre, this sum payable after twenty years, if so desired.

TONTITOWN, ARKANSAS. Father Bandini took a group of Italian fugitives from Sunnyside twenty years ago to this region in the Ozark Mountains which he had previously carefully examined. The land was a wilderness of scrub pines. The Italians cleared the land and are now, after two decades, successfully raising apples, peaches, grapes, and all kinds of vegetables. Each of the eighty families owns its own land and house. Each family possesses from 20 to 160 acres. The community life centers about Father Bandini, the church and the parish school he has built there. In strong contrast with Sunnyside, there is here good air, good water, and a climate similar to that in Italy.

ST. ELENA, NORTH CAROLINA. This is another agricultural colony of fifteen Venetian families induced to come to this region by the North Carolina Truck and Development Company. Each family was sold ten acres at an average price of $30 an acre, a sum far above the land's value at that time.

VALDESE, NORTH CAROLINA. A colony of 400 Italians from the Waldensian valleys in Italy, who went there to found a religious colony. Uncleared pine land was sold the pioneers by a land improvement company. The Italians made the best of the situation, cleared the land, and now raise corn, grapes, fruits, vegetables, and cow peas for fodder. About sixty families are there at present, most of them owning their land. Shortly after the establishment of the colony, a cotton mill was built which now employs 500 young men and women, a good many Americans among them, who prefer the factory to the farm. Consequently the farms are not so well tilled as formerly. The Waldensian Church, which was built by the Italians themselves (the only work done by an outsider was that of a certain section of the roof), is the center of the community life.

VINELAND, NEW JERSEY. This region has forty square miles of territory occupied by 7,000 Italians, each family holding from ten to 160 acres. This colony is one of the oldest in the country, having been established by Cavaliere Secchi De Casale, an Italian patriot, in 1873. The sandy soil is adapted to grape culture, garden truck, and fruit. The farmers find their markets in New York and Philadelphia. The Italian houses are well built, furnished with carpets, American furniture, and pianos. These homes are worth from $1,000 to $7,000.

There are also innumerable smaller groups of ten to fifteen and even thirty families scattered through the South and West. Near San Francisco these groups are engaged in market gardening, and the women and children work in the fruit canneries. About Salt Lake City, Utah, are also to be found small groups of Italians engaged in market gardening. In Louisiana there are ten small towns near New Orleans containing from ten to one hundred families engaged in market gardening and cultivation of sugar cane and cotton, while in the regions of Tampa and Pensacola, Florida, there are numerous small Italian settlements devoted to peach-growing or making of cigars.

L. DIRECTORY OF PROTESTANT ITALIAN MISSION STATIONS OR FIELDS IN UNITED STATES

I. BAPTIST

Massachusetts
1. Boston (First)
2. Boston (Second)
3. East Boston
4. Framingham
5. Franklin
6. Haverhill
7. Hyde Park
8. Lawrence
9. Lynn
10. Mansfield
11. Milford
12. Monson
13. Springfield
14. Wakefield
15. Worcester

Connecticut
16. Ansonia
17. Bridgeport
18. Bristol
19. Hartford
20. Southington
21. Meriden
22. Norwich
23. New Haven (First)
24. New Haven (Second)
25. Shelton
26. Waterbury
27. Wallingford
28. Winsted

Rhode Island
29. Providence (First)
30. Providence (Second)
31. Natick

New York
32. Batavia
33. Brooklyn (First)
34. Brooklyn (Strong Place)
35. Buffalo (First)
36. Buffalo (Second)
37. Buffalo (Cedar Street)
38. Gloversville
39. Mount Vernon
40. New York (First)
41. New York (Second Avenue)
42. New York (Judson Memorial)
43. New York (Bronx)
44. Ossining
45. Port Chester
46. Rochester
47. Syracuse
48. Utica
49. White Plains

New Jersey
50. Camden
51. Hoboken
52. Milburn
53. Newark
54. Orange
55. Passaic
56. Silver Lake
57. Trenton

Pennsylvania
58. Jeannette
59. Pittsburgh
60. Philadelphia
61. Philadelphia (Settlement)
62. Scottdale
63. Uniontown

Vermont
64. Barre

Michigan
65. Detroit

West Virginia
66. Boomer
67. Longacre

Ohio
68. Youngstown
69. East Youngstown
70. Cleveland

Florida
71. West Tampa

Louisiana
72. Amite
73. Independence

Texas
74. Beaumont
75. Dickinson
76. Galveston
77. Houston

Wisconsin
78. Racine

California
79. Los Angeles
80. Fresno

Oregon
81. Portland

District of Columbia
82. Washington

II. CONGREGATIONAL

California
1. *San Francisco (Green Street)

Connecticut
2. Branford
3. *Bridgeport
4. *Hartford
5. Kensington
6. New Britain
7. *New Haven
8. Saugatuck
9. Stony Creek
10. Torrington

46

CONGREGATIONAL—(*Continued*)

Connecticut
11. *Waterbury
12. Winsted

Illinois
13. *Chicago (Ewing Street)
14. *La Salle
15. Oglesby
16. *Spring Valley
† Maine
17. Biddeford
18. Hallowell
19. Livermore Falls
20. Lewiston
21. Mexico
22. Millinocket
23. Millinocket (East)
24. North Jay
  ‡Portland
25. Rockland
26. Riley
27. *Rumford
28. Smith's Crossing
29. Stonington
30. Virginia
31. Westbrook

Massachusetts
32. *North Plymouth
33. *Pittsfield

New Jersey
34. Cliffside
35. *Grantwood
36. Jersey City
37. *Northvale

New York
38. Brooklyn
39. Buffalo

Rhode Island
40. Providence (Silver Lake Region)
41. §House of Good-will, Boston, Mass
42. §Endicott House, Worcester, Mass.
43. §Emerson House, Chicago, Ill.
44. §Bethlehem Institute, Los Angeles, Cal.

* A regularly constituted church.
† Missions in Maine are branches of American churches without Italian workers.
‡ A union enterprise.
§ Settlements under Congregational auspices without attached missions, yet serving Italian groups with religious purpose.

III. EVANGELICAL ASSOCIATION

Illinois
1. Chicago

Wisconsin
2. Milwaukee
3. Racine and Kenosha

IV. LUTHERAN
1. Philadelphia, Pa.

V. METHODIST EPISCOPAL AND METHODIST EPISCOPAL, SOUTH

New York
1. Albany
2. Astoria
3. Buffalo
4. Dobbs Ferry
5. Elmira
6. Frankfort
7. Jamestown
8. New York (East Side Parish)
9. New York (Five Points)
10. New York (Corona)
11. New York (Jamaica)
12. New York (Jefferson Park)
13. New York (People's Home)
14. New York (Bronx)
15. New York (Washington Square)
16. Rochester
17. Schenectady
18. Syracuse
19. Troy
20. Utica
21. Yonkers

Pennsylvania
22. Altoona
23. Clearfield
24. Hillsville
25. New Castle
26. Oakmont
27. Philadelphia
28. Pittsburgh
29. Reading
30. Scranton
31. Wilkesbarre

New Jersey
32. Jersey City
33. Newark
34. Paterson
35. Rahway

Connecticut
36. Middletown
37. New Haven

Massachusetts
38. Boston
39. Fall River

Ohio
40. Youngstown
41. Columbus

Illinois
42. Chicago
43. Joliet

Maryland

44. Baltimore
45. Cumberland

Indiana

46. Indianapolis

Maine

47. Portland

Rhode Island

48. Providence

Delaware

49. Wilmington

Florida

50. Tampa

Louisiana

51. New Orleans

Colorado

52. Pueblo
53. Denver

Montana

54. Butte

California

55. San Francisco

Alabama

56. Birmingham

Missouri

57. Kansas City
58. St. Louis

Texas

59. Thurber

West Virginia

60. Welch

VI. PRESBYTERIAN (U. S. A.)

New York

1. Auburn
2. Binghamton
3. Brooklyn (Gregg Chapel)
4. Brooklyn (Elton Street)
5. Brooklyn (Central)
6. Endicott
7. Middletown
8. Mount Kisco
9. New Rochelle
10. New York (Labor Temple)
11. New York (East Harlem)
12. New York (Holy Trinity)
13. New York (Ascension)
14. New York (Calvary)
15. New York (Sea and Land)
16. New York (Spring Street)
17. New York (Madison Square)
18. New York (Covenant)
19. New York (John Hall Memorial)
20. New York (Bethlehem Chapel)
21. New York (Church of the Gospel)
22. Nyack
23. Pleasantville
24. Port Chester
25. Rochester
26. Rome
27. Schenectady
28. Solvay
29. White Plains

Pennsylvania

30. Berwick
31. Bristol
32. Chester
33. Clairton
34. Dunmore
35. Easton
36. Edge Hill
37. Germantown
38. Greensburg

Pennsylvania

39. Hazelton
40. Johnstown

41. McKeesport
42. Midland
43. Norristown
44. Old Forge
45. Philadelphia (First)
46. Philadelphia (Second)
47. Philadelphia (Tioga)
48. Pittsburgh
49. Pittston
50. Roseto
51. Salemville
52. Scranton
53. Windber
54. New Alexandria

New Jersey

55. Asbury Park
56. Bernardsville
57. Beverly
58. Burlington
59. East Orange
60. Elizabeth
61. Garfield
62. Hammonton
63. Jersey City
64. Montclair
65. Newark (East Side)
66. Newark (Olivet Chapel)
67. Newark (Friendly Center 4)
68. Newark (Friendly Center 5)
69. Paterson
70. Plainfield
71. Princeton
72. Red Bank
73. Riverside
74. Trenton
75. Vineland

Minnesota

76. Chisholm
77. Virginia
78. Eveleth
79. Gilbert
80. Hibbing
81. Keewatin
82. Mountain Iron

VI. PRESBYTERIAN (U. S. A.) —(*Continued*)

Illinois
83. Chicago (Olivet Institute)
84. Chicago (Italian Christian Institute)
85. Chicago (First)
86. Chicago (Church of Our Savior)
87. Chicago (Samaritan House)
88. Chicago (Center Mission)
89. Chicago (Burr Mission)

Ohio
90. Cincinnati
91. Cleveland (West Side)
92. Cleveland (Beckwith Memorial)
93. Bellaire
94. Steubenville

Indiana
95. Clinton
96. Gary

Massachusetts
97. Quincy
98. Somerville

Michigan
99. Calumet
100. Detroit

West Virginia
101. Clarksburg
102. Follansbee

California
103. San José

Colorado
104. Trinidad

Delaware
105. Wilmington

Maryland
106. Baltimore

Wisconsin
107. Hurley

VII. PROTESTANT EPISCOPAL

Massachusetts
1. Boston
2. East Boston

Connecticut
3. Hartford
4. New Haven

New York
5. New York (San Salvatore)
6. New York (Sant' Ambrogio)
7. New York (Saint Mark's)
8. New York (Ellis Island)
9. New York (Calvary)
10. New York (Grace)
11. New York (Bronx)
12. New York (Saint John's Cathedral)
13. New York (East 111th Street)
14. New York (Stater Island)
15. New York (Brooklyn)
16. Oyster Bay

Pennsylvania
17. Easton (First)
18. Easton (Second)
19. Philadelphia (First)
20. Philadelphia (Second)
21. Philadelphia (Third)

Maryland
22. Baltimore

Michigan
23. ....

Illinois
24. Chicago

VIII. REFORMED IN U. S. A.

New York
1. Newburg
2. Union Hill

New Jersey
3. Hackensack

IX. UNITED PRESBYTERIAN

Pennsylvania
1. Mount Pleasant
2. New Kensington
3. Pittsburgh (First)
4. Pittsburgh (Second)
5. Wilmerding

Rhode Island
6. Providence

California
7. Los Angeles

Washington
8. Tacoma

DENOMINATION	Number of Churches or Missions Doing Italian Work.	Number of Italian Church Members	Number of Church Schools with Italian Pupils	Number of Italian Church School Pupils	Salaried Italian Workers engaged in Italian work.	Total Contributions of Italian members for all purposes.	Total expenditure of the denomination for Italian work.
Baptist (Northern Convention) ..	82	2,750			60	$9,000	$69,030
Congregational	44	983		1,000	19	961	13,279
†Evangelical Association	3						
Methodist Episcopal and †Methodist Episcopal, South.....	60	5,241‡	42	4,927	52	7,357§	45,000
Presbyterian in U. S. A..........	107	4,800		8,000	70	14,253	100,000
†Protestant Episcopal	24						
†Reformed in U. S. A.............	3						
†United Presbyterian	8						
Total	326	13,774	42	13,927	201	$31,571	$227,309

* Table does not include many fields cultivated, and large sums of money expended by local churches are not reported.
† Statistics not included, except for the number of churches or missions.
‡ Of this number, 1,839 are probationers.
§ The sum reported by 46 churches.

N. SURVEY OF ITALIAN WORK IN NEW YORK CITY, 1912

By Rev. Howard V. Yergin

This is the latest available summary of Protestant work for Italians in Greater New York. While made five years ago, it will serve as a basis in measuring the growth of work with Italians since that time.

DENOMINATION	Total number Missions	Number Reporting	Form of Work			Founded			Added last year	Total Membership	Sunday School	Annual Cost	Congregational Contributions	Type of Building			Value of Independent Buildings	Paid Workers	No. Native Pastors	
			Mission	Department	Organized	1904	1904-1909	1910-1912						Stone, etc.	Dept.	Independent				
Presbyterian	11	11	0	7	4	0	7	4	270	1,114	1,493	$22,440	$2,282	2	6	3	$130,000	14	11	Also have neighborhood house.
Baptist	7	6	1	3	2	5	0	1	55	946	680	9,537	717	1	4	1	45,000	14	4	One mission (Harlem) now discontinued. Strong Place Baptist, Brooklyn, has a colporteur for Italians; work not reported here.
Methodist	9	9	1	4	4	4	4	1	184	897	951	17,000	1,345	3	4	2	125,000	6	5	York St., Brooklyn, soon to be discontinued.
Episcopal	8	5	0	1	4	2	2	1	239	1,190	610	9,373	1,637	1	1	3	320,000	14	6	St. Mark's Chapel, 10th St. and Ave. A, has a new work not included in these figures. Two not reporting. Also have a Neighborhood House.
N. Y. City Mission	3	2	0	0	2	2	0	0	54	775	780	20,000	550	0	0	2	35,000	12	2	New work at Olivet Mission not included in these figures.
Brooklyn City Mission	2	2	0	0	2	0	1	1	70	190	205	1,900	200	1	1	0	......	2	1	
Waldensian	1	1	0	0	1	0	1	0	0	350	0	600	600	0	1	0	......	0	1	
Independent	1	1	0	0	1	0	1	0	57	62	22	2,000	25	0	0	1	3,700	2	1	Presbyterian, but supported by private enterprise.
United Presbyterian	1	0	0	0	0	0	0	0	0	0	0	0	0	0	0	0	0	0	0	One mission, not reporting.
Congregational	1	1	0	1	1	1	0	0	14	60	0	2,600	315	1	0	0	......	1	1	
Total	44	38	2	15	21	14	15	9	943	5,584	4,741	$85,450	$7,101	9	17	12	$868,700	65	32	Three new works not included; three not reporting.

Selections From
THE ASSEMBLY HERALD

THE ASSEMBLY HERALD

An Easter Prayer

COME, Lord, for thy people are
    praying;
Thy chariot wheels are delaying;
A world is rocking with gloom.
Oh! Steady the faith that is shaken,
In our spirits expectancy waken
Of the pledge of the empty tomb.

OH! 'List to thine orphans crying,
    To a world in its weariness
        dying,
Come back to thine own.
Put thy hand on the nations' mad-
    ness,
Speak thy word to the people's sad-
    ness,
Oh! Master ascend thy throne.

—*Charles L. Thompson.*

Vol. 24, No. 3

MARCH, 1918

They of Italy Salute You

Rev. Howard V. Yergin

After graduation from Auburn Seminary, Mr. Yergin spent a year in Italy, under a Home Board Immigration Fellowship. Upon his return to America, he became Superintendent of Boyle Center, a community church in St. Louis.

I WRITE of a land sore wasted, and of men long suffering,—of Southern Italy, "the Garden of the Gods," but for thirty centuries the bloody battleground of race upon race of men. Never until the coming of the red-shirted Garibaldi and his immortal Thousand in 1860 was the South master of itself. And worst of all the tyrannies was the last, the rule of the Bourbons, whose kingdom was described by Gladstone as "the negation of God set up into a system of government." Bourbon law forbade improvements, even the removal of a stone from the road; declared it treason for more than three persons to meet together; stuffed reeking prisons with rotting prisoners, cast there on suspicion, untried and left to die as best they might amid the cold and wet and vermin of the dungeons.

Only as one carries in his mind this background of centuries of misrule, oppression and cruelty can he do justice and deal fairly with the heavily afflicted people of the sunny Southland of Italy. Such antecedents have rendered the Southern Italian individualistic, a bit fatalistic perhaps, stolid, uncommunicative, often a law unto himself, illiterate, unprogressive, unreligious. Through the centuries it has been literally "every man for himself," and a very real devil of the government to take the straggler. Whatever he might do, the government was quite apt to undo. The peasant learned to accept things as they come. "Diu guverna," said a farmer near Girgenti in reply to my question why he did not make certain improvements— "God runs things; what's the use of my trying?" Stolid and uncommunicative is he, because centuries of government spies and secret agents have forced him so to be; a law unto himself, because the government took no account of justice and judgment, and vengeance and justice must be sought by individuals. The Mafia in its inception and original purpose was identical with the Vigilantes and the Ku-Klux of the United States.

The Southern Italian is illiterate, not only because the government provided no schools, but because it, aided and abetted by the Papal Curia, discouraged and even penalized education. The daughter of the Duchess of Cassano completed her education in a convent in 1850 without being able to read or write. The Southern Italian is unprogressive because it cost his fathers too much to be progressive—in fact it was ruination. All improvements were taxed beyond their value, as indeed was everything else. Chickens, for instance, were taxed as chickens; they were taxed also on their feathers, on their eggs, on their carcasses after death, and even on their bones!

The edict of Constantine in the year 313 made Christianity the official religion of the Empire, but did little more than change the labels, leaving contents undisturbed. By a simple change of name, prayers to Jupiter became forthwith prayers to Jehovah; statues of Cybele—otherwise known as Diana of the Ephesians—became statues of the Virgin Mary; monks and nuns of the old religion were ready at hand for the new religion, the tonsure and habit of Diana's priests continuing to the present day in the tonsure and habit of the priests of the monks of Rome. Through all the centuries following 313, the Roman Church has little concerned itself with the personal or social religion of its children.

147

One encounters among the Italians of the South unlovely conditions, physical, mental, spiritual; but always let him ask whether, if sprung from such antecedents, he himself would be as good or do as well as they. Picking one's way through the noisome streets of an Italian city, and finding that there is still more truth than hyperbole in Mark Twain's description of the Civita Vecchia, let him understand and pity. "The people live in alleys two yards wide, which have a smell about them which is peculiar but not entertaining. These alleys are paved with stone, carpeted with deceased cats and decayed rags and decomposed vegetable tops and remnants of old boots—all soaked with dishwater." It is thus that "Jumbletown" in Denver, Phelan Creek in St. Paul, the "horrible blocks" in St. Louis, the East Side in New York, and scores of other Italian Colonies in the United States become understandable. The Italian may seem stupid, indifferent to sanitation or hygiene, superstitious and spiritually blind; but let us pause to understand him, then pity him, and help to right the wrong of centuries.

And the United States has done much to right the wrong. Perhaps unconsciously, or with little alturistic motive, the Italian has here been brought into contact with boundless resources of material, ideals and energy, with which none can come in touch without some degree of influence therefrom. Even in Termini-Imerese, a fishing village near Palermo, as long ago as 1900, almost every house was owned by its occupant, and every fisherman owned his own boat—thanks to careful savings in America. Before the present War, a steady stream of honestly hardearned American gold flowed back into every nook and corner of Italy, especially to the South. That gold was used to purchase many a small "terreno," to pay off hoary debts, to build homes, as well as to buy clothes or food and even some of the luxuries of life. In a hilltown in Umbria, I came one day upon a house with window sashes and frames. "Rinpatriati—returned emigrants" was the explanation. And inside were scoured floors, rugs, American furniture, and even an American range. All the impulse to

this cleanliness and better things had been born in Pittsburgh!

In South Italy in 1872 there was 85 per cent of illiteracy. Without school facilities and without funds, the new government with grim earnestness set itself to the tremendous task of modernizing Italy. But even where school opportunities were provided, the response of the people was at first discouragingly slight. Of late years the demand for

A SOUTH ITALIAN TOWN

schools has become general, and so insistent that even adequate funds cannot provide enough school facilities. Night schools and even holiday schools are being used to supplement the work of the day schools. Among the strong reasons for this is the desire to communicate with friends and relatives in America, and to prepare themselves for a possible journey hither. It has been discovered that even a small amount of learning is advantageous in America.

Spiritually too the United States has benefited Italy. But let it not be forgotten that the Waldenses, the world's oldest evangelical Christians, "faithful for centuries," promptly seized upon Victor Emmanuel's decree of religious toleration in 1870, and burst forth from their Cottian Alps to carry the light of the gospel into the remotest and darkest corners of the Kingdom. Such instances as the following are by no means few.

In 1912 a young man, Pasquale Calderaro, returned to his native village in the Abruzzi to marry. He had been genuinely converted in New York. "Most zealous," say the Minutes of the Waldensian Synod, 1913, "Calderaro commenced an active propaganda among his relatives and friends. There were already adherents when the Evangelist from Campobasso went there to hold his first service, at which he had about three hundred hearers." But with genuine humility, be it noted, Calderaro refused to become a professional religious worker, because he believed his education insufficient and preferred to work as a layman among laymen. He has since returned to America, and is laboring in a shoe factory in Cincinnati, faithfully witnessing for his Master as he works. Salle, in the Abruzzi, has now a strong church, founded in a similar manner, some eighteen years ago, by returned emigrants who had been converted in the Methodist Mission in Astoria, Long Island. Other Evangelical churches throughout the Kingdom have had similar origin.

But let us not be too complacent about the good we are doing Italy. There is a dark—a very dark—page in the record of our influence. An Italian writer, who has had exceptional opportunity for studying the question, says that twenty per cent of those returning from America to the Abruzzi have contracted tuberculosis in the United States. Before 1887 tuberculosis was practically unknown in Southern Italy. Since then it has gradually decreased in the North, but alarmingly increased in the South.

The same writer (Amy Bernardi, in Italia Randagia) also asserts that the effects of immorality are spreading throughout Italy as a result of emigrants who return from America. Her pictures of Italian lodgings in the United States, with their numerous boarders and consequent lack of privacy, with the inevitable decline in morals and growth of attendant evils, are not pleasant, but not overdrawn, as any mission or settlement worker can testify.

"They of Italy salute you." They ask your sympathy, your prayers, your co-operation, as they struggle into the light of today, out of the long dark past.

Six Years in Little Italy

Rev. Norman M. Thomas

Mr. Thomas is the Chairman of the American Parish, a federation of Presbyterian churches and social agencies on the Upper East Side of New York City, a new adventure in City Missions, and the pioneer of the Industrial Parish as fostered by the Home Board.

WILL the reader please consider the difficulty of writing the short article the editor demands on this subject? The possibilities are many. For example:

We could try the picturesque approach, and begin by describing the great throngs which crowd the streets on the day of the Feast of Our Lady of Mt. Carmel. Arches of light then transform the tenement streets. There is a strange procession of chanting women behind a banner or image of the Virgin. Children are held up to pin money on that banner and win the Virgin's favor. Street stands display wax models of diseased parts of the body, and painted candles, great and small, to be given as votive offerings within the church.

Or we might try the sentimental style, and fall to musing upon the pretty Italian faces of many of the little girls, and the great contrast between their lives and the lives their parents lived in many a picturesque village of Sunny Italy—villages whose beauty was but slight consolation for the bitter poverty of the people. Then there are the women so often old before their time. How many of them can look back on that "long road of woman's memory," of which Jane Addams has recently given us a glimpse.

Or we could talk in terms of statistics, and tell of a colony of some 90,000 Italians of the first and second generations; of blocks peopled by those coming from one particular district in Italy, which usually have their own stores and druggists and saloons. In some cases more than 3,000 people live in one of these blocks. More significant still, we could try to find out the average income of our neighbors—an income which in a very great majority of cases falls from $150 to $200 short of the income of $980 estimated by social investigators to be necessary in New York for the proper support of a family of five, and many of the families here have more than five! These figures are not dry, if one considers them with sympathy and with understanding. In them you will find no small share of the explanation of juvenile delinquency, of the retarded development of children, and of all the ills that weigh so heavily upon our neighbors.

star athlete, a good student in a certain preparatory school, a real force for Christianity wherever he is. Alas! most of the tales of crime in our district are more serious, and to few of them can we add a record of conversion. The district has had an unenviable supremacy in the percentage of crimes of violence for all too many years; and the gangs and individual criminals reveal the terrible workings of man's passions and greed. It is fair to add that the intelligent action of the police and their co-operation with social agencies have, within the last few years

GIRLS AT SAMARITAN HOUSE,
A NEIGHBORHOOD WORK IN AN ITALIAN COMMUNITY, CHICAGO

Or there is the sensational approach to the problem, thus: It was the night before Christmas. A working man was taking his small wages to buy food and some simple presents for his children. Suddenly from out the shadows of a tenement leaped two boys, only fifteen years old, armed with guns. They forced the man to stand and deliver. As he turned over his little roll of bills, he remarked sorrowfully: "Boys, that's all I've got, and tomorrow is Christmas!" The boys' hearts were touched, and they gave back the money. As they did so, the man said: "God bless you boys, and give you luck!" And, added one of the boys some months later, "God did. We went over to the Park, and stuck up a guy for $100." The best part of the story is that one of the two boys who thus started on the road of crime is today a

brought about a change for the better.

Any short article about one of our so-called immigrant colonies is at best much like a caricature, because of overemphasis upon this or that aspect. Here are people, often ignorant, illiterate, dazed by the life of the new world, with no sense of economic security, forced to live in barrack-like tenements, supplied with cheap commercialized amusements, unused to democracy in Church or State, yet filled with tremendous possibilities of development. They are men of like passions, desires and hopes with the rest of us, but perhaps more generous, more willing to share with their neighbors. Just before I wrote these lines, there came word of a big family too proud to ask help anywhere. The father was sick. They had no furniture. One neighbor lent his own mattress—he was an anarchist somewhat notorious for his gospel of hate of existing conditions in Church and State. Another neighbor lent a bed—he was a member of our Church of the Ascension, but so poor that his family are continually undernourished. A third took some of the children to live for a time with him. It is a spirit like this that will help to make the new world we seek.

From a missionary standpoint, an Italian colony is on the whole an encouraging field for work. Competent and energetic Missionaries get excellent results, both in numbers and in character-building. The Church of the Ascension, in the heart of the Italian colony of which I have spoken, is a notable proof of this statement. Under the efficient leadership of its Pastor, the Rev. Francisco Pirazzini, it has in some ten years of life attained an active membership of over 700.

The justification for Protestant work is to be found in the moral and spiritual conditions of the colony. There is too often no choice for the people between rapidly increasing agnosticism, religious indifference, or open hatred of religion on the one hand, and a particularly superstitious form of Roman ecclesiasticism on the other. Of course the Roman Church, here as elsewhere, has its better side, and Protestantism has itself too many faults to assume a harshly critical or intolerant attitude. Nevertheless we are abundantly warranted in preaching here the religion of Jesus as we understand it. The indirect results of our witness are, perhaps, more important than the direct. The good we do is measured not by the number of church members but by the higher ethical standards and the new spirit of understanding, sympathy and religious tolerance in the community.

These six years in Little Italy have taught me two lessons which (at first sight, though not upon longer thought) may seem contradictory. First of all we Americans—especially Christian Americans—who want to be of service to immigrants or to our own country and Church, must have a sympathetic understanding of these foreign people, of their historical backgrounds, and if possible of their language. City streets are schools of pseudo-americanism, which makes children

talk rather contemptuously of their fathers as "dagoes" and "wops." Real Americanism is a process not of tearing down but of building up. The important facts, however, for consideration regarding the life of industrial workers in New York or elsewhere are not racial but economic. I have lived these years as neighbor not only to a large Italian colony but to a polyglot community, and to small Hungarian and Slovak groups. The colors of the picture vary with the language and racial inheritance of the different people; but in every case the lines are the same, and are determined by our political, economic and social conditions.

As Christians, our deepest concern is to bring the spirit of Christ to bear upon those conditions of fundamental injustice in our industrial life which keep men from earning a living wage; which deny them any sort of democracy in industry, and then expect them to use political or religious democracy wisely. Mission churches can do much good, but they can never Christianize our communities until the Church itself and (through it) the social order are Christianized. Christ's religion is profoundly revolutionary, and none the less so because the instrument He would have us use is love and not hate.

The supreme justification of our missionary efforts is in the degree in which we can promote and make effective the love of God and of one's neighbor, in no sentimental sense but as a cleansing, inspiring, organizing principle for the rebuilding of our social life the world around. Ours is the faith that God "hath made of one blood all nations of men to dwell on all the face of the earth"; and ours must be the difficult practice of universal brotherhood. It is in these great matters that the Church has failed to live up to its duty and opportunity. In the sight of Jesus who told the Pharisees that publicans and sinners would enter the Kingdom of God before them, the responsibility for the sin and misery about us lies far more upon us comfortable folk than upon those toilers upon whose bent backs the structure of our civilization so largely and so cruelly rests. God help us to meet by loyal endeavor our opportunity to remake life in the spirit of Christ!

Training an Italian Ministry for America

Rev. Professor Agide Pirazzini, Ph.D., S.T.D.,

DIRECTOR OF ITALIAN DEPARTMENT, BIBLE TEACHERS' TRAINING SCHOOL, NEW YORK CITY

THERE are times in the history of the Church when God sees fit to use and to bless an ignorant ministry; but nowhere in Scripture is such a ministry represented as normal. Far too much has been made of the fact that the Apostles were "ignorant and unlearned men." The days in which they lived and the conditions under which they preached were strictly exceptional. Least of all in such an age as this, when "the schoolmaster is abroad" as never before, can the ministry afford to be mentally unfurnished. Students and thinkers ministers must ever be, no matter among whom they labor, knowing their Bibles from beginning to end, and knowing as much of related truth as time and talent will allow them to learn.

All these considerations apply particularly to those who would labor among Italians, a race whose intellectual power is prominent, even in those individuals who may not be able to read and write. "Contadino—scarpe grosse, cervel fino!" says the Italian proverb, which means: "The peasant—thick shoes, keen intellect!" Success in the evangelization of Italians demands an educated ministry. The educated lay-worker is sometimes as necessary as the minister himself. Whatever subjects may be considered necessary, the curriculum for all such workers ought to include, first of all, the study of the Bible, not merely in English and in the original languages, but above all in the language in which one is to minister to his own people.

Italian theological students have even more need to study the Italian Bible than Americans have to study the English Bible, because, as a rule, the latter come from Protestant homes and Sunday-schools, in which they have been taught the Bible from early childhood. The Italians come from Roman Catholic families. When they begin their preparation for the ministry, they very often know less of the Bible than American Sunday-school children know. Such ignorance

of the Bible is not by any means limited to Italians of the lower classes, but is just as common among young men of college or university training. A few years ago, an Italian member of the senior class of a prominent theological seminary, who was doing evangelistic work among his own people, asked a fellow worker, in all earnestness, to show him in what part of the New Testament the Apostles' Creed is contained, confessing that he had never been able to find it himself.

It is very essential that the Italian preacher should know intimately the Standard Italian Protestant Version of the Bible, its history and peculiarities, as contrasted with the Vulgate and the Italian Catholic Version. He should do this not in order to engage in controversy with Roman Catholics, but to be able to give intelligent and adequate answers to the many inquirers who will be sure to ask explanations along these lines. Not long ago at the examination of a seminary graduate for ordination, it was found that he did not even know the name of Diodati, the famous translator of the Italian Protestant Bible, and had not the least idea when he lived. He could not tell correctly the name of the translator of the Italian Catholic Bible. Such matters never had come up in his studies. Just imagine what would have happened to him if he had come face to face with an intelligent Roman Catholic, especially if in the presence of members of his own church! The Italian minister should also know the difference between the Canonical and the Apocryphal Books, the Roman Church basing several of its doctrines on the Apocrypha, while accusing Protestants of mutilating the Word of God by leaving them out.

Italian students for the ministry are generally divided into two great classes: Those who have lived and studied chiefly in Italy, and who therefore need to be Americanized; and those who have lived and studied chiefly in America, and therefore need to be Italianized. It is therefore a great mistake to segregate foreign students in institutions where few, if any, real Americans are found, or where they must meet other foreign races with different national peculiarities. Such conditions will surely prevent or greatly retard their Americanization. Those also who were either born or bred in America need to come into contact with teachers and fellow-students who represent the best characteristics of their own race, and speak their native language fluently and correctly. Most of the Italians who were born or brought up in America, who have studied in the schools of this country, find it very difficult to learn the Italian language correctly. This may seem strange, but is due to the fact that Italians (of the working classes in particular) always speak among themselves abominable dialects, which differ in the different Provinces, though they all understand and like to hear good Italian spoken. Children whose only Italian consists of such jargons with the admixture of English forms find it almost impossible to avoid using them in their public utterances, even after completing creditably a college or a seminary course in English, including perhaps elective courses in Italian, such as are now offered in every college of good standing. Those who would prepare to preach to Italians in their own language must either start the study of the language early or give it their close attention for several years under competent teachers, in connection with their other studies.

As soon as a young man of this class becomes a theological candidate he ought to be sent to an institution where provisions are made for such teaching, if possible during both preparatory and theological stages of his education. This necessitates a department of Italian Homiletics and Pastoral Theology, as theory and practice must go hand in hand. The way to learn to preach to Italians is by constant practice in their language under the guidance of competent teachers. Those who wait until they have finished their studies in English and then try to preach in Italian will soon find out that they cannot win the respect of their congregations. Their hearers are very critical, and apt to think their Pastor's college degree and diploma not at all evidences of learning. In the institution the writer represents it has been found necessary to keep some young men studying Italian five or even eight years before they are allowed to graduate.

It is of course just as important that those who have had most of their preparation in Italy should come into contact with American teachers and students representing the best in American Christianity. Thus only can they learn not only how to speak but especially how to act as American gentlemen. The development of the Christian personality, which after all is the essential thing, can come in only one way—by personal contact, not by any curriculum of study. Our Saviour did not merely send us a book of precepts from Heaven; He came to earth Himself. If we are to speak to life, we must have a life of our own from which to speak!

The Italians are an emotional people, quickly responding to the preaching of the gospel when backed by strong convictions and a holy enthusiasm. These can be created or developed only in a proper atmosphere or spiritual environment. To this end those who teach and those who learn ought to be men enthused with their message, embodying it in their daily conduct, radiating their influence all around. In this, after all, is the secret of success.

Training an Italian Congregation in the Support of the Church

Rev. J. W. Vavolo

Mr. Vavolo, Pastor of the Presbyterian Church of the Holy Trinity, New York, contributes a suggestive article on one of the most important phases of our work among Italians.

SOMETIME ago, at a conference of workers on Italian Evangelization, I stated that the hope of ever having an entirely self-supporting Italian Church ought to be renounced altogether. This assertion I now reiterate, without mentioning the reasons so well known to all familiar with Italian work. As before, however, I declare my personal belief that members of an Italian church can be made to understand that it is a duty as well as a privilege to give to the support of the Church, whose Head they have confessed, and for whose moral and material support they have implicitly pledged themselves. All training implies a gradual process. It cannot, of course, be expected that financial contributions will be obtained from people who have just begun to attend a newly started mission; but it does not look right when we see a church, duly organized and officially recognized, doing practically nothing to meet the financial obligations of their church.

Generally speaking, the lesson that "it is more blessed to give than to receive" is a hard one to learn. In the case of Italians it is harder than usual. Those of Evangelical faith have come either directly from the Roman Catholic Church or from an attitude of indifference or antagonism, after opening their eyes to the many inconsistencies of the faith of their ancestors. In the Roman Church there is no such thing as systematic giving. The head of a Catholic parish is paid out of general Church funds, his assistants deriving their living out of the proceeds of masses, free-will offerings, baptisms, weddings, funerals, and religious festivities altogether too numerous.

When one passes from the Roman to the Protestant Church, he already has the idea that, whereas in the former all privileges are subject to a financial tariff, in the latter everything is free. Italian converts learn easily and quote often the verse: "Freely ye have received, freely give." The majority of them believe this "the" difference between the two religious systems. This fact, and the further fact that the labors of an Italian Pastor are often reckoned only by the number of names added during the year to the church roll, make the financial question most delicate and difficult. Many Pastors regard as paramount the consideration that an Italian's income is in many cases inadequate to meet the demands of his large family; but this difficulty ought easily to be set aside by the consideration that the training of Italians to give is not so much for the sake of getting money out of them as it is to ascertain whether their faith is an innermost reality or merely a cloak to hide secondary ends.

To me it seems that the solution of the whole problem of the relation of Italians to the finances of the church which with pride they call "their church" may be obtained by enlightening them and granting them greater confidence than they have ever before enjoyed. Ordinarily they know nothing either of the amount of money invested in their church property and maintenance or of the manner in which the money is raised. This happens because in many an Italian church an autocratic spirit dominates, which is contrary to the democratic spirit of Presbyterianism. The Pastor is the church; the people are nothing. This keeping of the people in darkness or considering them unworthy of confidence does not help in the least to rouse them to the full realization of their financial obligation to their church, even though this obligation were to be fulfilled by a contribution resembling the famous "widow's mite."

How can we remedy this state of affairs?

Let the people feel that the church is theirs. Imbue them with the feeling that every true follower of Christ has some financial obligation toward the carrying on of Christ's blessed work. Make them realize that their opinion is valuable and appreciated in all church matters. Cause them to see that the little they give is wisely spent and carefully accounted for. A great deal will thus be accomplished toward their living up to their Christian duty of giving.

But in order to have a quicker solution of the problem, the co-operation of Americans is also needed. The system heretofore obtaining in the organization of Italian churches ought to be reformed to the extent of allowing representatives of the congregation to take part in the meetings of the Session. In other words, our Italian Presbyterian Churches ought to have a mixed Session. In every congregation there is one at least who is worthy of the honor and dignity of the eldership. It may be contended that, in cases where an American Session administers both spiritual and material matters for an Italian congregation, it is sufficient to give them a Board of Deacons. But such a Board can have only a nominal existence, for it has no power whatever, not even that of administering the funds for the poor, for in ninety-nine cases out of a hundred there are no such funds to be administered. Italian Elders should not only supervise the spiritualities of the church but also, at periodical congregational meetings, enlighten the congregation and keep it posted on all decisions arrived at in the sessional meetings.

Besides the representation on the Session of the church, a lay committee ought to be chosen by the congregation, from amongst its most influential and representative members, to co-operate with the Pastor in securing from each member or from entire families financial pledges, redeemable within a year, toward the covering of the amount which the Session, in co-operation with the Italian Elders and Pastors, has deemed reasonable and just to assess the congregation. This lay committee ought to organize, and

have a monthly meeting at which to review the monthly account of moneys received and deposited in bank, and of bills to be approved and settled by the church. Every three months there should be distributed to the congregation a detailed, printed account of all moneys received and expended during the quarter. At the end of the ecclesiastical

ITALIAN PRESBYTERIAN CHURCH
OF THE
HOLY TRINITY
253 E. 153 rd St.   Bronx, New York

RESOCONTO FINANZIARIO del TRIMESTRE
Luglio – Settembre 1917

INTROITI.

Rimanenza trimestre precedente		$ 43.36
Lug. Colletta col can.	$ 10.80	
Contribuzioni Trimestrali	5.50	
Matrimonio	4.00	
Scuola Domenicale	2.27	22.57
Ago. Colletta col can.	6.32	
Contribuzioni Trimestrali	15.00	
Scuola Domenicale	2.50	23.82
Sett. Colletta col can.	11.10	
Contribuzioni Trimestrali	12.25	
Scuola Domenicale	2.50	25.85
Offerta speciale		6.75
	TOTALE	122.35

ESITI

Luce Elett Luglio	6,94	
Agosto	5.03	
Settembre	2.77	14.74
Abbonamento Mag. e Giug. all'Era Nuova		3.00
Beneficenza (Mrs. V.)		4.40
Riparazione ad un Organo		4.00
	TOTALE ESITI	26,14
	Residuo in Banca	96,21
	TOTALE	122.35

A QUARTERLY ACCOUNTING OF RECEIPTS AND DISBURSE-MENTS, ILLUSTRATING MR. VAVOLO'S METHOD OF BUILD-ING UP INTEREST AND CONFIDENCE ON THE PART OF HIS ITALIAN CONGREGATION.

year, a still more detailed report should be put into the hands of all members and adherents of the church, giving the names of all those who have pledged and redeemed their pledge, and of those also who pledged but did not give.

I have suggested this plan because, in my experience, it works out most successfully. I do not assume, however, that it is "the" plan.

Looking Forward

The Second Biennial Conference on Italian Evangelization

Rev. Vincent Serafini, Trenton, N. J.

In June, 1916, the first Presbyterian Conference on Italian Evangelization was held at Princeton, N. J. The Conference was attended not only by Italian-speaking workers and ministers from all parts of the country, but by Chairmen of Presbyterial Committees, Executives of the Synods of New York and New Jersey, and others interested in this broad field for constructive Home Mission Work. The Conference received the hearty support of the Synods of New York and New Jersey, the Board of Home Missions, the Board of Publication and Sabbath-school Work, and other agencies of the Church. A permanent organization was effected, and a Committee instructed to arrange for another Conference in the spring of 1918. In view of the unusual conditions in our Italian communities created by the War, enlarging the opportunities for service, the Conference this year is most timely. It is furthermore a forward step in unifying Presbyterian work among our recent-immigrant populations. Mr. Serafini, Secretary of the Conference, writes hopefully of the next Conference, and reflects the attitude of eager desire to co-operate on the part of our Italian-speaking ministry.

W. P. S.

WITH great interest and enthusiasm, we are all looking forward to the next Conference to be held in Princeton. We know that much that is practical will be considered, and encouraging reports will be heard from the different fields throughout the United States. If the first Conference was an inspiration and a revelation to all who attended, what may we not expect from the second?

It was with great trepidation that we called the first Conference, even though the suggestion came from the officers of the Association of Presbyterian Italian Ministers and Missionaries of the U. S. A. We did not know how the workers in general would take the idea proposed, nor whether they would vote to perpetuate the Conference. Then we had hope only to encourage us; now our hope is crystallized into reality, for we are organized, and have well chosen committees of different kinds, actually at work. We have also a well defined idea of the necessity for such an organization. All friends of Italian Evangelization, whether workers or otherwise, Italians or Americans, should be present without fail, and participate in the exchange of suggestions for the development of this very successful and promising work.

It is absolutely necessary that Italian workers all feel that we are engaged in the same kind of work. My mission and some-one's else, no matter how widely separated, are part of the same great movement,—the evangelization of the Italians. Until now, each has worked by himself, unconscious of the actual relation of his work to that of other fields. Such unconsciousness of relation is a great hindrance to the proper development of almost any enterprise, but much more so to the advancement of Christ's Kingdom on earth. Think of the encouragement that comes when one realizes that he does not stand alone, that other congregations like his are doing the same work, that other Missionaries faced by the same problems are solving them all, by the grace of God. Many other prayers like his ascend to the great Mercy Seat, whence, according to the faith and perseverance of each, the Almighty will send to each at the proper time such showers of blessing as he never knew before.

After three and a half years of fighting in the great World War, the Allied Powers have just come to the realization that they have common interests at stake and a common foe to overcome. Though their armies may be facing enemies in various parts of the world, the many battlefields are to be considered as one front. That is exactly the idea we expect every attendant at the next Conference to carry home with him. The interests of one mission field are the interests of every mission field throughout the country.

The foe which in the name and by the Spirit of Christ we try to conquer is common to all. The present key-word of the friends of Democracy is co-ordination. Our key-word must be co-ordination and co-operation. And it is in Conferences like this next one at Princeton that the workers and friends of Italian Evangelization meet and learn to know and appreciate one another. It is there that leaders are discovered, and the intellectual and spiritual forces may be co-ordinated. From the fellowship resulting from consideration together of the common problems there will spring a brotherly co-operation which the forces of evil may well fear. There will undoubtedly come a deepening of our own spiritual life, and a great ingathering of souls for God's Kingdom.

An Italian Year

William P. Shriver

DIRECTOR OF CITY AND IMMIGRANT WORK, BOARD OF HOME MISSIONS

NO movement of population in recent years is more likely to make its impress upon our American community life than the quiet, persistent yet friendly invasion of the Italians. In the single year preceding the War nearly three hundred thousand of these industrious folk from Sunny Italy came to America. A most careful approximation, including children born of Italian parents, would indicate the Italian population in this country as in excess of three million. There is scarcely a community in the East or Central West that does not have a "Little Italy." None among our recent immigrants are more approachable. None are more eagerly taking their place in the industry and community life of the new America. None are making so ready a response to the gospel of Christ. There are more than three hundred Protestant churches and missions in this country using the Italian language, Baptist, Congregational, Methodist, Protestant Episcopal and others. There are over a hundred Italian Presbyterian churches and missions.

For the year 1917-18, the Protestant denominations have united in a great friendly drive in the interest of a more neighborly and Christian service among these new Americans. In the early stages of this work the point of contact was ordinarily established through missions and churches in Italian communities; but with the growing up of a generation of young Italians, born in this country, educated in our schools, the field of service has broadened. The Italian is a part-

ner with us in the new democracy. He has a contribution to make out of his own heritage and temperament. We need to appreciate him in the same measure as we are desirous that he should know us.

The Immigrant Work Committee of the Home Missions Council has in the first place prosecuted a general survey of Italian communities in this country with particular reference to the religious situation and the work of the churches. Rev. Antonio Mangano, who made this survey, is a graduate of Brown and Columbia Universities, and director of the Italian Department of Colgate Theological Seminary, Brooklyn. His long residence in America, and his sympathetic understanding of both the Italian and the American viewpoint, well qualify him for this service. The findings of the survey are published in a pamphlet *Religious Work Among Italians in America*, which also contains statements concerning the work and policy of leading denominations engaged in work with Italians, a list of Protestant Italian churches and missions, and much other valuable information.

Mr. Mangano has also written for this Italian year *Sons of Italy*, a study book syndicated by the various Home Mission Societies through the Missionary Education Movement. In its discussion of the social and religious needs of the Italians in this country, and in its suggestion of modes of service, this little book is thoroughly helpful. I have known Mr. Mangano intimately for fifteen years. In his sterling Christian character, in his fine grasp of the social and religious problems which inhere in our immigrant communities, and in his program of constructive service, I do not know of anyone better deserving the confidence of the Church.

At Work with the Italians, by W. P. Shriver, is a pamphlet with further suggestion as to ways of co-operative service. It will be mailed to anyone who will send postage. Other literature has been issued in connection with this friendly drive.

This year is a highly opportune time to press forward in our work with Italians. There is the finest spirit of co-operation among the various denominations. Quite apart from the work of distinctive Italian-speaking churches and missions is the social service to be rendered in every community, and the manifold opportunities for personal acquaintance and mutual helpfulness. The Presbyterian Board of Home Missions is disbursing $30,000 annually in work with Italians. The Synods of New York, Pennsylvania, Ohio, and New Jersey, and many of our City Presbyteries (New York, Philadelphia, Newark, Cleveland, and Chicago, among others) are steadily enlarging their interest in this field of finest promise.

The Evangelical Movement
Among Italians in New York City

A Study
By HENRY D. JONES

●

For the Comity Committee of the Federation of Churches
of Greater New York and the Brooklyn Church
and Mission Federation

1933-34

SURVEY COMMITTEE ON ITALIAN EVANGELIZATION

*Of the Joint Comity Committee of the Federation of Churches
of Greater New York and the Brooklyn Church
and Mission Federation*

Rev. CHARLES H. SEARS, Chairman
Rev. JOSEPH BRUNN
Rev. PAUL L. BUFFA
Rev. PETER CAMPO
Rev. JOHN CASTELLI
Rev. J. H. CARPENTER

Rev. W. R. JELIFFE
Mr. ANTHONY LONGARZO
Rev. F. H. NEWELL
Rev. THEODORE F. SAVAGE
Rev. ARNALDO STASIO
Rev. F. T. STEELE

*Published by the Unit for City, Immigrant and Industrial Work Board
of National Missions of the Presbyterian Church*
156 Fifth Avenue, New York
January, 1935

INTRODUCTION

IN the Autumn of 1933 the Unit of City, Immigrant and Industrial Work of the Board of National Missions of the Presbyterian Church, U. S. A. felt the need of a careful appraisal of Presbyterian work with Italians in New York City. It was clear, however, that an inclusive study of all evangelical work with Italians was of much greater importance. It was accordingly proposed that such a study be made under the auspices of the joint Comity Committee of the Federation of Churches of Greater New York and of the Brooklyn Church and Mission Federation. The Presbyterian Board agreed to furnish the necessary service.

The Comity Committee gave its support to this proposal and a Committee for a Survey of evangelical Italian work was appointed. This Committee in addition to denominational executives concerned included leaders from among the churches nominated by the Italian Ministerial Association of New York and environs. The cooperation of all the denominations and of the Italian churches was thus assured.

The plan of the survey and its procedure was guided by the Survey Committee as thus constituted. This final report has been submitted to the members of the Committee and is published with its full understanding and approval. Separate recommendations bearing on adjustments on the field have been made to the Comity Committee. Rev. Henry D. Jones has been responsible for the field work and for writing the report. About eight months in the winter and spring (1933-34) were devoted to the project.

In 1912 Howard V. Yergin, then a student at Auburn Theological Seminary and with a summer scholarship granted by that Seminary, made a survey of "Italian Evangelization in New York City" This study carried out under the direction of the then Department of Immigration of the Presbyterian Board of Home Missions was the first comprehensive study of Italian work in New York and has furnished a valuable background for the present study. Mr. Yergin subsequently was appointed to an Immigration Fellowship by the Presbyterian Board, resided in Italy, and thereafter took up work among Italians in New York. As minister of the Church of the Covenant he continues to this time an active interest in the Italians and has given his counsel in the making of this survey.

Again, in the summer of 1926, Miss B. Therese Voorhis, holder of a Fellowship for Social-Religious Work granted by the Presbyterian Board, resurveyed the field of work with Italians in New York and visited forty-two projects. This study, also, has been of great help in taking the measure of the progress of the years.

The present study is particularly meaningful in its development of the early history of the work. The situation both in Italy and in this country furnished fertile soil for the new mission to Italians, and the fact that the initial drive came very largely from the awakened purpose and passion of the Italians themselves has led to the conclusion that what we have is an Evangelical Movement among Italians and not a missionary project thrust by Americans from outside on an unreceptive population. It is the hope that a recognition of this characteristic phase of evangelical work with Italians will continue to inspire the Italian language churches to carry on and with the flaming zeal that marked the initiators of the movement. The future of the work must increasingly rest in the leadership which these churches command.

It is the persuasion of this study that there are great numbers among the four and a half million Italians in the United States of the first and second generations who sustain no vital relation to a Christian church, who are deprived of its fellowship, support, and encouragement to service. From the standpoint of urgent social and religious need there is now, as in former years, a wide though confessedly difficult field to be cultivated. Work with Italians today must be carried forward with fresh adaptations of the Christian message. New and resourceful methods must be employed and with particular reference to the younger generation. The conviction that there is still something of vast importance to be done is the first thing that matters.

New York City, January, 1935.

WILLIAM P. SHRIVER

Chapter I

HISTORICAL BACKGROUND OF ITALIAN IMMIGRATION

The Italian people have shared the life of America since the Italian navigator Christopher Columbus discovered the new land and the German cartographer Waldsemiller of the College of St. Die named it on his early maps for Amerigo Vespucci, his correspondent. Italian noblemen and peasants were in Washington's army during the American Revolution (1). Throughout the development of this country the citizen of Italian birth or descent has played an important part. This fact we have not generally recognized as we have considered the Italian in America. The number of Italians in our early history was small. Their descendants have lost identity with things Italians through the amalgam of American life. However, their tradition is influencing young Italo-Americans today who want to feel that their people have made and can continue to make real contributions to our nation's life.

Any study of the Italian in America must begin in Italy. This story quoted by Jacob Riis (2) will introduce us to many a family in our cities.

"In the month of July, 1902, I stopped on a march by a threshing floor where they were measuring grain. When the shares had been divided, the one who had cultivated the land received a single tamolo (less than a half bushel). The peasant, leaning on his spade, looked at his share as if stunned. His wife and five children were standing by. From the painful toil of a year this was what was left to him with which to feed his family. The tears rolled silently down his cheeks."

The government, the landlord, the padrone, had had their share and only a single tamolo remained for the worker.

Another story from this same period tells of the mayor of a village in southern Italy welcoming a government official with this speech:

"I welcome you to our village in the name of its eight thousand citizens, three thousand of whom are already in America and the rest of us eagerly awaiting an opportunity to go." (3)

This economic poverty is somewhat explained by the density of population for this primarily agricultural land. With at least 30 per cent of the total land

---

(1) "Italy and the Italians in Washington's Time" — Five essays by five scholars published to honor Washington's Centenary.
(2) Jacob Riis — "The Battle with the Slum" quoting an Italian correspondent in the New York Evening Post" - 1902.
(3) Samuel McLanahan — "Our People of Foreign Speech."

area incapable of development the density of population in Italy today exceeds 340 per square mile (1), being practically the same as industrialized Germany. It may be compared with the agricultural State of Iowa with 44.5 persons per square mile. Lack of political franchise also was a factor in discontent. Italian parliamentarianism was slow in developing. Up to 1919 there were only three million voters out of a population of forty million.

EMIGRATION

There have been two main streams of Italian emigration directed toward this country. One came from the Northwest section of the Italian peninsula and the other from the Southwest. The "Genoese" came first and were pioneer merchants. Today they are leaders in many communities and are rarely thought of as having come from the same land as the large group from the south. In the far west, especially California, these early immigrants attained an enviable position, both economically and socially (2). Throughout the period of this early migration (1850-70) Italy was in her struggle for national independence and unity. Many of the patriotic leaders from noble families were obliged, as fortunes turned, to flee for safety and some found refuge in America. The great Garibaldi lived in seclusion on Staten Island, New York. for two years. Although the total immigration from these northern states has exceeded 50,000 only one year (1907) and has dropped very low recently, it has never stopped. The present quota is very favorable to this northern Italian group. Fifty per cent of the skilled weavers in the factories of Astoria, New York, and Paterson, New Jersey, are from Piedmont and Lombardy.

From Naples, Calabria, Basilicata and Sicily came an increasing stream of immigrants until the World War which began the succession of changed social and political conditions that reduced the number entering this country. In the early decades of 1870 and 1880 the movement grew slowly but the years 1906, 1907, 1913 and 1914 each brought approximately a quarter of a million newcomers from these southern states. Our crowded cities, the shawled immigrant woman and itinerant peddler of plaster-of-Paris statuary and the strolling musician made older Americans aware of the presence of these new neighbors.

Intense interest in the Italians developed during the period from 1904 to 1907. Magazines sent feature writers on extended study tours here and abroad. Others devoted whole issues to the Italians. The leading periodicals carried serious discussions of the "problems" connected with the coming of these new groups to our shores. Books by social workers, journalists and college professors, appeared constantly on the subject. It was during this wave of interest that many fine projects began in which new and old Americans shared.

Close to five million immigrants from Italy have come to the United States since 1871. Over four and a half million in our population today have either been born in Italy or have one or both parents who were born there.

ITALIANS IN NEW YORK

Although these newcomers are dispersed in every state in the union the largest number remained in New York City. In 1930, with 1,070,355 Italians of

---

(1) C. D. H. Cole — "An Intelligent Man's View of Europe".
(2) A. Mangano — "Sons of Italy."

foreign birth or foreign parentage, this metropolis became a larger Italian city than Rome. From 1880 to 1910 there was a steady growth in the per cent of the city's population that came from Italy. In the later year it was 7.1 per cent of the whole. The total number of persons of Italian background has contined to grow so that today approximately one-sixth of the city's population are first and second generation Italians.

With the practical doubling of this population from 1910 to 1930 many changes have occurred. There has been a spreading into new colonies, but even more marked a dispersion into new communities not distinctly Italian.

The Rev. Howard Yergin in his study of "Italian Evangelization in New York City", 1912, gives us this picture:

"The foreigner, on arriving in New York, hies him amid his fellow countrymen where he can speak his native language and be understood and where he can eat his native dishes. This results in the formation of very definitely bounded foreign communities. Sometimes the width of an avenue spans the distance between a 'Ghetto' and a 'Little Italy'; the tenement dweller on 110th Street east of Second Avenue, New York, is in the heart of Italy so far as language, ideals, and customs are concerned."

The Italian in New York twenty or thirty years ago was a stranger in a strange and rather bewildering world. He was poor, ignorant of the laws, customs and habits of this land and without much opportunity of learning about them except as he observed. His contact with Americans was ordinarily with those who exploited his labor for as little as they could pay him; with the landlord who took as much as he could get, and others who drew away from him as being objectionable. He was forced by his poverty to have his children work. The only protection which the immigrant had was in his community. These were generally village colonies with many of the mores of the old land transplanted. the social organization and social controls operating (in face of handicaps). Padrones from Italy still dealt in the labor of their fellows by acting as employment agents. Men of higher social position took political leadership in the colony. The Italian immigrant believes in American citizenship. Jacob Riis puts it well when he says that their viewpoint was: "One dollar a day for a shovel with a man behind it, two dollars a day for a shovel and a citizen behind it. He got his papers and took the two dollars." Rarely has it been noted that there were strong socialistic tendencies in the Italian colonies of twenty years ago. Coming from the oppression and poverty of the old land where resentment had driven many to think of revolt and where they had been a part of the growing socialist movement of the time in Europe, it was natural that they brought this philosophy with them. Faced with democracy in its happy prosperous days the revolt philosophy died. but in depressions and strike situations it grew.

"It may be worthy of note that, contrary to public opinion, it is the northern Italian weavers in Paterson, New Jersey, and the stonecutters in Barre, Vermont, who are the most fiery and irreconcilable anarchists, and strikes are frequent among these justice-loving workers." (1)

---

(1) "Religious work among Italians in America" - Antonio Mangano.

There were in 1910 ten well defined Italian colonies of between 5,000 to 100,000 persons in Manhattan and the Bronx and a similar number in Brooklyn. What changes have taken place? There is a rather definite pattern which the immigrant community follows in its process of adjustment. The description quoted from Mr. Yergin typifies the first stage in the process, that of gathering together and building its social organization. Then comes the development of its social controls; supervision of its youth, organization of benefit societies, celebration of town festivals, religious sanctions urged, all in an attempt to become a self-sufficient social group. But while this development is taking place the seeds of disintegration have been at work; the youth have American ideas rather than Italian; the social classifications are destroyed by American ideals of equality of opportunity; the colony within a city is far different from the agricultural village pattern, and finally new ways of living contradict old world ideas. The last stage in the process of adjustment of the immigrant colony to American life is seen in many German, Welsh or Scotch communities. There is just a semblance left of what had been built up in the way of religious, social, benevolent, or educational institutions. Certain activities lingering on, some as mere forms, others as occasional social functions to keep alive the memories of older days.

THE SITUATION TODAY

In New York today we find the communities in different stages. The size of some colonies with their continued importation of Italians from Italy and from colonies throughout this country will tend to keep them in the second stage longer than any others in all America. Nevertheless the seeds of disintegration are there and working. No colony in Brooklyn can be said to be in this second stage but rather in the third, and some in the fourth stage where "the good old days when this was a real Italian neighborhood" are gone forever. Scattered colonies, very slightly integrated, are now in every section of the city. Thousands of young Italian families are located in areas quite apart from any social demarcation as Italian. These scattered colonies and families of young people are American with merely the accident of birth connecting them with the Italian group.

When we talk of the Italians in New York today, we have to consider some few who have only recently arrived; the older folks who came here in their youth and have lived in the colonies, "Little Italys," all their lives and consequently know little of America or its language; the youths born in these colonies, reared in American schools, faced with difficult personal and social adjustments, some conquering, others failing; and finally, Italians of the third generation as well as the second who are American in mode of life, thought and conduct,—Italians only in heritage.

Chapter II

RELIGIOUS BACKGROUND OF THE ITALIAN IMMIGRANT

Italy's forty-two million people are generally considered entirely Roman Catholic. This is an assumption which is unfounded as a little study reveals.

IN ITALY

With regard to religious inclinations, there are four definitely discernible groups in Italy:

(1) "The devout Roman Catholics, the majority of whom consist of peasants, largely illiterate, plus the decreasing 'black aristocracy' or noblemen who gave themselves to an ecclesiastical career and the clergy.

(2) A smaller number of free-thinkers, agnostics, atheists, and materialists who are for the most part workingmen in large cities, and also professional men.

(3) The millions, apparently indifferent, who go through life without religious feeling or spiritual experience." (1)

(4) The Protestants, native Waldensians and converts of Protestant missions numbering more than 60,000.

To understand the evangelical movement we must see something of Catholicism in Italy. The Church has represented temporal power as well as spiritual leadership. This was based on the philosophy of the Church that religion had to do with all of life, that it could not be segregated to a special function. But the temptation of the material gains was strong and abuses of temporal power grew as it had in Germany earlier. The Church, however, felt the imminent danger of another Reformation movement and constantly held up in horror the examples of individual Protestants in every community. The power of the military force of the Church and of the State were used periodically to suppress the Waldensians, the primary evangelical group of Italians.

Finally Italy was united by the combined efforts of the House of Savoy (Kings of Piedmont and Sardinia) and the independent forces of Giuseppe Garibaldi, linked together by the statesmanship of the Count of Cavour. He was like Garibaldi greatly inspired by the philosophy of Giuseppe Mazzini. The Church

(1) Philip M. Rose — "The Italians in America."

opposed the uniting of Italy because it would take away its Papal States and reduce its function as a temporal power. Also its kingly supporters in France and Austria had interests and possessions which would have to be relinquished to the united peoples. The Roman pontiff declared himself "the prisoner of the Vatican." The Church lost in its support of the foreign powers and in its opposition to Italian Unity. The Church afterwards supported several other enterprises that met defeat. It had lost its temporal power and was now losing swiftly its moral power with the masses.

There was a strong movement in the Church on the part of some priests toward a more personally helpful relationship between Church and people. This was illustrated by such a notable character as Alessandro Gavazzi, known by all as Father Gavazzi. He lived close to the people, loved them dearly, had their cause at heart, supported earnestly the movement toward uniting Italy, was excommunicated for this espousal, organized (1854) the Chiesa Libera Italiana and continued to preach. This Free Church of Italy at one time had congregations and institutions in every important city of the land. It was not only the result of the dynamic power of the one who was known as "the greatest Italian religious orator of his generation," but also a symptom of the changing temper of the Italian nation in regard to religious matters. An earlier indication of this change was the Edict of Emancipation by Charles Albert, King of Sardinia declaring that on February 17, 1848 the Waldenses might hold their first legal religious service in Italy after centuries of persecution, dispossession and exile.

Then began the missionary activities of Protestant groups from other lands to Italy. In 1861 the Moravians from Southern Germany came; in 1865 the Weslyan Methodists from England; in 1870 the Presbyterians from the United States made their first approaches and in 1873 the Methodist Episcopal and Northern Baptist representatives, just preceding the Lutherans. From these missions in Italy many of the leaders of the Evangelical churches in America came. From the churches here much inspiration and many reinforcements went to the work in Italy. The Italian government's publication concerning its relations to "the cults" lists twenty groups working evangelically among the Italians. The most important of these groups today are:

	Parishes	Ministers	Members	Souls	Work begun
Waldensian	96	—	22,000	40,000	—
Weslyan Methodist	—	—	—	—	1865
Methodist Episcopal	61	47	3,453	—	1873
Baptist	50	50	2,500	—	—
Salvation Army	16	39	—	—	1887
Pentecostal	148	—	—	—	1910

Drs. Adolph Keller and Robert Stewart in their book, "Protestant Europe," conclude the chapter on the work in Italy:

"The Protestant Church in Italy has a service to perform for the entire Italian people. Free speech, free press, free worship, spiritual independence and the open Bible are values which Italy and Christendom can ill afford to lose in these days of reaction and dictatorships."

After the Concordat between the Vatican and the Government had been signed and rights of the minorities were guaranteed by a similar agreement between the

Government and the non-Catholic cults. This law of June 24, 1929 and its ordinance affirm liberty of conscience and of worship for non-Catholics; also their full equality as Italian citizens before the law.

IN AMERICA

So interwoven is the work of evangelization in Italy and the evangelical movement among Italians here that it is impossible to separate them. Let us look at the beginnings here. In the basement of an Irish Roman Catholic Church in lower Manhattan an Italian priest was holding services for his people. When the new doctrine of the Infallibility of the Pope was declared he and his people withdrew from the church and became part of the Old Catholic movement. In 1872 they held services in old Grace Chapel as the San Salvatore Protestant Episcopal Mission. In 1889 the Church of San Salvatore was taken into the Diocese of New York and has continued under the guidance of the Diocesan City Mission Society.

Going back to Italy again, we meet a drummer boy in the Army of Garibaldi. Antonio was captured in the seige of Rome, sent to the galleys as a slave, escaped and came to America. Here he joined some fellow countrymen and started to tramp across the country selling plaster-of-Paris statuary to the villagers and farmers of Pennsylvania, Ohio, Indiana, Illinois and Iowa. In Fairfield, Iowa, he began to work in a store, met and became staunch friends with an American harness maker who through his Methodist Church introduced Antonio to a new way of life. Antonio grew. He wanted to share his new life with others. He went on to school, graduating from Ohio Wesleyan University, and Boston Theological Seminary before he began to preach. In the old Five Points Mission, New York, Antonio Arrighi first preached in Italian. This was in 1881. Broome Street Tabernacle is one monument to this soldier of the new freedom.

The freer atmosphere of American life, the resentment against the organization which opposed the uniting of Italy, the break down of the immigrant colony with its social controls, all contributed to the failure of the Roman Church to hold its people. More and more Italians became indifferent to religion, because this church was the only spiritual guide they had ever known. Antonio Arrighi and his followers found fruitful soil for their Gospel of freedom and of a new liberty in Christ.

The *Catholic Citizen* of Milwaukee said in 1913 that "the Italians of today are of a generation whose ideals of political liberty collided with the established order and temporalities of the church" and it further admitted that at least one million Italians had already been lost to Catholicism. "Out of the 600,000 Italian people of Greater New York, the Roman Church by its own figures lays claim to only 180,135 members of Roman Catholic Italian churches. This includes children, and even so, it is less than one-third of the total Italian population." (1)

Father Shaughanessy in his book "Has the Immigrant Kept the Faith?" says that "the Italian Protestant churches in the United States in 1916 had a membership of 53,073." "Probably the greatest single racial loss is to be found among the Italians where the drift away from the Catholic church and into Protestantism has been amazing." (2)

---

(1) Sons of Italy — Mangano.
(2) "Will America become Catholic?" — John F. Moore.

There is need for us today to understand these facts in any discussion of the religious work among Italians in America. The four groups present in Italy are found also in America.

(1) The loyal devout Roman Catholics make up about one-third of the Italian population of our cities. As is true with immigrants from every country where an established church exists the drop in enumerated members is heavy.

(2) The active free-thinkers and atheists are a small group but they have an important influence. The *Catholic Citizen* of Milwaukee in 1913 complained, "Among eighty Italian newspapers in the United States not one is religious or Catholic." In 1921 there were 190 papers of which six were Roman Catholic.

(3) Millions are unchurched. Prof. Sartorio holds that 60 per cent are unreached and states that a leading Italian Roman Catholic prelate put the figure even higher. (1)

(4) The Protestant Italians according to Father Shaughanassy in 1916 numbered 53,073. The most recent report gives 240 Protestant churches with 25,731 church members, which definitely supports the estimate of 100,000 Protestant Italian adherents. (2)

Certainly with this estimate of the situation among these people no charge of proselytizing is supportable.

---

(1) "The Social and Religious Life of Italians in America" — Sartorio.
(2) National Italian Evangelical Conference - 1934.

Chapter III

HISTORY OF ITALIAN EVANGELIZATION IN NEW YORK CITY

"The first man of whom we have any record of having preached the gospel among Italians in the United States was Alessandro Gavazzi." (1) While in this country speaking for the Italian struggle for freedom he preached at Broadway Tabernacle in English and in his own tongue to a group in lower Manhattan. This was in 1853. He left no organization here, continuing with his lectures throughout the land.

The first protesting group of Christians to be organized was the San Salvatore Mission in 1872. Antonio Arrighi began his evangelical work in 1881. In the year 1890 Michele Nardi was a padrone dealing in the labor of his fellow countrymen with the railroads, mine owners or other contractors for their brawny muscles. An American friend in Philadelphia gave Michele a copy of the New Testament one day. It gripped him so as he read it that he left the mining camp to spend weeks in solitude and study. When his vigil was over he returned to the camp, preached to his workers, left his work and began the life of a missionary. He was never ordained. He evangelized his people and organized churches in Philadelphia, Vineland, Chicago, St. Louis, San Francisco, as well as New York. Street preaching, persecution, tent meetings, and finally organization of a little church with a pastor is the story of Michele Nardi in every city and community that he entered. From the report of "Home Missions and Synodical Missions, October, 1907" in the New York Presbyterian Handbook we take the following paragraphs, "During the past year two new Italian missions have been established and have been blessed with almost phenomenal results. The one in East 106th Street in the colony known as "Little Italy" was opened November 7th with the noted evangelist, Mr. Nardi in charge. He labors without compensation. From the first the room, which accommodates only 114, has been crowded to overflowing at all the services on Sabbath and week-days. The doors have been locked to prevent overcrowding, and sometimes policemen have to be called to prevent eager people from forcing an entrance. In June Mr. Nardi was succeded by Mr Pirazzini, so that he could give his time to Summer Tent Work. These two brethren preached every night from June 1st to September 15th to crowds in the Italian tent and at the same time kept alive and flourishing our mission.

"Last January (1907) a delegation of Italians from the Bronx brought a petition signed by forty-three Italians asking to be organized as a Presbyterian Church. They had listened to the preaching of Mr. Nardi and Mr. D'Anchise.

---

(1) History of Italian Work in the United States - Jos. Brunn, MSS.

Your Committee established a mission for them in Morris Avenue, with young Mr. D'Anchise in charge."

To illustrate the relationship of the missions of American denominations to Italy and the work among Italians here we may quote from 1889 report of the New York City Mission Society of the Methodist Episcopal Church: "There came to this country in May last, in company with Dr. Vernon and Dr. Gay, a local preacher of our Italy Conference, by the name of Vito Calabrese. He offered himself for work among his countrymen. The Rev. O. R. Bouton opened his chapel at the Five Points to use free of charge. In October Dr. Vernon, returning from fourteen years of work in Italy, visited this humble mission at Five Points and told me that in the line of gathering a congregation willing to hear the gospel, more had been accomplished there in four months than could be accomplished at any point in Italy in four years."

No story of Italian evangelization in any country can be told without recognizing the leaders contributed to the movement by the Waldensian Church of Italy. Some lay leaders but particularly ministers of this church have contributed to the leadership of the evangelical work of practically all the denominations.

It was in 1889 that English-speaking workers at Mariners' Temple started a Sunday school and week-day meetings for Italian children. In 1897 a church was organized there under an Italian pastor. The great Judson Memorial Church recognized an opportunity for Christian service in its own neighborhood. The church letter of September 18, 1896 to the Southern New York Baptist Association reports, "We have inaugurated a work among the Italians." In 1897 the Rev. Car. A. Dell'Erba and his wife were received as church members by letter from the Mount Pleasant Baptist Church, Newark, New Jersey, and he was authorized "to administer the ordinance of baptism to his brethren." Before the end of that year over one hundred Italians were received by baptism into the church fold. Another great Baptist Church entered the field of Italian work through this feeling of Christian privilege—the Second Baptist Church beginning in 1900.

The Church of the Sea and Land had a devoted, saintly church visitor in Mrs. Eliza E. Rockwell, who felt at a loss to help many families on whom she was calling because of the barrier of language. She presented her difficulty to the Session and they asked Mr. Arrighi to help them. He sent a young man, converted at Broome St. Tabernacle, to work with Mrs. Rockwell. In 1906 the Home Missions Committee of New York Presbytery reported "We have but one mission among the vast and steadily increasing multitudes of Italians in our midst. This is at the Church of the Sea and Land, where Mr. Villelli has done a good work."

And so we might go through the list of the beginnings of work in various ways of all the eleven denominations at work in the city among the Italian peoples, until we come to this significant entry, "In 1910 a survey of the Italian communities on Staten Island was made and two centers started there."

AN EVANGELICAL MOVEMENT

Denominational societies did not begin the work among Italians in this country. Mr. Arrighi and Mr. Nardi were the evangelists who started the work. They were supported, encouraged and sponsored later. This significant statement is found in the reports of one denominational committee at this time. "Opportunities are abundant and inviting for new work in the Italian colonies of this city. We are restrained only by the lack of accommodations, or the money to provide them." The leadership came from the Italians themselves. The accommodations came as churches felt the opportunity of acting as Christian neighbors to these newcomers. It was in 1904 that the first missionary education book dealing with "Our People of Foreign Speech" was published. It was written by Rev. Samuel McLanahan of Lawrenceville, New Jersey. Later as the City Mission Societies grew to be recognized as expressing the cooperative principle in church planning some centers were started by them, as illustrated by the Staten Island entry. Nor was it until after the members of churches using the foreign speech had grown to large numbers that the national missionary organizations established departments of immigration of bi-lingual missions. The most important method of establishing Italian work has been and still is that of the missionary activity of the Italian pastors and people. This is illustrated today by the eight mission outposts sponsored and led by members of the Italian churches themselves. The second significant way of establishing Italian work has been that of American churches inviting an Italian leader to help it do its neighborly task. This is illustrated by the New Utrecht Reformed Church of Brooklyn which secured Mr. Sylvan Poet, a Waldensian by birth, educated for the ministry both here and abroad, to reach its new Italian neighbors. The church has asked the Women's Board of Domestic Missions to help it meet the financial obligation. Historically the least important, but growing in significance, is the place of the denominational city mission society in starting, planning and conducting the work in all missionary areas of the city.

A study of the dates on which new enterprises were begun gives us a valuable insight into the work itself but also an index of the interest in the work during the successive periods. From the beginning in 1872 to 1900 eleven centers were started. In the decade 1905-1914 thirty-three centers of work were begun. After that there was the almost inevitable dropping of interest which has, however, seemed to revive since 1930. The significant thing in this revival is that it has come from the Italian churches themselves. Seven of the ten centers that have been started since 1930 are being supported and conducted entirely by the Italian churches. None of these are large, nor do they have much expense, but they are an expression of the zeal of these congregations to meet the needs of their people in new communities.

CLOSED CENTERS

One of the saddest chapters in the history of this work has been that of the closing of churches and centers without an understanding of what it meant to the people. Zealous to share with these new Americans the possession of greatest value, we open a center and invite them to hear and accept Jesus' way of life. Accepting this new way means that the displeasure of friends, often times ostracism from the homes of relatives is directed against the new convert. It is only with faith and the sense of a greater security in the new found Friend that he is able to withstand the taunts and jibes of old friends or persecution of others. After a year or two of earnest effort the missionary may have fifteen or twenty families ready to withstand all for the sake of their new faith in Christ. Then the center is closed and these brave souls are left without their leader and their place of worship and fellowship and are open to still greater persecution. "What's the matter? Why did they close the church? Did Jesus die?"

So far as we have been able to secure the data we find that thirty-four centers have been closed during the past 30 years for various reasons. Many figures can be gathered from the table recording the data on these centers but the following seem to be the only significant facts. Twenty-two of these closed centers were under the direction of local churches, as missions or departments, and received their support from them, while twelve were under denominational city or national organizations. Of the thirty-four dropped only seven were merged or united with another church so that the congregation might continue its Christian fellowship while twenty-six were merely closed. One continues under consecrated volunteer leadership. Of the twenty-six dropped, eight were under the guidance of denominational agencies while eighteen were under the wings of some local church. It appears that the best planning and the most understanding guidance and leadership have come from the mission organizations rather than the local churches. There are exceptions, of course, to this statement, but generally the wider vision of the task of the church in the city is in the leaders of the city's mission societies.

It would seem logical from this experience to suggest that an advisory council of some sort be set up from which guidance and advice on procedure in cases of removal or closing of Italian work might be expected. This seems a reasonable suggestion when we realize that twenty-eight administrations are responsible for the operating of the fifty-one centers of eleven denominations in this city. This council might be a clearing house for policies and plans on Italian work, to meet only when needed.

Chapter IV

LEADERSHIP

During the period of greatest influx of Italian immigrants and greatest interest on the part of the Church in this group the breadth and variety of the program of the churches was praiseworthy. It is from this period too that we have reports in all the records concerning the great crowds in attendance at tent meetings, church services and even prayer meetings. What were the factors that created this situation?

"I was a stranger, and ye took me in; naked, and ye clothed me. I was hungry, and ye fed me." This recognition of the duty to serve the stranger in our midst was the strongest motive in the whole movement so far as the American Protestant churches were concerned. How many times these verses from the 25th chapter of Matthew were used as the basis for an appeal we shall never know. The poverty of the Italian immigrant, his bewilderment at the new life, his disillusionment, and his helplessness at the hands of his exploiters made a Christian friend one whom he loved. So the program of the churches in that era included the teaching of English, assistance in securing citizen's papers, mother's clubs and classes, many activities for the boys and girls, visitors and nurses who assisted in the homes and straightened out many troubles, defenders in the courts, and providing a meeting place for the benefit societies and lodges. The program of the churches in this period was particularly progressive and well adopted to the needs of the Italian immigrants.

The preaching which attracted the attention of such large numbers was vigorous and impassioned, true to the best tradition of Italian orators. The message had two main lines, first, polemic declarations against the theology or practice of the Roman Catholic Church, and second, the presentation of the gospel of Christ, bought with His blood and free to all for the asking. The message was a strange one to all and many came out of curiosity. The denunciation of the Church was not publicly done in Italy. Often too the preachers used the patriotic appeal, for had not the Roman Church opposed the unification of Italy. The Protestants were of the people and for them, they shared and helped the needy and troubled. Finally they offered a gospel that was free, that need not be paid for every time the services of the church were needed.

In reviewing the purpose and method of this enterprise we can do no better than quote the estimate of one with twenty-five years of intimate and discerning contact with the work. Dr. William P. Shriver in speaking to the Italian Ministerial Association of New York and vicinity said in effect, "Evangelical Christianity as promoted by its missionary agencies has had three major interests:

(1) The reconditioning of individual life, according to the pattern of the life and spirit of Jesus; (2) Disinterested service to the people everywhere, which is inherent in the very nature of Jesus' own ministry; (3) The building of a new society on the earth, a brotherhood of men, the Kingdom of God. The Church has largely centered its energy in recent years on the first interest. The service which has been given through the Church's missionary enterprise however is outstanding—the beginning of schools, hospitals, neighborhood houses and social programs in churches. The weakness of the whole program has been in its failure to work with a real sense of direction for the third objective."

TRAINING

This large social service program and popular preaching appealed to the Italians and Americans alike. There was a very rapid growth of centers all over the country and an insistent demand for men to lead the work. The insistent calls for leaders for new fields led to one of the greatest mistakes in the history of the movement. Unqualified, unprepared and sometimes unscrupulous men were placed in positions of responsibility and the work suffered a severe set-back. The original leaders of the movement, Arrighi, Nardi, Mangano, Pirazzini, Buggelli and others were trained, capable men. They set themselves to the task of training young men to fill the new places. In rapid succession 1905, 1906 and 1907, Italian Departments of Colgate University, Bloomfield Theological Seminary and the Biblical Seminary of New York were organized.

The ranks of the ministers today have been generally purged of men untrained for the ministry. The pastors of New York Italian churches measure, in training, well above the average pastors of urban Protestant churches throughout the country.

	New York Italian Pastors	Ministers of 17 white Protestant Denominations in the U. S. A.
	Per Cent	Per Cent
Seminary Trained only	32.	12.7
College Trained only	11.	14.7
College and Seminary	57.	52.3
Neither College or Seminary	0.	20.3

Not only do the statistics give something of the educational training of these pastors but the length of their pastorates speak for their leadership ability and the personal esteem in which they are held by their people and the administrations governing their work. One could scarcely pick a group of churches in which the average length of the present pastorates was more than the 10.3 years indicated here.

NEW DEMANDS ON LEADERS

The task of the leader in these Italian centers is a very different one today from that of twenty years ago. Social changes have come rapidly and demand much of the minister. No longer are the people arriving in boat loads from poverty stricken Italy seeking the economic haven of opulent America. Today thousands are annually leaving this depressed land to return to the old land revived by the leader of the Fascisti. No longer are these people strangers in the land needing a friendly interpreter. They are citizens, indeed one of their own group is the mayor of this largest city in America. No longer are there Italian community units in which the social controls of the villages are effective. Nor is the Italian language used by the entire community. A surprisingly large number of the young people in our churches professed an inability to speak the language. Educated in American schools, the youth is rapidly dissevered from these traditional bonds of unity. No longer is the Roman Catholic Church an enemy of the united Italy, she is today the staunch supporter of the state. A lay representative of the Vatican attending the Ecumenical Conference in Chicago happened to meet a member of the Italian Consular Service in a hotel there. The interest of the two men in history and statecraft soon led their conversation to the most puzzling problem of Italian statesmen. "How can the rift between the state and the Church be settled?" The report of their informal conversation started the long series of conferences which led ultimately to the Concordat. Add to these changes peculiar to the Italian communities all the social changes in America during the last quarter of a century and we shall begin to understand the problem of adjustment with which the ministers of our Italian language churches are faced.

Men trained in the era of polemics find it difficult to meet the educational demands which their young people are making. Men trained in the era of the self-sufficient Italian colony find it hard to cope with its disintegrating forces. Men trained in Italy are with real difficulty facing the need of a positive, constructive educational program in their churches. Few American ministers face such difficulties. Our Italian pastors are making the adjustments but they now and will for some time need understanding and helpful guidance in making the necessary changes.

The transition is rapidly coming. The distinctly Italian church of today will become the church of a whole community, with possibly an Italian service in its program. The church in the oldest and most distinctive Waldensian colony in this country (Valdese, N. C.) has now an American minister with no Italian language service. The cultural, racial and family bonds will keep these primarily churches of Italian Christians long after the Italian language has been dropped from the services. The ideal of this transition is not the replacing of Italian services by English but rather the ability, willingness and success in serving as *the church* of the whole community.

Chapter V

THE PENTECOSTAL MOVEMENT

In the year 1906 an Italian laborer in Chicago was converted and received the baptism of the Holy Spirit according to the method usual in the Pentecostal Assemblies. He felt compelled to preach the message among his own people. In a store in the Italian colony of Chicago's Northwest side this movement had its humble beginnings.

The best available information estimates that there are today in the United States 275 congregations, in South America 70 churches and in Italy, principally in Sicily, about 150 churches of Italian Pentecostals. In New York City we have listed 33 with approximately 2,840 members. In the whole New York Region there are approximately 40 congregations.

In the year 1912 a number of denominations had active missions and churches. The Salvation Army had started an Italian Post and was urging its various Posts to reach their new Italian neighbors. Mr. S. Margadonna, a laborer, had joined the Army and was earnest in his professions of loyalty to his Master. Two men from the Pentecostal Church in Chicago felt the call to come to New York and share their joy. They found the home of Mr. Margadonna and taught him there. He received "the baptism and spoke in tongues." This was the beginning of the Italian Pentecostal movement in this city.

A warm-hearted, fervent Baptist preacher was reaching a goodly number in his two churches. But he wanted to be an evangelist and not be held to a pastorate. He tried, with some of his friends, to organize an evangelistic committee through which evangelistic campaigns might be arranged. But the invitations to speak were very few. He was touched by the enthusiasm of the new Pentecostal movement and joined it. He became its itinerant evangelist. His consecrated zeal and persuasive sermons gathered together groups of people in city, town and village as he traveled about the country. The Rev. J. Petrelli was the flaming evangelist of the Pentecostal movement and a large share of the 275 churches of this group in this country owe their initial stimulous to his preaching.

Mr. Petrelli is not an administrator, so he did not attempt to organize these churches into a denomination. A lay leader was left in charge of each group and urged to carry on. Occasionally these elders or leaders in various sections of the country would gather together for inspiration and fellowship. The attitude toward the denominations was one of hostility for "they had killed the spirit of Christ by organization." The Pentecostal groups therefore shunned organization. Among the elders, however, some had more ability than others, some had an interest in correspondence and records, some had inclinations toward theological discussion and debate, so the usual division of function according to the interest and ability of the respective personalities began. For example,

Elder M. Tosetto of Niagara Falls, New York, has published a list of churches with the names and addresses of their leaders. It is the first directory of these Italian Pentecostal Churches. Mr. Tosetto, through his interest in correspondence and ability has come into a position of recognized leadership over many congregations.

Some of the leaders recognize the need for some kind of organization eventually. This group through its meetings of elders has come to an agreement that each local church adopt the name "The Italian Christian Church." Elder Rosario Italiano, pastor for twelve years of the strong self-supporting Italian Christian Church of Jersey City is the leader of this more progressive group.

Often the question is asked, "Do these groups live on members taken from our regular Italian Protestant churches?" After seeking the answer to this question with many of the groups in various sections of the city the response is "No." In the beginning the Italian evangelical movement was an exciting, aggressive enterprise. Its leaders needed supporters who would stand in the tent or on the street corner to sing or speak. Certain types of personalities are able to do this better than others and they joined the evangelical pastors happily. During the last decade the out-door work of our organized Protestant churches has all but disappeared with the growing emphasis on the slower educational task of training the converted families. The expansive personalities felt cramped in this new atmosphere and left to take leadership in the new growing Pentecostal movement. Most of the leaders in the Pentecostal groups were first reached by the Protestant church missions and have had their training in them. However, the 2800 "members" of the Pentecostal churches have generally come from among the great group of Italians who are indifferent to all religion. They have discovered in it a vital force that they had never before thought existed in religion. It is conservative to state that 90 per cent of the persons reached by the Pentecostal groups have not been reached by our Protestant churches. There is a rather large percentage of turnover in these groups, for the level of the religious experience is generally little above that of the emotional. Some persons grow weary of it and "fall by the wayside," others take leadership in the group and attempt to raise the educational level of the services; others join the Protestant churches as they afford opportunities for a growing Christian life. Many pastors say that they gain from as well as lose to the Pentecostals in their neighborhood. Some say that their strongest people have come to them from these Pentecostal churches.

The opinions of the various ministers of our Protestant churches in regard to this movement are important for they come in almost daily contact with it in their work. Like every other subject there is a great diversity of opinion. We record here some of the statements regarding it: "Work of the devil"; "lives only on the Protestant churches"; "should be considered a part of the evangelical movement;" "doing good work, but not up to our standard": "the most significant indigenous evangelical movement among Italians in this generation."

This movement of Italian Pentecostals is one of the most significant of our day. It is reaching tens of thousands in the various colonies of Italians throughout the world and this with no financial or sympathetic encouragement from Protestant forces. It is now our privilege to express confidence in the work and mission of these people and offer our encouragement to them in their task. Those Italian and American pastors who already have the confidence of various Italian Pentecostal groups should keep a close relationship to them so as to guide them into an educational program for their youth while encouraging them not to relinquish their zeal for souls.

Chapter VI

PROGRAM

In any statement of the program of as large a number of churches under the direction of a varied administration the first recognition should be their diversity of aims and consequently their variety of methods and program. There are surprising differences in stated purposes. One institution's stated aim is "to share the good life" through neighborhood activities and services for the children. Its program is rich in the finest character building qualities,—(It could be desired that others might have its spiritual depth and truly educational technique) but it is limited to children by policy so that the organization of worship services for adults and young people shall not become a part of its program.

Another institution has an evangelical church for adults and young people but its Church School activity is planned for the "religious education of Roman Catholics and Jews, to make them better Roman Catholics and Jews rather than evangelical Christians." And the children of the Italian Protestant parents are expected to attend!

Still another Italian Protestant Church advertises the following program on its bulletin board: Sunday 10 A. M.—Mass; 11 A. M.—Mass; 3 P. M.—Benediction; Saturday—Confession. The pastor says, "This is a Catholic Church but we do not recognize the Pope."

At the other end of the list might be placed the program of one of the Pentecostal groups with three Praise services on Sunday, Testimony and Evangelistic service every week night. Diversified as these examples are the majority of the churches have a pattern of organization sufficiently alike to give ample basis for comparison and study.

TYPE OF ORGANIZATION

These centers are classified generally in three groups: 1) independent, self governing churches; 2) departments within large English speaking churches; or 3) missions of city societies or local churches. From the studies made of these Italian centers we have the following data:

	1912	1933
Churches	20	26
Departments	16	17
Missions	2	13
	—	—
	38	56

The Baptist and Episcopalians seem to favor strongly the independent church arrangements while the Methodists and to a greater degree the Presbyterians prefer the departmental method. The only Baptist groups listed as missions are those which are outposts of self-governing Italian Baptist Churches. Of the thirteen missions listed in this report seven are missions of Italian churches, indicating something of the virility and missionary zeal of these churches today. The Baptist preference for independent churches is understandable as being a result of their polity. Separate congregations cooperate in the use of a single building held as the property of one of the worshipping groups but used quite freely and harmoniously by several self-governing churches. Generally the Baptist City Society supports the idea of separate buildings as well as independent congregations for its Italian churches. The Presbyterian agencies in New York after beginning with independent organizations shifted to the departmental organization and have developed most of their enterprises this way. It is not due to the polity of the denomination nor is it the general practice (nationally there are three organized churches to one department) but grew out of the conviction of the leaders here that this method is the best adapted to the needs and circumstances of the Presbyterian Church in New York City.

The mission is generally a young organization started by a local church, English-speaking or Italian, in temporary quarters awaiting results before it is given larger place and responsibility as an independent church. Some missions have remained so for almost thirty years and although some sudden growths in membership are recorded in their life histories they have failed to gain permanency and strength because all responsibility is held by the parent organization. A Mission should be thought of only as a temporary stage in the development of a more adequate organization. Some might be only experiments in discovering the possibility of growth and after an adequate trial be discontinued. This is particularly true of the seven mission outposts of the Italian churches. One of these at present seems to be growing into a department of an English-speaking church, and at least one other is ready to become an independent church.

CHURCH MEMBERSHIP

Are the Italian churches growing? Can the record of statistics prove their success? Before we discuss the figures it would be well for us briefly to look at some of the results in the personalities who are leaders in this Italian colony of over one million people. In Brooklyn one of the leading pastors of an English-speaking church is a boy from an Italian church. In other American churches are several directors of Religious Education. The President of the Youth of New York Presbytery is an Italian young man from an English church. On the rolls of officers of Baptist, Methodist and Presbyterian churches in the city are Italians, some reached by the missions here, others in Italy, others by the American churches. Conservatively we estimate 2,000 persons of Italian background as members of English-speaking churches in New York City. The director of the Italian Welfare Society, the organizer of the Italian Chamber of Commerce, and a vice president of the Corn Exchange Bank are Italian Protestants. Mr. Ferdinand Pecora, County Prosecuting Attorney and Mayor F. La Guardia are members of Protestant churches. If this group of undisputed leaders in the Italian colony of this city came from the small fraction (3%) of the population known as Protestant, it seems that Italians do not lose status by their contact with

Evangelical institutions, nor can those who come to these institutions be held as coming because of "bribes," "loneliness" or "a peeve at the priest."

The figures on church membership as given by the three reports fail to give much light on our question (Are the Italian Churches growing?) because they are of too varied a group of churches. Many centers closing, others opening, still others merging makes it difficult to get meaningful data.

	1912	1926	1933
No. of churches reporting	38	42	51
Church membership	5581	4803	6676
33 Pentecostal Churches membership			2840
			9516

In order to give us some fair basis of judging the growth of individual churches over a sufficiently long period we have taken all the churches for which we had data for the years 1922 and 1933. Eighteen churches, chosen from the 51 reporting for the sole reason that data was available for these two years, showed an increase over the ten year period from 1,829 church members to 2,810 or a gain of 53 per cent. Taking them separately we find that 13 definitely gained in membership during this period, while 3 were static in their development and only 2 showed decline. The older churches in Manhattan and lower Brooklyn and the Bronx did not show such progress. But what neighborhood institutions did show progress in these areas that lost from 20% to 53% in population during the two decades 1910-1930? It might be more understanding to take the record of one of these churches in the heart of a disintegrating lower Manhattan community and see that while it reports 381 members today, its record shows 2,006 members received in the church during its 50 years of life. Also to note that 90% of those who have taken their letters have transferred to English speaking churches. To the definite knowledge of the church, forty-one of its members have gone into Christian service as ministers or missionaries.

We have included above the 2,840 members of the 33 Pentecostal congregations in our total membership figures. This group comprises almost 30% of the total number of members in Italian Evangelical churches. They are a part of the growth of the Evangelical movement and need to be considered as such.

We might also have added our conservative estimate of 2,000 Italian members of English speaking churches but as it is an estimate we have preferred to record it here only.

ADHERENTS

Various discussions regarding the number of persons who might be considered "adherents" of a church have given a wide variety of answers, depending on the type of church studied, its community, its program, its leadership, etc. The Baptist City Mission Society has its centers report the most carefully of any administrative agency on the number of adherents. They show·6,572 adherents to the 10 churches which reported 992 members. This indicates 6.5 adherents per member. The two largest Methodist institutions claim 9 Italian adherents to each member of the Italian congregation.

One other group of agencies not counted in our statistics because of their cosmopolitan enrollment but which nevertheless are an important part of the evangelical influence in Italian communities are the church neighborhood houses. Some have no church services, or Sunday school only, others have English services but no specific work for Italians, nevertheless, God's Providence House (Episcopal), Goodwill Center (Brooklyn City Mission Society) and others reach into many Italian homes in the spirit of the Master.

Thus it is conservative to state that there is a constituency of 30,000 Italian Protestants in New York City.

SUNDAY CHURCH SCHOOL

The enrollment of the Sunday church school in Italian language churches has changed very little during the last twenty years.

1912	1926	1933
4,741	4,906	4,942

Judging merely on the basis of the growth of the population of Italian youth in the city these figures show a disappointingly small growth in number of children reached by the Sunday church school. Our responsibility to show the child life of the community Jesus' way of life is not limited by any fences of "church families only" or "children assigned to our spiritual care." The change in our churches in the past twenty years into adult institutions is one of the most distressing. The warning cannot be too sharply sounded that we must reach the children if we are to build for the morrow. The table below indicates the trend that must be checked:

	Total		Presbyterian		Meth. Episcopal		Baptist	
	1912	1933	1912	1933	1912	1933	1912	1933
Church members	5581	6676	750	2348	292	1104	761	992
S. S. enrollment	4741	4942	1020	1529	630	1200	680	1126
No. S. S. enrollment per 100 ch. members	84.	74.	136.	65.	215.	92.	89.	113.

Mr. Yergin's figures in 1912 indicated that there were 84 children enrolled in the church schools of all the Italian churches of the city for every 100 church members. During the twenty years the percentage of children has dropped to 74. The Presbyterian and Methodist churches indicate a radical change from child-centered programs to adult-centered institutions, while the Baptists have moved toward being more child-centered. A healthy growing family has more children than parents; a healthy growing society must have more youths than adults, so a church if it is to grow healthily must have an emphasis on its program for youth.

It might be pointed out that the tendency in all city churches is toward a loss in the Sunday church school as compared with the church membership. The figures support this statement. However it is generally explained that English-speaking Methodists and Baptists have moved to the suburbs where they help to make the Sunday schools large. This leaves a still heavier responsibility on the churches that still find their constituency in the city. If the child life of our cities is to be reached, if Protestantism is to live in the cities of our land, these churches must reach them. Ten Methodist Episcopal churches were at one time located within a half mile of the present Church of All Nations. All of these churches have moved or closed and their responsibility is now the charter of this noble institution. The whole strategy of Protestantism it at stake in this phase of the work of our city churches. Only as our Italian churches and others like them are able to reach the growing life of the city can the message of the Christ live in the most densely populated centers of these urban communities.

STAFF

The basis for building the program of any institution is its staff whether paid or volunteer. Eight of the missions and churches among our 56 have no paid leadership, but are conducted entirely by earnest volunteers who seek to promote the interests of the Kingdom in their communities. These leaders are connected with some one of the older, more established churches and call upon their pastors for assistance and occasional service. There are 42 pastors in charge of the work with 48 other paid staff members assisting them directly. In such an institution as Labor Temple we have counted only the pastor of the Italian department for the other members of the staff of the institution are not directly assisting him in the work of the department although the staff is a unit in its common purpose. On the other hand all of the workers on the staff of Broome Street Tabernacle are counted because here the common objective is the building of the church led by the Italian pastor. The paid leadership is distributed thus:

9 institutions with ½ (part time) of one worker
23   "   "   1   worker
5   "   "   2   workers
3   "   "   3   "
1   "   "   5   "
1   "   "   6   "
2   "   "   7   "
2   "   "   8   "

This averages less than two paid workers per institution which is a low average for institutions trying to meet the needs of the great Italian population of this city.

PAID WORKERS

1912	1926	1933
65	126	90

There has been a decided reduction in staff workers since the boom days of 1926. The huge reduction in staff workers indicated in the Methodist figures may be accounted for by a different basis for counting the workers in such institutions as Church of All Nations, Five Points Mission, and People's Home Church (now discontinued as Italian work).

MINISTERIAL LEADERSHIP

Institutions	Total
No minister	8
Part time minister	10
Full time of minister	38

The 42 ministers engaged in the evangelical work among the Italians of New York City have charge of work in 48 centers with 8 missions which they serve voluntarily as needed. This corps of men who fellowship together in the Italian Ministerial Association of New York and vicinity are the very heart of the whole enterprise. We have discussed previously their qualifications for this leadership. Here we note that the policy of departmental work emphasized by the Presbyterians seems to carry with it the idea of one minister dividing his time between two centers . With the Baptists the men have specific relationship as pastor of one church but they seem very ready to volunteer their time to missions begun by their church members or even suggested by themselves.

One of the vexing questions which executives raise in regard to the minister and his relationship to his constituency is, "Does the pastor live in his parish?" The implication is that unless the minister does live in his parish he fails to identify himself completely with his people, prefering not to live in his own parish. In studying the question we found no advantage in dividing the group according to their denominational connection but found a suggestion toward the answer in a borough classification of the churches:

Location of Church	Pastor lives in Parish	Pastor lives out of Parish
Lower Manhattan	5	8
Upper "	1	5
Bronx	4	1
Brooklyn	11	1
Queens	2	0
Staten Island	5	0
	28	15

On Manhattan Island we find that the majority of ministers live away from their parish while pastors in all other boroughs (with two exceptions) live in the community of their church. Those who do live in their parishes on Manhattan all have their homes provided in the church building, which allows them some freedom from the neighborhood environment in building their own home life.

Chapter VII

ACTIVITIES

The following summary of the activities includes reports from the 48 centers with paid leadership. We have not included the 8 mission centers whose program is simply that of a small gathering in a home for a prayer circle, a Bible study period or a Sunday school for children of a few families who find it impossible to pay the expense of traveling regularly to their own church.

There are forty-four types of activity indicated as a regular part of the program of these centers. They vary in frequency from 45 Sunday church schools to 2 health clinics. The list below gives the activities in the order of their frequency in the program of the church

PROGRAM

Sunday church school	45	Daily Vacation Bible School	8
Morning worship	42	Basket ball for Girls	7
Girls clubs	36	English classes	6
Mothers clubs	31	Civics or citizenship	6
Mid-week service	30	Kindergarden	6
Church choirs	30	Italian classes	5
Young Peoples Societies	30	Glee clubs	5
Boys clubs	28	Piano instruction	5
Week-day R.E. or catechical class	19	Young Men's clubs	5
Vesper services	18	Boy Scouts or equivalent	5
Adult Bible classes	17	Girls Scouts or equivalent	5
Junior children's groups	15	Leadership Training	5
Basket ball for boys	13	Lectures or Forums	5
Handwork groups	11	Young Married Peoples Club	3
Gymnasium	10	Pre-school nursery	3
Evening services	10	Orchestra	3
Group meetings in homes	10	Visiting nurse	3
Camp	10	Library	3
Men's Clubs	10	Children's congregation	2
Young women's organizations	9	Street preaching	2
Dramatic groups	9	Clinic	2

Several items in this list are of interest and attract attention. Adding together the various music opportunities, such as choirs, glee clubs, instruction, orchestra, we have forty-three, indicating a real interest in music. Volunteers, trained paid directors and F.E.R.A. workers were used in the various centers in this program. On the whole the music work is not of the high quality which the interest shown indicates that it might be. One well-trained director of music could work with the music groups of three or four centers and immeassurably improve the singing and the whole worship program of the churches.

Thirty young people's societies exist in 48 centers. There is room for the M.I.P.U. to work with the pastors in attracting young people and building strong young people's programs.

When one considers that one church like the Church of San Salvatore alone has seven boys and girls clubs, the total of seventy-nine such clubs for 48 churches does not indicate an extensive use of the club method for reaching boys and girls during the week. The Boy Scouts and Girl Scouts or equivalent types of organ- ization do not seem to thrive in these centers with only ten indicated.

The mothers' clubs are an important factor in the program of the older churches, carrying something of the tradition of the earlier type of program. Rarely is it referred to as the Ladies Aid Society or Women's Organization as it would be in the English speaking churches.

Only six centers report English classes while five report classes in Italian for the children or young adults who wish to retain something of the cultural herit- age of their parents through the medium of the language.

Five groups report lectures and forums as a part of the regular program. Most of these are lectures by invited guests to young people's groups. There is no really active forum for the free discussion of problems in any of our centers. The Italian Department of Labor Temple a few years ago did conduct such a forum, true to the traditions of the institution, but that has been dropped in the last year or two. It would seem that some one center should be assigned the mission of presenting the gospel to socially or radically minded Italian groups in the city and that the funds available to that institution be used in conducting forums, discussion groups, classes, etc.

The program of the Italian centers which were started in the period from 1905 to 1914 was generally laid on the broad base of meeting the needs of the new strangers. Whether the need was social, educational, physical or spiritual an attempt was made to meet it. It was a progressive social program. As the Italians have become acclimated to our social life the needs for these special services de- creased and sometimes disappeared entirely, as for instance, the decrease in the number of classes in English and the disappearance of provision for baths. The need has either disappeared or it has been met by the institution of govern- ment specifically designated to meet these needs. Our centers, however, in- stead of continuing the pioneering program by searching for the new and growing social problems and experimenting with solutions to them have generally lapsed into the conventional church program. They say, "There is no need for us to do the social work any longer, we have been relieved of it by the other agencies, so we can give ourselves completely to the spiritual work."

May we analyse this statement briefly by examining some distinctive problems of our day? At the time this study was being made almost 20 per cent of the fam- ilies in New York City were on relief. The Italian population was a fair share of that group, yet not one of these institutions was providing activities, reading rooms, discussion groups, clubs for the building of the morale or the retaining of the physical powers of those unemployed persons. Thousands of young men and women are unable today in this city to find work and are lapsing because of the lack of stimulous into attitudes not conducive to attainment of the highest values in life. Yet only one center suggested that some use of their institution was being made during the day to meet the needs of three such young men who wanted a place to study.

Juvenile delinquency is more prevalent among children of Italian parents than among children of any other group. This is no prejudiced statement, it is a fact. Are churches interested in saving boys and girls? Further, we find in New York City the lack of family adjustment which produces juvenile delinquency is considerably higher for Italians than any other national group. Are the churches interested in Christian homes? Yet in no center was there a studied experimental attempt to meet these immensely important problems of the people. Crime prevention study and activities should be a part of the program of centers interested in the salvation of the Italian people of this city, for individually and socially the cancer of crime is destroying the moral strength of the family and the church.

Ten per cent of the men that attend the missions on the Bowery are Italians. Yet not one of our Italian churches makes provision in its program for the encouragement in Christian life of these men rescued by the missions, wanting to grow into wholesome Christians but failing so often because no opportunity is provided.

We might suggest the place of the Church in supporting the movement for better housing. It is with joy that we report that certain of our pastors have taken an active part on committees pushing this program. But we must study further. The members of our churches are feeling the pinch of the unbalanced economic system under which we are operating. Should all of their discussion and information concerning its workings come from the daily papers or street corner harangues? If we are to change our system should the ideals of Jesus have any place in its remaking?

These are merely suggestions of a few ways in which the progressive, experimental tradition of these centers might search for an expression of the good life. If we are to find the abundant way of life which the Master of joyous living has taught us we must continue eagerly the search. Our Italian churches are among those which are located in the communities where our society is sickest. The ills of our social body show first in these congested areas. If then in these places we can diagnose the disease while it is incipient, try various remedies applied with love and an insatiable desire to cure the body in order to save the soul, the greatest service to mankind can be rendered.

TRANSITION

Rapidly the transition from a distinctly Italian mission or church to that of the church of the community is taking place. The church will, of course, have its background of Italian work and will probably have services in the Italian language for some time but its place in the community will be that of serving all groups in its parish. Just as former Dutch, German, or Scotch churches are today serving all groups in their parish while still cherishing their old tradition with probably an occasional service in the old language, these Italian churches will meet the changing needs. The best examples of the progress of this transition are the Borough Park Baptist Church in Brooklyn and the Astoria Methodist Episcopal Church in Queens. In both of these the Sunday school and morning worship services are in English. In the community interchange of pastors and interchurch activities the Borough Park Church is as active as any, creating thereby an entirely new attitude toward "the church that turned Italian."

The following table indicates the extent of this change throughout the churches of the city. Language used in Sunday services:

Churches		English only	English & Italian	Italian only	French	Latin
42	Morning worship	9	7	23	1	2
24	Evening Service	4	1	18	1	—
45	Sunday Ch. School	30	Joint session with American School 13	0	2	—

YOUNG PEOPLE

It is natural that this change should be taking place and it is fortunate that the majority of the leaders in the churches are meeting the transition wisely. Inquiry into the number of young people who could read, speak and understand the Italian languague so as to be able to take part in the Italian services of their churches revealed an astoundingly low percentage in even the largest and most representative churches.

The sense of nationality or pride in heritage does not, however, disappear as does the use of the language. Therefor, it is not surprising to see the young people of these churches unite their societies in a Metropolitan Italian Protestant Union, where they feel a sense of common bond in their heritage but never use a word of Italian in their conversation, business or public meetings. "We, Protestant Young People of Greater New York of Italian origin and descent, believing in Evangelical Christianity and believing that its benefits can best be served and extended through the organization of young people for Christian service, do establish" this union. It is the presamble of the constitution which goes on to outline the method by which they feel Evangelical Christianity can be most adequately promoted among Italian young people. Assisting local societies to build stronger programs, cooperating with pastors in starting young people's societies and providing rallies or other united functions for the inspiration that comes from larger gatherings, are basic in the program of the Metropolitan Italian Protestant Union.

It is young, it has enthusiastic and capable leadership.

NEIGHBORHOOD CENTERS

The line between the neighborhood houses under Protestant auspices and the churches is sometimes very difficult to draw. It cannot be said that one is a more positive evangelizing force than another. We have therefore made an arbitrary division on the basis of whether the staff includes an Italian minister whose duties would be assumed to be those of building or directing an evangelical group.

The five neighborhood houses listed are all doing a fine piece of work with a thoroughgoing six day a week program. Young People's groups in which the problems of the day are discussed are perhaps the closest these centers get to a church or evangelical program. The spirit of the Christ is present in the whole purpose of the work and the Christian motive that impels the workers in their service. By their very presence these people interpret the very meaning of the fuller ,happier and more abundant life, but either by personal conviction or policy of the institution they are restrained from sharing with the adults or young people the very experience which motivates their own life. Despite the fact of the organizational set-up these institutions are unquestionably factors in the total impact of the evangelical movement.

COOPERATING AGENCIES

The New York Bible Society and the New York Tract Society are large contributors to the evangelical movement through their gifts of Bibles, Testaments, portions and tracts to the workers. The Bible Society has three Italian ministers as part-time colporteurs in Manhattan, Bronx and Staten Island. These men are expected constantly to make new contacts and distribute the Word so that it might do its own effectual work in the changing of life. But not only do these colporteurs receive all the materials they need, either in the Italian or English language, for distribution, but all ministers officially connected with home mission churches can get all they can use in their work. One pastor reported that he used Gospels and Testaments so regularly that his requests amounted to at least $50 for materials per year. This is a service of inestimable value to our missionary pastors.

The New York Tract Society is a similar agency, making available tracts in various languages interpreting simply the gospel message for the use of colporteurs, missionaries and pastors. It is compelled to sell at a very low price, however, the materials prepared. There are at present two Italian colporteurs officially connected with this Society working in the city.

That tract material, giving experiences of converts, histories of growing evangelical fellowships, sermons, and controversial discussions, is an important part of the evangelical method is shown by the editorial policy of the veteran journal "L'Aurora" and the expressed purpose of the new publication "Il Rinnovamento." These papers sponsored, edited and largely supported by the evangelical pastors and their congregations are further evidence of the growth and independence of this movement.

The active Italian Ministerial Association of Greater New York is a fellowship, clearing ground and stimulus to all those ministers who take advantage of the opportunity it offers. The usual monthly program is an inspirational talk or a discussion of some common problem to which some member has a suggestion for solution. Occasionally some problem is presented on which a common opinion is needed. Here concerted action gives a sense of solidarity and unity important to the spiritual life of these men. It would seem wise to at least once a year enlarge the fellowship by inviting in the pastors of American churches which either have Italian groups meeting in their building or have a large number of Italian families coming into their church fellowship. This would strengthen still further the sense of spiritual unity in the task of meeting the needs of this great Italian colony.

The thirty thousand Italian Protestants of this city are an important group in the social life of the colony. Nevertheless they are only about 3 per cent of the total number of Italians and they are constantly aware of their being in the minority. The M.I.P.U. did a fine thing in their "Italian Protestant Day" program with a huge rally and radio program. An occasional gathering of this sort is stimulating. Vision, devotion, zeal of missionary executives, pastors and lay folks have made possible this triumph of faith. It will live and grow because of their earnest faith.

Chapter VIII

FINANCES

Over $100,000 of Home Mission aid is expended annually by the eleven denominations which are working in this evangelical movement of the Italians in this city. In the 23 buildings which are used exclusively for work under Italian leadership over $1,360,000 has been spent in construction. This is a significant Home Mission enterprise. It needs to be guided as a whole, an integrated enterprise, to most effectively accomplish its end.

BUILDINGS

	1912			1926			1933		
	Bldg.	Store	Dept.	Bldg.	Store	Dept.	Bldg.	Store	Dept.
Totals	11	7	21	20	3	27	23	4	25
Total		39			50			52	

There has been a steady and decided gain in the number of church buildings devoted entirely to the work under Italian leadership. The number of stores used has always been small, as it should be. The unfortunate fact is, however, that two of the four stores used at present have been used continuously for twenty years. No work can command the interest or respect of Italian citizens in this way. The number of departments or church buildings shared with another congregation is slightly higher than twenty years ago.

BUDGETS

The distribution of budgets for the Italian work at the various centers is always of great interest. In 1926 Miss Voorhis made such a distribution. It differs so decidedly from the one for this year that we hesitate to assign all of the difference to the "depression." It is quite evident that she had a base for her figure somewhat different from the one which we use. We have only the statment that this is "the distribution of Italian budgets in all of the centers." Our aim has been to determine the actual cost of the Italian work alone in each center.

	Total	Less than $2,000-	$4,000- 3,999	$6,000- 5,999	$8,000- 7,999	$10,000- 9,999	$15,000- 14,999	over 19,999	$20,000
1926	38	2	17	4	4		6	3	2
1934	51	19	22	5	1	2	2		

The shift into the "less than $2,000" class is noticeable and regrettable. The movement out of the "over $15,000" group is a clean sweep. The total cost of operation of this work annually again gives us a wide range of costs.

	1912	1933
Annual cost of operation:..................................	$85,450	$158,225

Again the great disparity between Miss Voorhis' figures and both the 1912 and 1933 figures raises doubts. She commented in 1926 thus, "This large increase may be explained in part by the more adequate equipment involving great overhead expense." The same "adequate equipment" is being used today but is being manned more and more by volunteers or cut down in total program. Let us examine these figures still further.

PER MEMBER COSTS AND GIFTS

The usual per member cost of operation of churches is approximately $20 annually. In New York Presbytery the average is $26. In the light of this we can look at the cost of these mission centers with small memberships but great tasks to perform. We can analize it best by taking the whole picture of costs and gifts together:

	1912	1926	1933
Annual cost of work..................................	$85,450.00		$158,225.00
Per member cost..................................	$ 15.31		$ 23.70
Annual contribution to current expense.....	$ 7,101.00	$35,227.00	$ 43,414.00
Per member contribution..........................	$ 1.27	$ 7.33	$ 6.50
Ratio of contribution to cost......................	8.3		27.4

The per member cost of operating these 52 centers is $23.70 annually. When we realize what this means on the basis of the median church membership (98) we can judge the adequacy of these centers to cope with the problems of this city. The median budget is $2,960. May we make a comparison so as to see more clearly this matter of the adequacy of the institutions? Generally when "city churches" are discussed some great churches like the Madison Avenue or Fifth Avenue groups come to mind. We have picked at random four Fifth Avenue churches and we present them in comparison here:

	Fifth Avenue Churches	Italian Centers
Number Institutions	4	52 (27 separate buildings)
Total membership	4,908	6,676
Total S.S. enrollment............	781	4,942
Total cost of work............	$275,491	$158,225
Per member cost............	$ 56.13	$ 23.70

With seven times as many buildings to keep in working condition and twice as many definite enrollments the Italian centers operate on 60 per cent the budget of the four adequate city churches.

The growth in the support of the work by the Italians is reassuring. Had it not been for this steady growth, even in the depression period, the work would have fared sadly. While in 1912 the Italians contributed 8.3% of the total cost of the work, in 1933 they shared 27.4% of it. That there is a real movement toward self-support is indicated by studying the percentages of its total cost which each congregation contributes.

Percentage of total costs contributed by congregation	No. congregations
100 per cent	6
40-60 "	5
30-39 "	14
20-29 "	2
10-19 "	11
0-9 "	12

The above table can be qualified by saying that only two of the congregations in the 100 per cent class have buildings to support. These two are under the leadership of one pastor who has been able to achieve this standing. It is also illuminating to use the denominational division:

Percentage of Contributions Toward Total Costs

	Over 30 per cent	Under 30 per cent
Presbyterian	8	9
M. E.	4	3
Baptist	4	6
Protestant Episcopal	3	2
Others	6	5
	—	—
Total	25	25

The operation of Baptist centers is the highest cost per member, but they receive almost twice as much support per member as any other group. Is this due to the policy of separate buildings and self-governing congregations? The Presbyterians are low in costs influenced by the departmental nature of their work, but they likewise receive very little support.

The question of why the support is what it is from these various centers cannot be answered by the denominational analysis, or by studies based on geographic areas. It must be done on the study of the economic areas from which the constituency is drawn. This too is the answer to those who ask why the Italian centers are not supporting themselves. Churches of any nationality with as small a median membership fail to support themselves in the lower income areas. The newspapers of the city made a Market analysis in 1932 and divided the city into what they termed "income areas." There are five groups based on the family income in thousand dollar steps from "under $2,000" to the "over $5,000." Four boroughs were so analyzed, Staten Island evidently being considered too small a market to be studied.

Family Income Area Analysis of Church Support

Areas	Family Income	No. churches in Area	Medium giving	Median cost	Per cent of cost contributed
1	Under $2,000	15	$4.15	$26.24	11
2	$2,000-2,999	15	5.40	26.90	25
3	3,000-3,999	13	8.50	21.42	34
4	4,000-4,999	none	—	—	—
5	5,000 & over	none	—	—	—
S. I.		5	6.90	23.43	32.

As the family income rises from below subsistence level to one of health and decency the amount of giving rises rapidly. The people are willing and can be taught and encouraged to support their own work when they are able. One of the definite signs of this willingness is in the amount of volunteer work which these people, especially the young people, are now giving to their churches in order to continue the work begun by paid workers who have had to be dropped.

THE FUTURE

In the future we shall need to see the work of the evangelization of the Italians in the terms of three general problems. There is no one Italian type of church any more than there is one American type. Nor is there any one approach to the Italian. The suggestion is that the first type of work is distinctly missionary in the older colonies of Italians which will in the future become less and less Italian while becoming more cosmopolitan. These colonies will be made up of those persons and families which for various reasons, physical, mental or social, are forced to remain or wish to remain in these areas of low social status. These churches must be thought of as missionary, be endowed or supported for a long-time progressive experimental program.

The second type of work will be with the second generation in the Italian colonies everywhere. Here the problems of adjustment between the older and younger generation, old and new cultures and traditions present a challenge to the Church. Most of our churches are in this class. They are growing in their responsibility for their own work. They should become self-supporting within twenty years.

The need here is to give these congregations more and more of the responsibility for the church's program and financing. Annually the total program of the local church should be built by its lay people in conference with the paid leaders. Annually also the basic financial budget of each congregation should be made and planned for by the congregation. As a result of these plans they might request assistance in meeting their own needs from the mission society. The imperative need in these churches is more responsibility and leadership in the democratic growth of the fellowship. As more of the leadership for the spiritual growth of the group comes from within the group itself the more sturdily will it grow.

The third type of work is one yet little realized although it is the largest field. There is no district of the city where Italians do not live. We can say that there is probably not a Protestant church that does not have Italians in its parish. The work of making these Americans an integral part of our parishes is the next important step. It has begun without the guidance of the missionary agencies. It needs now their support, study and encouragement.

Many Italian families who have been in contact with evangelical churches throughout the years are now in new communities away from Italian churches. Our funds should be consecrated to giving additional leadership to churches that might reach many of these new Americans as a regular part of their task of being churches for the whole of the community. This has been done by a few churches but it needs to be recognized as a more definite policy. Young Italian Americans trained in American seminaries and schools of religious education can help our English speaking churches enlarge their service in this direction. Thus a new cycle of the task of the evangelization of the Italians in New York City can move just as the first one. Started by individuals and churches with the vision to serve their neighbors, then supported by the missionary agencies until it flourishes into its own strength.

Our job is not done. For fifteen to twenty years we shall need to hold services in the Italian language in many communities in this city. For much longer than that we will be supporting home mission enterprises in communities now primarily Italian. While a goodly number of the Italian people in this city have found strength, inspiration and fellowship in the Evangelical churches yet thousands are without a spiritual outlook on life and need the grace and love of the Fellowship to raise them from the despair and doubt of an unanchored life. Many have found their fellowship within the Roman Church, many have found it in the Evangelical churches of either American or Italian tradition, but many still are unreached. Having lost faith in the church of their homeland they are adrift in this perplexing new land. "A Christian nation is a nation of Christians, of individuals won to discipleship of Jesus Christ, unted in Christian fellowship and Christian service, accepting the full implications of their discipleship, creating for themselves Christian institutions and a Christian influence. That such an end is above all else worthy of our united effort and that it can be achieved through Christ is the dearest conviction of Home Missions and of the Church it represents." (1) Seeking to achieve this goal, we press on toward the mark of presenting to our fellow citizens of Italian birth or heritage this high calling of life made vivid, full, exuberant, through Christ.

---

(1) Home Missions Today and Tomorrow p. 5.

Centers of Italian Evangelization of Protestant Denominations

With their ministers as of the time of this survey, Winter of 1933-34

C—*Church*   D—*Department*   M—*Mission*

Church	Denomination	Type of Organ'z'n.	Address	Minister
Borough of Manhattan				
Church of San Salvatore	P. E.	C	359 Broome St.	Rev. John Castelli
Broome St. Tabernacle	City Miss'n	C	395 Broome St.	Rev. Joseph Brunn
Five Points Mission	M. E.	D	69 Madison St.	Rev. V. Carulli
Mariners Temple	Baptist	C	3 Henry St.	Rev. C. Pagano
Church of Sea & Land	Presby.	D	61 Henry St.	Rev. J. A. Villelli
Bethlehem Mem'l.	"	C	34 Charlton St.	Rev. Gaetano Lisi
Church of All Nations	M. E.	D	9 Second Ave.	Rev. O. Schiavoni
Olivet Memorial Church	City Missn.	D	59 Second St.	Rev. A. Hugon
DeWitte Mem'l Church	" "	D	280 Rivington St.	" " "
Second Ave. Baptist Ch.	Baptist	D	164 Second Ave.	Rev. R. Mingioli
Labor Temple	Presby.	D	244 E. 14th St.	Rev. A. Mangiacapra
Christ Church	Un. Luth.	C	406 E. 19th St.	Rev. C. D. Del'Osso
Judson Mem'l. Church	Baptist	D	55 Washington Sq.So.	Rev. J. Di Tiberio
Waldensian Church	Presby.	D	7 West 11th St.	Rev. B. Tron
1st Waldensian Church	Waldensian	C	409 West 41st St.	Rev. P. Griglio
Christ Church	Presby.	D	336 West 36th St.	Rev. R. Valenti
Church of the Covenant	"	D	310 East 42nd St.	" " "
John Hall Mem'l. Chapel	"	D	342 E. 63rd St.	——
Church of the Ascension	"	C	340 E. 106th St.	Rev. A. Stasio
St. Ambrose	P. E.	C	236 E. 111th St.	Rev. F. DeCristoforo
Italian Church	7th Day Adv.	C	307 E. 112th St.	Rev. A. Catalano
Jefferson Church	M. E.	C	407 E. 114th St.	Rev. P. Campo
Borough of Bronx				
Holy Trinity	Presby.	C	253 E. 153rd St.	Rev. A. Zaccara
St. John the Baptist	Baptist	C	2411 Lorillard Pl.	Rev. Paul Buffa
Church of the Evangel	Presby.	C	204th St. & Villa Ave.	Rev. G. Verdesi
Williamsbridge	"	D	732 E. 225th St.	Rev. N. Testa
St. Mary's of the Angels	P. E.	C	729 Cranford Ave.	Rev. L. Di Sanno
Olmstead Avenue	Presby.	M		——
Mission (St. John)	Baptist	M	2428 Matthews Ave.	——
Borough of Queens				
1st Italian, Astoria	M. E.	C	14-54—31st Road	Rev. A. Sartorio
Resurrection	M. E.	C	58-43r Ave., Corona	Rev. D. Rossi
Mission	M. E.	M		" " "
Mission	Baptist	M	2352 95th St. Corona	——

Centers of Italian Evangelization of Protestant Denominations

With their ministers as of the time of this survey, Winter of 1933-34

C—*Church*   D—*Department*   M—*Mission*

Church	Denomination	Type of Organ'z'n.	Address	Minister
Borough of Richmond				
Trinity	Moravian	C	Third St., New Dorp	Rev. E. Barletta
Holy Trinity	M. E.	C	12 Eunice Pl. Graniteville	Rev. S. Buzzalini
Calvary	Presby.	D	23 West St. W. New Brighton	Rev. J. DeRogatis
Rosebank	"	M	St. Mary's Ave. Rosebank	" " "
Holy Redeemer	P. E.	C	43 Jewett Ave. Port Richmond	Rev. C. Di Sanno
Borough of Brooklyn				
Nostrand-DeKalb	M. E.	D	Nostrand & Quincy	Rev. A. Signore
Church of the Brethren	Un. Breth.	C	266 Twentieth St.	Rev. G. Allegri
St. Peter's	Un. Presby.	C	171 Hopkinson Ave.	Rev. Baradelli
New Utrecht	Reformed	D	18th Ave. & 84th St.	Rev. Sylvan Poet
Italian Church	7th Day Adv.	C	176 Atlantic Ave.	Rev. A. Catalano
Mission	7th Day Adv.	M	Coney Island	" " "
St. John's	Presby.	M	53 Central Ave.	Rev. D. Colaneri
St. James	"	M	Elton St. & Arlington	" " "
Gregg Chapel	"	M	190 Fourth Ave.	Rev. A. Malinverni
Canarsie	Baptist	C	1186 Remsen Ave.	Rev. B. Franconi
Strong Place	Baptist	D	491 Henry St.	Rev. Stabelli
Our Saviour	"	C	444 Liberty Ave.	Rev. G. Basile
Borough Park	"	C	1105 67th St.	Rev. G. Dellutri
First Italian	"	C	16 Jackson St.	Rev. A. Mangano
Mission (1st Italian)	"	M	1446 South Ave.	Rev. G. Basile
Mission (St. John)	"	M	1215 61st St.	——
Mission (Borough Park)	"	M	1004 Avenue X	——
Emmanuel House	"	M	131 Steuben St.	Rev. Zibelli
Neighborhood Houses or Christian Centers				
God's Providence House	P. E.		330 Broome St.	Manhattan
Grace Church N. H.	P. E.		415 East 14th St.	Manhattan
East New York N. H.	Presby.		2030 Pitkin Ave.	Brooklyn
Goodwill Center	City Missn.		York and Gold Sts.	Brooklyn
Children's Center	Cong.		118 Fourth Place	Brooklyn

Italian
Evangelical Pioneers

by

JOHN B. BISCEGLIA, Th.D. (*Magna cum laude*)

Author of "Italy's Contribution to the Reformation"

1948

BROWN-WHITE-LOWELL PRESS, INC.

Kansas City, Missouri

Printed in United States of America

To My Children
MARY ELIZABETH, KATHRYN MARIE,
FRANCIS PAUL and THOMAS JOHN

TABLE OF CONTENTS

Introduction

"He whom a dream hath possessed
knoweth no more of doubting."

The story of the evangelization of the Italians in America has all the necessary elements for a first class book, which would meet a ready public made up not only of old converts who were thrilled and won over by the message of salvation coming from the lips of the pioneers, but of the new generations, blessed and fascinated whenever they hear the story of that noble galaxy who, in obedience to the Lord's command to go and preach the Gospel, became kindred spirits with all the pioneer missionaries whose heart yearning was expressed by the Apostle Paul: "Woe unto me if I preach not the Gospel."

These noble pioneers are not different from all those who have enriched the life of the world, except in this respect, that they sought no personal gain. They blazed new trails with prophetic vision, they met difficulties with stout hearts, they were motivated by sacrificial spirits, they knew in advance that when the promised land was in sight, they would not be permitted to enter in, that their task was just to prepare the way and then relinquish the torch to others.

No great church buildings, no large congregations, no self-supporting organization would crown their herculean efforts; there would be no adequate returns for their labor, no monument was to perpetuate their memories, no poetry to sing their accomplishments, no canvas to immortalize their deeds; their task was simply to build stout foundations that no one would see, their glory was to work in real Christian humility, their reward was to be the "well done" from those sacred lips and the crown of everlasting life from His scarred hands.

These are just brief pen portraits of some of the Italian pioneers and evangelical workers. Had we contemplated a

more comprehensive work, many others would have been
included. We trust that someone else with greater ability and
more time, closer to the sources of information, may be inspired by this feeble effort to undertake such a work of love.

If it is true that the man who has vision and no task is a
dreamer, and the man with a task and no vision is a drudge,
then the man with the task, a vision and a determination is a
hero. Judged by this measuring rod, these men and women
are the real unsung heroes of the Cross.

> Speak, History! Who are life's victors?
> Unroll the long annals and say,
> Are they those whom the world calls victors?
> Who won the success of a day?
> The Martyrs, or Nero?
> The Spartans who fell by Thermopylae's tryst?
> Or the Persians and Xerxes?
> His Judges? Or Socrates? Pilate? Or Christ?

No one will ever know the sufferings, the heartaches, the
privations and the martyrdom of these humble pioneers, who
depended not directly upon a congregation that saw the problem, appreciated the efforts and was able to supply the need,
but on boards whose members visited the work occasionally or
on superintendents who, directing by remote control, were
often misled by large figures and loud talk.

1

The Religion of the Italians

Sometime ago I had the privilege of meeting a prominent surgeon, well known in several states and much loved in his city for his charitable work. I wish you could have seen his surprise when I was introduced to him as a Presbyterian Minister serving an Italian congregation. Had he not been a scientist, accustomed to inhibit his emotions, he would have remarked, as hundreds have during my ministry, "Why, I thought that all the Italians were Roman Catholics!" Such ignorance on the part of otherwise intelligent men and women becomes less shocking when I am reminded that the non-protestant Italians are on the whole equally uninformed, and almost unaware of this vital movement outside the Roman Church, which, albeit small numerically, has exercised tremendous influence in the history of our country, and in the life of our people here and abroad.

New Testament Italians

Several years ago, in order to clear the minds of my own people, I spent many delightful hours with them in the study of the Italians of the Gospel. Beginning with the four Gospels, we made the acquaintance of the centurion whose servant was sick, and we learned from the lips of the Master that He "had not found so great faith, no, not in Israel." We blushed somewhat as we traced the life of Pilate, a politician and an opportunist, who tried to wash his hands of Jesus, but as we knelt at the Cross we met a fine captain of the guards who was first to confess Christ after His Crucifixion, and we heard him exclaim, "Truly this was the Son of God."

In the book of Acts our hearts rejoiced in finding that the first Gentile to be converted was none other than our countryman Cornelius, a centurion of the Italian band, "a devout man and one who feared God with all his house, who gave much alms to the people, and prayed to God always." We were agreeably surprised to discover Sergius Paulus, governor of the Island of Paphos, a man of understanding, who was converted by the Apostle Paul. However, our rejoicing came almost to an end with the discovery of Gallio, pro-consul of Achaia, who is a good representative of many of our people today in his utter indifference toward religion. Nor were we very much complimented by the ignorance of Claudius Lysias, even though he succeeded in saving Paul's life.

As we proceeded with our study we made the unpleasant acquaintance of Tertullus, the orator, who literally covered Paul with calumnies; of Felix, who was very much impressed with the Gospel message but would prefer to wait for a more convenient season, and of Festus, who ridiculed Paul. But our spirits were lifted up by Julius, who treated Paul kindly and gave him leave to go to his friends and refresh himself, and by Publius, prefect of the Island of Malta, who was benefited by Paul and who in turn was very kind to him and received the Gospel in his household. Our journey ended with a very brief study of the letter to the Romans. We were challenged by the Apostle Paul, and we accepted his challenge when he reminded us that the faith of our ancestors was spoken of throughout the world.

All Roads Start from Rome

We had been so fascinated with such a study that we decided to make a very brief survey of church history, and our hearts went out to the men and women, young and old, as they worshipped in the catacombs, and as they defied ten fierce persecutions in three brief centuries. We wept as we pictured them devoured by hungry beasts, burned alive to light the gardens of Nero and to satisfy his thirst for blood; and we were tempted to imitate our youngest boy who, when he saw the moving picture "The Sign of the Cross" and heard the cries of a boy emanating from a torture chamber, broke a very tense moment in a full house with the shout, "Stop it!"

We felt anew the urge to take up the battle cry of Christianity, as voiced by John R. Mott, Sherwood Eddy and Robert E. Speer three or four decades ago, "The evangelization of the world in this generation." Our hearts were thrilled as we saw legions of foreign and home missionaries marching on the same roads and bridges constructed by the legionaries, this time, however, not under the eagles to conquer or to destroy, slaughter or exploit, but under the banner of the Cross to free from sin and superstition, and to preach Christ and Him Crucified.

REFORM MOVEMENTS

Christianity has demonstrated over and over again an enormous digestive ability, and has accordingly absorbed and assimilated much from other sources. But even such stupendous capacity reaches a saturation point sooner or later; so we find that Romanism, having taken up much objectionable paganism foreign to the mind and spirit of Christ, found itself in sharp contrast with His teachings and in the direct line of His fiery invectives, addressed during his earthly ministry, to those who had contaminated "pure and undefiled religion."

As Christianity became the religion of the state, and as wealth poured into the coffers of the Church, she became corrupted with idolatry, simony and superstition. It was then in Italy that many voices were raised protesting against the wrong. We saw the glorious pre-reformers in action, sealing their faith with their blood, writing one of the most glorious pages in the history of the Reformation. We can only give here a glimpse of the triple contribution made by Italy, in preserving the documents which were indispensable in the fight for religious freedom; through the Renaissance she discovered the documents and furnished the tools for the Reformation, and with the pre-reformers she organized the protest and laid the foundations which paved the way for the Reformation.

Four centuries before the Lord summoned Luther in Germany and Calvin in France, almost three centuries before Huss in Bohemia and Wycliff in England, Arnaldo Da Brescia (1105-1155), the first martyr of the Reformation, denounced with irresistable eloquence and courage all the abuses of the Roman Catholic Church. He was accused before the Lateran Council and in the year 1155 was hanged and then burned, pierced by a spear, and his ashes scattered on the Tiber River.

Marsiglio Di Padova (1280-1340) was in many ways the mind of the Reformation in Italy. The Roman Catholic historians Dollinger, Pastor and Riezler called him Calvin before Calvin and the forerunner of Luther. Dr. Philip Schaff says his program was a proclamation of complete changes such as the sixteenth Century witnessed. His protest may be briefly stated as follows:

1. Religious tolerance.
2. The Church is made up of all believers.
3. The Church must not own temporal goods.
4. It is the right of the people to elect or depose the pope.
5. The pope has no more authority or jurisdiction than other Bishops and Priests, because they are all equal by the Institution of Christ.
6. Neither the pope nor any other for him can exercise any act of coercion against any heretic, this power belonging only to the emperor.
7. The ruler must be elected by the people.
8. The pope is subject to the state.
9. The pope is not infallible.
10. St. Peter was never in Rome
11. The function of binding and loosing is not judicial, but a declarative one.
12. The general councils may err and laymen should sit in them.
13. The Scriptures are the ultimate seat of religious authority.

In our book on *Italy's Contribution to the Reformation* we have demonstrated in detail how Dante and Petrarch denounced openly the vices of the Roman Catholic Church, how Laurentius Valla (1405-1457), whom Bellarmine called the forerunner of Luther, and whose works Luther esteemed very highly, made a fine contribution to the Reformation. We presented Francis of Assisi as a real son of the Church universal; Peter Waldo, founder of the great and glorious Waldensian Church; and Savonarola (1498-1542), who was the Italian prophet and organized an independent government in Florence which had as a motto "Christ is our King," who having incurred the hatred of Alexander VI, who wrote "Even if he be John the Baptist he must die," on May 23, 1542, was burned alive with two of his companions. To the Bishop who, tearing his garments, pronounced the sentence, "I separate thee from the militant and triumphant church," Savonarola said: "Not from the triumphant." Of his martyrdom Catholic historians have said that this prophet, who like Elijah preached righteousness, was unjustly condemned. His statue since has been placed in the gallery of 500 in Florence (Westminster Abbey) and a place has been given him in the Reformers statue at Worms.

Someone said that when the Germans were converted the leader, in being immersed, extended his right arm, holding the sword, above the waters, and that this explains the belligerent nature of the Germanic people. If I were to offer an explanation for the superstitious and idolatrous nature of many of our people, I would say that the idols were converted but not the hearts of the people. The Romans during the days of the empire permitted all the conquered people a great deal of freedom in religious matters and allowed them to bring their gods to a very inclusive temple in Rome which was called the temple of all the gods. As you recall, they had a god of war and a god of peace, a god for the fields and a god for the sea, a god which would protect them from the tempest and one who saved them from sickness; in a word, they had a god for every need in life. The Roman Catholic church adopted all these gods, changed their names, and called them saints, thus causing Dante to exclaim:

> Ye have made yourselves a god of gold and silver;
> And from the Idolator how differ ye,
> Save that he one, and ye a hundred worship?

The well-known historian and politician, Nicholo Machiavelli, remarked, "The Roman Catholic Church, in order to make her people believe so many impossible things, ended in making them believe in nothing."

PRESENT DAY ITALIANS

The Roman Catholic Church has four different groups among our people living in Italy or in our immigrant communities. The first group is made up of people whose connection with the church is due only to the fact that they were brought there to be baptized, led there to be united in marriage, and will be carried there for their funeral service. Another group maintains its connection with the church because it is the religion of the state. A third group, intellectual but spiritually indifferent, is composed of those who feel that since Rome lost her political supremacy they must help preserve her spiritual power in the world. Finally, there is a considerable group which is sincerely, though wrongly, convinced of the adequacy of the teachings of the Roman Church.

Italian Protestants in Italy today are still confessing their faith in spite of discriminations, moral and spiritual sufferings, and persecutions. The governmental census of 1931 gave the Protestants of Italy a membership of 83,618. These figures include, of course, only those who were baptized in Protestant Churches during their infancy, excluding all those who have been converted. Had the latter been included, the figures would have mounted well above 50 per cent more. The Waldensian Church, which is Presbyterian both in doctrine and in government, is the largest group, followed in order by Methodists, Baptists and smaller groups.

There are about five million Italian-born, or of Italian extraction, in America, most of whom are at least nominally

Roman Catholics. Coming chiefly from the farming districts of southern Italy, they have been the victims of social and economic discriminations, of priestly graft and idolatry. In consequence, many of them have grown indifferent to religion. As these masses of Italians came to the United States they congregated in our large cities on the Atlantic and Pacific coast, but some gradually moved toward the central states, until now they are to be found scattered more or less all over the country. Different Protestant denominations soon became interested in these newcomers, and missions were started in many centers, whose varied success was determined by the interest of the sponsoring groups, the competence and consecration of the workers, proper equipment for this important task, and the constancy with which committees and workers remained at a particular task.

An Interdenominational National Conference of ministers of Italian extraction was held in the Broome Street Tabernacle, New York City, during the first week of November, 1946. This Tabernacle, which has been in use for sixty-four years, is the oldest church building erected for the Italian work in this country. At this meeting three hundred churches and missions were reported, with over twenty-five thousand communicants, as many as forty thousand Sunday School pupils, and many young people's groups, which brought the aggregate number to over one hundred thousand. In this country and in Canada the Presbyterian Church is in the lead, followed closely by Methodists, Baptists, Lutherans, Episcopalians and many smaller groups.

From this seemingly negligible number of Italian Protestants in America is coming fine leadership in education and politics, in social and charitable institutions. This fact will be much more clear when I say that at one time, out of four congressmen of Italian extraction, two were Protestants; that the first mayor of Italian extraction of the largest city in America, the late Fiorello H. LaGuardia, was a Protestant. The Hon. Charles Polletti, Lieutenant-Governor of New York and later the head of the military government of Italy; and Ferdinando Pecora, one time special counsel for the Senate Investigation Committee, and now Judge of the Supreme Court of New York, are also Protestants.

Our people today are called to give up fathers and mothers, brothers and sisters, friends and relatives in order to follow Christ. We are accused of being renegades and deserters as in times of old, and we join Clement of Alexandria who, belonging to a second century cultivated pagan family, described his steps from paganism to Christianity as "taking the noble risk of a desertion unto God." We leave it to your imagination to understand some of the pathos and heroism in a great experience so modestly expressed. Our faith is challenged by ridicule, a spirit of intolerance, and all sorts of discriminations, taboos and persecutions, but we trust most will come out purified, our stature made more heroic by the ordeal, and our lives more worthy of a crown.

The work among the Italians has not been pursued as it should have been by the various denominations for two chief reasons; first because Boards become discouraged for lack of apparent results, and secondly because they cannot find sufficient qualified workers willing to undertake the task and make it their life work. To the first objection we would remind our friends that the standard of measurement must not be the success achieved in American communities, where the work is among Protestants and the task consists chiefly in gathering the people together and reviving their spiritual interests. Our work, instead, is with people who have grown indifferent to religion because of a thousand abuses and superstitions; therefore by its very nature it is slow, discouraging, heart-breaking at times, but worth-while and, if we compare results with similar enterprise, most heartening. To the second objection, we would suggest this remedy, that young people of vision, ability, consecration and training be enlisted, given special training, furnished with adequate up-to-date equipment, and be considered on equality socially and economically with our ministerial brethren who serve larger and more prosperous churches.

Our claim is just and I firmly believe that we have something worth-while, something which affects the lives of people for time and for eternity. It is our sacred duty, in obedience to His command, to share it with all those who have it not. In order to be consistent, *we must either shout our beliefs from the house tops*, especially on controversial subjects, or rewrite our history, confess that the Reformation was a mistake, that all the martyrs during and after the Reformation died in vain, and that their sacrifice is a colossal blunder. We should recall at once our missionaries from Cuba, Porto Rico, Mexico, South America and the Philippine Islands. Since the Roman Church believes and teaches that there is no salvation outside of the Roman Church, and hence that you and I are lost, like Henry IV we should go to Canossa and stand in penitence until we are admitted; yes, we should seriously become concerned about the souls of our departed loved ones and buy their way out of Purgatory.

2

The Pioneer as a Soul Winner
(Antonio Andrea Arrighi)

The Protestant work among the Italians in America was started in New York, where the East meets the West, where the peddlers sell their wares in ancient carts, and where the motley crowd strives for expression in a babel of tongues. The story of the man who started this work has the ingredients of a first-class novel. Almost adolescent he ran away from home, fought for the freedom of Italy, was made a prisoner, escaped, came to America, ventured in the Middle West, and after his conversion prepared for the ministry, was ordained in Rome and returned to start the work among his countrymen in this country. He was the first Italian prophetic voice in America calling the new immigrants to God.

Loaded with plaster of Paris toys, images and ornamental works, and crying in a rich musical voice: "Beautiful toys very cheap," a most handsome young man with an abundant crop of curly black hair peddled his strange assortment through the streets of Des Moines, Iowa. Sunday arrived, he did not know what to do with himself, since all amusement places were closed, selling was prohibited by law, and he had very few acquaintances, so he decided to take a walk, perhaps find a church; therefore it was not surprising that he entered the first one that he happened to come by. You can imagine his feelings when he discovered that he had been in a Protestant church, his conscience accused him of having committed a mortal sin, and he found comfort only after promising himself "after this I will see to it that the devil shall not lead me again into such a trap."

From Des Moines, Antonio moved to Fairfield, Iowa, where

in partnership with a friend he had purchased a meat market. This venture did not prove successful because in a short time they saw all their savings vanish away. He was lodging with Cyrus D. Carpenter, a harness maker, who through his clean life, religious zeal and enthusiastic concern about lost souls made such an impression upon the young man that he felt impelled to attend revival services and later accept Christ as his personal Saviour.

As soon as he had been saved, he began to feel a deep compassion for the souls of his countrymen, and, having received a definite vision for service he decided to prepare himself for the Gospel ministry. In his book, "The Story of Antonio, the Galley Slave," he related how in the fall of 1858 he entered Iowa Wesleyan University with $65.75 to his name with which to pursue eight years of studies. His struggle for an education, his recurring sickness which he had contracted during his incarceration, his poverty, were matched only by his faith in God, his eagerness to preach the Gospel and his passion for the salvation of souls. From Iowa he went to the Ohio Wesleyan University, from there to Dickinson College at Carlisle, Pennsylvania, and thence to the Boston Theological Seminary.

This assignment might have proved disastrous for a lesser man, but not for Antonio, who had been schooled in hardships from early childhood. At fifteen he had run away from his home in Barga near Florence, and jeopardized the future of his entire family by enlisting as a drummer boy in the army of Garibaldi, who was then considered the arch enemy of the church. After several engagements he was captured in Rome and made a galley slave. He escaped after three years, then he took enough time to say goodbye to his parents and came to America. New York accorded him a rough welcome but he was not dismayed, and now that he had found his life work, had received a definite vision of what God wanted him to do, there was no obstacle too great to stop him on his forward march toward the prize for the high calling to preach the Gospel of Jesus Christ.

While he was attending college in Ohio, he became acquainted with "the best young lady in the town," Miss Emma Vining, daughter of the sheriff of Delaware county, and he felt that God had guided him to that place to find a companion for his life. "I was not mistaken," he wrote later, "for our married life has been happy indeed. Her wise counsels have been a great help to me in my work."

In 1871 he sailed for his native land with two burning desires: to preach the Gospel in Italy, now that Rome had been freed from the Popes and the new Italy, according to the maxim of Cavour, was to enjoy "a free church in a free state;" and to see his parents, from whom he had not heard for a long time, because, due to the teachings of the local priest, they had disinherited him and declared him dead.

The local priest wanted him arrested for escaping as a galley slave and for preaching now against the Holy Father, but fortunately Italy's new government's love for Garibaldi was equalled only by its antagonism for the Pope, therefore, he was not molested.

He opened a Chapel in Florence and after the initial persecution by a mob, instigated by the local priest and quelled by soldiers, the ringleaders, two young men who were later converted, were discharged on the recommendation of Dr. Arrighi, while the damages were assessed against the priest. In 1880, after preaching the Gospel in Italy for several years, he was sent by the "Free Italian Church" to the Pan-American Presbyterian Council meeting in Philadelphia, Pennsylvania, and there he was asked by the New York Mission and Tract Society to evangelize the Italians in that great city. On Sunday, June 21, 1881, he preached his first sermon in the beautiful chapel of the Five Points House of Industry. Here he labored for fourteen years.

The Rev. Antonio Arrighi organized the first Italian Church in America, known as the Broome Street Tabernacle, which celebrated its sixtieth anniversary in 1941. He had the joy of serving this Church until his 90th birthday. Most of our people should read the volume entitled, "Antonio, the Galley Slave." During his very fruitful ministry he received more than 2,000 persons on Confession of Faith, fifty-three preachers and Christian workers went out from the Broome Street Tabernacle, and over 100,000 different individuals heard the Gospel of Jesus Christ preached in their native tongue. Those who found the Saviour here were instrumental in starting many missions on three continents.

The writer had the privilege of meeting the present pastor, Dr. Joseph Brunn, at the celebration of his twenty-fifth anniversary. He had a twinkle in his eye, and his heart was aglow as he related how he had been directed into the ministry by the Rev. Arrighi, how he labored first in Hazelton, Pa., for seventeen years, and then was called to succeed his mentor at the Broome Street Tabernacle.

3

The Pioneer as the Moody of the Italians
(Michele Nardi)

"There goes the man who was born with a golden heart," remarked a mother to a boy about fifteen years of age, as she gently pushed him through the door of an Italian grocery store on the old Mulberry steet of New York, pointing to a kind gentleman going by with a basket under his arm. "That man," she continued, "is the patron saint for the Italians in our city, for he feeds the hungry, he visits the sick, he helps those who are in need and in distress, he sets free those who are imprisoned unjustly and counsels the others, and by his example and his teachings many bad boys and mean men have been made good. I hope and pray that some day you may become just like him."

The man who had passed by was none other than Michele Nardi, who like Francis of Assisi was a merchant's son of Savignano Romagna on the Rubicon River, immortalized by Caesar when he made his historic decision to cross that boundry line, march on Rome and place himself at the head of the Republic. He had come to this country when he was about twenty-one years of age and acquired at once the contagious disease of "get-rich-quick." To achieve this goal he entered the new business of furnishing laborers for the railroads which were then trying to span the continent. But the Jay Gould failures ruined his business and he heeded the advice to go west. In Pittsburgh, Pennsylvania, he introduced the first large group of Italians to coal mining, after overcoming considerable opposition from the famous Molly McGuire gang which was supreme at that time. Although he won a victory, yet he was later greatly disappointed, and returned to railroad contracting and the production of charcoal, at which the Italians were past masters.

In 1878 he went back to Italy for a visit to his parents, and at the Exposition of Paris he became acquainted with an American who was to change his entire life. The American friend, upon returning home, had been converted through the prayers of his sister, and Mr. Nardi, who was successfully playing the stock market in Philadelphia, remembered his friend and went to pay him a visit.

The American offered him an Italian copy of the Bible but he promptly refused it, saying that he had no time to read such a large book, but the former was not discouraged and begged Mr. Nardi to read only the verses he had marked. When he went home he was so impressed with the promise and privilege of becoming a son of God found in John 1:12 that he began to pray, "If Thou wilt give me power to become Thy son, I want to be Thy son right now." God answered his prayer immediately, and he jumped to his feet and said, "Praise the Lord." Then he heard the call to forsake all and follow Him, he went to the stock exchange, asked that his name be stricken from the list, notwithstanding the fact that he would have made a large fortune in a short time. His friends thought that he was crazy.

He returned to Pittsburgh, closed up his business affairs and went to Economy, with his English Bible and a couple of blankets, settled in a small shanty to study the Word of God, and there discovered for himself the will of God for his life. After his preparations he went to New York and while walking on 23rd Street he saw a sign, "Gospel Tabernacle." He attended the meeting, met Dr. Simpson, accepted the invitation one evening by going forward to the altar, he received the imposition of hands and considered himself set apart for the Lord's service. He never accepted another ordination.

Soon after he came under the influence of Dr. Arrighi, the first minister among the Italians in America, and of Miss

Blanche Phillips, a fine Bible student, who later became his wife. After a few months, Mr. and Mrs. Nardi left for Pittsburgh to visit her sister, and having found several hundred Italians in East Liberty, he began to hold services in the Methodist Episcopal Church for his countrymen. The seed sown then developed into the Italian Presbyterian Church of East Liberty, served so long and so ably by the Rev. Fragale.

Like flaming evangels, husband and wife went from the Atlantic to the Pacific, preaching the gospel to his countrymen and founding a string of missions in New York, Philadelphia, Pittsburgh, New Castle, River Falls, Chicago's Hell's Half Acre, St. Louis, Denver, Los Angeles, San Jose and San Francisco. His plan was to establish a work, then call a minister or a missionary, and like

" . . . the race of hero-spirits
Pass the torch from hand to hand."

Like the Apostle to the Gentiles he had greatly desired to preach the Gospel even to those who were in Rome. The Lord granted him his wish and many cities of Italy heard the message of salvation from the lips of one who had fought for the political freedom of Italy and now was ready to give himself, his all, for the spiritual freedom of his countrymen.

For this journey to Italy, since his constant companion was totally blind, they decided to take along a young woman who might serve in the dual role of a reader and of a companion. The selection fell upon a young woman whose mother had been converted to the Gospel, but she herself had not only shown her displeasure by going to a convent for her education but had only one purpose in life, to become a nun. A trip to Italy fascinated her as it would any young woman with dreams and vision, and in her case it was more so because she would see Rome, visit the Vatican, receive the benediction from the holy father, and enrich her mind and heart with religious treasures with which Italy is filled.

Mr. and Mrs. Nardi made no attempts to disturb the faith

of the young woman. Since she was to read for Mrs. Nardi, she was obliged to read several chapters of the Bible each day. While visiting one of the Cathedrals in Rome, she heard priests, who were in large numbers among the worshipers, making fun of those who were celebrating the mass, the light shone in her own heart, she reached the same conclusion of Martin Luther that *"the just shall live by faith,"* and before returning to America she was baptized and received in the Protestant Church. She became a Missionary and worked for many years for different churches, then married one of the ablest ministers among the Italians in America, the Rev. John Allegri of Brooklyn, New York, sharing with him the joys and the sorrows of a home missionary life. She closed her earthly ministry in 1939.

Nardi's work was first in Genova, later in Florence, and Lucca. He happened to be in Rome during "Holy Year" and he opened a Gospel Hall near the great Cathedral of Santa Maria Maggiore, which was filled night after night with many visitors, some even mistaking it as a side show of the celebration, thus giving our missionaries an opportunity to distribute Bibles and tracts. From Rome they went to Naples and Capri, preaching in missions and private homes, they visited the Italians of Switzerland, and from there they descended into the Waldensian Valleys where they attended the Waldensian Synod at Torre Pellice. Mr. Nardi preached in the old historical church of Ciabas where in the time of persecution the cry was, "fight or flight," and, of course, they decided to fight for the faith once delivered to the saints. He preached in Milano, from there he returned to Rome, and later conducted services at Monte Carlo and on the Riviera.

From Italy they crossed into France and arrived in New York on October 12, 1903. They started on a pilgrimage, visiting churches from New York to Chicago, when they received a call to take over the small church of Hammonton, New Jersey, and there they were able not only to establish peace and harmony, but conduct meetings in the near-by beautiful Vineland. In 1904, he accepted a call to initiate the "open tent work" among the Italians of Philadelphia during the summer, where later a lot was bought by the Presbyterian Board and a church building was started. After some months, Mr. Nardi felt that he should return to his work in New Jersey, and the Rev. A. Pirazzini of Rhode Island was called to Philadelphia. Rev. Mr. Stasio and his wife, who had just come from Italy, were helping him in the work which extended as far as Atlantic City.

From Vineland he went to Washington, D. C., to preach in a mission started by Miss Margaret Mauro. From there he went to New York where he was instrumental in erecting the first tent for the Italians in Harlem on 112th Street, later he was asked by Dr. Schauffler to take charge of the work on the west side in lower New York on Charleton Street. Here he induced Mrs. John S. Kennedy to erect a beautiful building, known as Charleton Memorial Church, in memory of her sister. While ministering to this church, Dr. Antonio Arrighi, who had been pastor of the Broome Street Tabernacle for thirty years, retired, and Mr. Nardi took over that work. During his seven years at the Broome Street Tabernacle he started several missions in New York City and continued as much as possible his summer tent preaching.

In 1914, he felt again the call of his native country. He had made very ambitious preparations for a vast program of evangelization, but as often is the case, the spirit is strong when the flesh is weak and before he was able to initiate such a program he was called to his heavenly reward.

The writer had the privilege of meeting Mr. Nardi in Pittsburgh, Pennsylvania, when he came there for his brother's funeral. I was a mere infant in Christian experience, nevertheless, I was deeply impressed by his gentleness, his faith and his strong character. I was a bit set back when I heard that he had conducted the funeral of his own brother. It was hard for me to understand how a man could conduct a funeral under such emotional strain, but I have since changed my mind on this score.

What appealed to me most at that time was his genuine humility. In a land where all the newcomers claim to descend from royal ancestors, or at least of having left a comfortable living, it was refreshing and revealing to find such modesty. He had fought with Garibaldi at Mentana, when he was only seventeen years of age, with such distinction that he was awarded two medals for distinguished bravery in action, and his name had been carved on the monument erected to the great hero in the Italian capital, and yet no mention had ever been made of this, until some of his friends in America discovered it by accident.

4

The Pioneer as a Loyal Soldier of Jesus Christ
(The Rev. Francesco Pesaturo)

"I came from Italy as a young man and I was fascinated and conquered by the oratory of Dr. Arrighi. After leading me to Christ he said: 'Francesco, you are young and full of life and my advice to you is that you go into the ministry, you could do much for our people who are now coming across in such large numbers'."

The Newark Presbytery claims the honor of having ordained to the gospel ministry the first Italian Protestant Minister in the United States, Mr. Francesco Pesaturo, who in turn claims the distinction of having been in the active pastorate longer than any other minister among the Italians in America.

Mr. Pesaturo was born at Prata Sanita, province of Caserta on September 20th, 1856, and came to America in 1884. He was in the banking business in New York when he was converted to the Protestant faith and felt at once a profound concern for the souls of his countrymen. He joined the Worth Street Presbyterian Church in New York, of which he became an elder and a volunteer worker. Later he decided to enter full-time service, and accordingly he enrolled at the Bloomfield (New Jersey) Theological Seminary for his theological preparation.

His first missionary work was in New York in 1884, as an assistant to Dr. Arrighi. From there he went to Port Chester and Rye, New York, and in 1884 he accepted a call to establish a Mission in Newark, New Jersey at the Bethel Mission on River Street. In 1891 a Church was organized with twenty-eight members and he was ordained by the Presbytery of Newark in the High Street Presbyterian Church and remained there until 1904. During this period of his ministry he received 303 members, of which only twenty came by letter. He organized several Missions in and around Newark and encouraged several young men to enter the ministry. A building was erected at 203 Plane Street (at a cost of $20,000) which was dedicated on November 23, 1893.

On November 7th, 1904, Mr. Pesaturo was called to New Haven, Connecticut, to take charge of the First Italian Congregational Church. Afterward he was called to the first Italian Presbyterian Mission of Patterson, New Jersey, to succeed one of his converts, the Rev. Carlo Altarelli, and in 1920 he returned to Newark as pastor of the First Italian Presbyterian Church.

Forty years in the service of our Lord is the proud record of this soldier of the Cross, moving among his countrymen in love and humility before God, living a life of self-sacrifice, and exemplary to all. Several of his converts consecrated their lives to the gospel ministry and several young women became Missionaries, among whom was his own daughter and faithful co-worker, Christina R. Pesaturo.

During all his years in the ministry, Mr. Pesaturo was the divinely-guided instrument of bringing into the Christian life many Italian families, some of them representing four generations. Among those converted through the preaching and work of this consecrated Italian minister are men and women prominent in the life of their respective communities. The Cavicchia family is perhaps the most notable.

Mr. and Mrs. Domenico Cavicchia and their two sons were brought into the Presbyterian Church by Mr. Pesaturo. Mrs. DePamphilis of Coral Gables, Florida, told us some time ago that as this man of God was visiting in the Italian community, two boys who had just arrived from Italy and had chosen the ambitious career of shining shoes, made fun of the Protestant minister as he went around in his ministry of love. In a spirit of humility and kindness he drew them to his heart and thence to the Christ. One of those boys is a distinguished professor of language at Brown University, while the other became a well-known lawyer, state inheritance tax collector, and later one of the four congressmen of Italian extraction, the Honorable Cavicchia, of Newark, New Jersey. The third generation of this family is in the Kilburn Memorial Presbyterian Church, Newark. Another example is the Corbo family, representing three generations. In the second generation, Mr. Alfonso Corbo became a Baptist minister, and Mr. Charles Corbo, a prominent lawyer.

A man with the ambition, energy, sympathy and love of the Reverend Pesaturo was bound to inspire young people not only to accept Christ as their personal Saviour, but to make the most of the new opportunities offered them by our great country. Like all his brothers in the Home Mission work among the foreign-speaking people in America, he was not only a zealous preacher of that Gospel of Jesus Christ which is the power of God unto salvation to all who believe, but a consistent teacher and a fine exponent of the highest and the finest Americanism. He was one of the very first to demonstrate what every home missionary among the Italians from Maine to California has since experienced, that what makes a good Christian makes also a good American.

Mr. Pesaturo, early in his ministry, purchased a stereopticon lantern, which he operated with kerosene oil, in the open air and in rented vacant stores. All around Newark where Italians lived he showed pictures of the life of Christ He organized the first Christian Endeavor Society, which went along with the minister and sang gospel songs. He organized an Italian Daily Vacation Bible School, and one of the teachers assisting was the Marquis Vitelleschi of Naples, a distinguished Protestant Christian. Among his other activities Mr. Pesaturo was owner and managing editor of the first Italian Evangelical Magazine, called "La Luce Evangelica." He organized the Italian Interdenominational Ministerial Association which for years met in the First Italian Presbyterian Church of Newark with Mr. Pesaturo as host.

Mr. Pesaturo retired from the active ministry at the ripe age of eighty on September 1st, 1936, and he has been followed by a distinguished ex-Dominican friar, the Rev. Reginaldo Bartolini.

5

The Pioneer as a Poet
(Thomas Fragale)

As soon as Thomas had reached his ninth birthday, he was called by his father, who, in a stern judicial countenance both by profession and temperament, informed him that they were leaving Serrastretta that next morning for the capital of the province, Catanzaro. The boy was duly enrolled in the provincial private school, and with the exception of his summer vacations, spent chiefly at the home of his married sister in the delightful seashore resort of Pizzo, he remained as if in a cloister for ten long years until his graduation from college, and his subsequent matriculation at the University of Naples Medical School.

All that he had heard and dreamed of Naples epitomized in the phrase, "See Naples and then die," was finally realized. The great metropolis of southern Italy was such a change from the monotonous provincial capital, that he drank freely of the gay Neapolitan life, but the sight of cadavers in the dissecting room almost scared him stiff, whereupon he ended his medical career, and enrolled in the Normal School of the University.

His real love, however, had been poetry. Just at that time there was a contest for the best poem on the death of King Victor Emmanuel II which attracted most of the numerous poets of Italy, and to his great surprise and joy, his "Ode" was awarded a gold medal. The prize and publicity were instrumental in reducing the fury and in mitigating the punishment of his father.

His own literary merits, the publicity received, his father's political influence opened for him a position as teacher and later as supervisor of didactics for the entire province. He applied himself with such unusual interest and zest to what he considered now his life's work, that he published a volume on pedagogy which became required reading for all the teachers of that entire region.

The current idea of a pre-arranged marriage between the two families was naturally repulsive to a university man, therefore, when he met a beautiful girl, albeit not a member of his own social stratum and an orphan besides, he proceeded to marry her. He had to pay dearly for his love because he lost caste with his friends, his relatives ostracized him, he was disinherited by his father, and there was nothing else for him to do but to leave his small world and go to the United States of America, where the Italians were immigrating in greater numbers day by day.

The young couple started for Naples, the city of many enchantments and of a thousand allurements, and there they basked in the sunshine of the rich inebriating life of that city before sailing for America. This was the age of rationalism, and the young husband was in perfect agreement with modern current ideas, so much so that, when they left for Naples, he did not even want to take the trouble of christening his first child, and convinced his young wife to leave it with his youngest brother and his wife, who were childless and were in line to receive all the parental wealth.

One evening, as he was showing his wife more of the magic attractions, they passed by an old building and heard some strange melodies coming from within, not a bit like the happy and carefree songs of the Neapolitans. They went by that evening without entering but they returned the next evening, the next and the next, and to the pleadings of the young wife he would say, "But these are Protestants." In so saying he was hoping to put fear in the heart of a provincial girl and avoid a religious meeting. The melodies, however, had such a strange attraction for her that one evening she pulled her husband in with the strong cords of love. The passionate preaching of the great Taglialatela had an immediate effect upon their tender hearts, private conversation and subsequent meetings brought a decision from them, and when they finally sailed for America, they had two definite purposes: to enter a new career and to live new lives.

As soon as they reached New York City in 1892, they went to live among people from their own province, who knew, loved, and respected them. His first venture was in banking. In those days the new immigrants did not know how to transact business with large banking institutions or were afraid of being swindled of their hard-earned savings, and as a result, many small banks sprang up within all foreign communities. His business prospered, and like many others with less ability he could have made a fortune and lived on easy street had he continued in such an undertaking. Encouraged by his wife, however, they attended Dr. Arrighi's church, and the spell of this man of God was so compelling that he felt impelled to exclaim with the Apostle Paul: "Woe unto me if I preach not the Gospel."

The need for workers was so great and so urgent in those days that ministers and missionaries were authorized after a brief period of self preparation, or under guidance of a local minister. Having satisfied himself that he had a definite call to the Gospel ministry, as well as having satisfied his friends that he was well qualified to preach, he became first a co-worker of Dr. Arrighi, later of Dr. Malan in the establishment of the Wanamaker Mission of Philadelphia, and then accepted a call to the Italian Mission of Hammonton, New Jersey, where he labored faithfully and diligently for over four years.

With such a fine cultural background, unusual oratorical abilities, a zeal for the conversion of his countrymen, and a profound love for his Saviour, so much more pronounced in neophytes, his fame spread all over the State and to larger immigration centers such as Philadelphia and New York. Many Italian communities vied for his services, and in 1899 he accepted a call from the rapidly growing Italian colony of

Pittsburgh, Pennsylvania. This new field presented a challenge for larger service and greater opportunities, since many people from the sunny shores of southern Italy, attracted by good wages and scarcity of labor, had begun to arrive in increasing numbers.

Going through Pittsburgh by night one receives the impression immediately of finding himself in one of those infernal bolgias, described in Dante's Inferno. He sees from a distance a thousand flickering lights which, as one draws near, are discovered to be giant foundries, steel mills, and coke ovens, which advertise graphically the smoky city as the industrial heart of America. Such must have been the impression received by this man, who incidentally, was one of the foremost students of Dante in the United States.

Two pastors had been called to start a Presbyterian Mission in East Liberty, after a visit by the Rev. Mr. Nardi, but one left for green pastures, and a young Waldensian minister, Mr. Ribetti, who married a well-to-do American young woman, Miss Buchanan, prepared himself for the more congenial and lucrative medical profession.

During his ministry in East Liberty, Mr. Fragale saw the fine brick building erected, a branch of the now famous Mellon Church, and was instrumental in starting several missions, chief among which is the first United Presbyterian Italian Church of Pittsburgh, and, indirectly, through some of his converts, one in Italy. He led many to Christ; he cooperated with Professor Agide Pirazzini in the translation and poetical arrangement of the Psalms in Italian for singing by the Italian United Presbyterians; he published a number of important pamphlets in Italian; he led several young people into full-time Christian service, including his own daughter, Mrs. J. B. Bisceglia, of Kansas City; he was co-editor of the Presbyterian Italian paper and of the Italian Sunday School publications; and he was always a favorite patriotic and religious speaker, even after his retirement from the active ministry. He left several volumes of sermons in Italian all written in clear, precise handwriting. His sermons were always garbed in beauty, patriotism, poetry and truth.

In his poetry he extols the greatness of Italy, the country of his birth, the love of God in Christ whom he served so well for so many years, and pleads for the needs of, and the prejudices against, his people. He reaches sublime heights when in the tenderest terms he speaks of his home, of his mother whom he did not see when she passed away, of his family, and of his two boys who were wounded in the war which was to save the world for democracy.

After over thirty-five years of active service in the ministry he was retired, but continued to preach wherever his services were requested, and it was during this period that he started the Missions of Washington and Coreapolis, two neighboring towns, both served now by two of his converts, the first by the Rev. Mr. Patrone and the second by the Rev. Mr. Pastore.

During the summer of 1929 he visited his daughter in Kansas City, Missouri, and preached every Sunday evening for eight weeks. Notwithstanding the heat, he showed as much vigor and zeal as a much younger man. He had an excellent memory and it was a literary tonic for the writer to hear him repeat by heart the entire Inferno, many portions of Paradise and Purgatory from Dante's Divine Comedy, as well as numerous passages from all the important Italian classics. He supervised the publication of a collection of his poems and returned to Pittsburgh during the first week in August. He died on the fourth of December.

High tributes were paid to his memory by all the Italian ministers of that entire region and by people of all creeds. For the Presbytery, Dr. Hugh T. Kerr, the beloved pastor of the Shady Side Presbyterian Church, spoke most eloquently of Thomas Fragale as a dear friend, a true missionary of the Gospel, and a man of letters; and for the Italian ministers, the Rev. Mr. D'Aliberti of Steubenville, Ohio, as Timothy would have spoken of the Apostle Paul.

6

The Pioneer as a Linguist
(Agide Pirazzini)

A seventeen year old boy, full of life, beaming with joy and ambition, his eyes sparkling with intelligence, had come to Rome to complete his college course and prepare for a profession. He was enjoying a walk in the spring sunshine, admiring the famous sights of the eternal city, rejuvenating with every new season. His fancy, like that of every youth, was turning to love, when his attention was caught by an open book in the window of a "store room mission." His curiosity having been aroused, he pressed his nose almost flat against the window pane, as he read these words: "Vanity of vanity, all is vanity." This verse became fixed in his mind, it gripped his heart and would not permit him to sleep that night.

As soon as he was able to make inquiries and learned that the book was the Holy Bible, the word of God, the entire course of his life was changed. In 1934, when he answered the summons from the house of many mansions, the bulletin of the Evangelical Theological Seminary of Jersey City, N. J., carried this significant paragraph: "In scholarship he was to be ranked with the late Dr. Robert Dick Wilson, for he was at ease in using any semitic language and could read the Assyrian Cuneiform and the Egyptian hieroglyphics. In evangelistic fervor he could be compared with J. Wilbur Chapman. In Christian humility, he did not hesitate to do the least service for the most obscure of God's children. In generous love, he manifested the very spirit of Christ himself."

Agide Pirazzini was born at Cotignola, Ravenna, on February 22, 1875. He was attending the Royal Giannasio-Liceo in Rome, when he passed by that obscure mission in Rome, which aroused in him such an interest in the book of books, that made him not only one of its most ardent students and a living example of its power, but made him by far the best linguist among the pioneers of the Italian evangelization in America. For although most of our pioneers have been linguists of some sort, since they all spoke more or less fluently at least two languages, Italian and English, Dr. Pirazzini excelled them all, because he was not only at home with Italian, English and French but, following the noble traditions of Pico della Mirandola and Diodati, he became one of the foremost scholars of semitic languages in America.

He went into Y.M.C.A. work first in Rome and later in Paris, and in 1894 he came to this country to take special courses at the Y.M.C.A. College of Springfield, Massachusetts, under the tutelage of Mr. Stokes. While young Pirazzini was still in training at the Springfield Institute, he heard and met the great evangelist, D. L. Moody, who inspired him with a burning desire to preach the Gospel among the Italians in this country, and to this end he began his preparation for the ministry at Drew Seminary. But since he had pledged himself to Mr. S. Stokes, who was helping him in his preparation and who had bought a building in Rome for the first Y.M.C.A., to do secretarial work in the capital of Italy, he returned there and devoted three years in the establishment of that Center.

The Italians in America, however, were continually pulling the strings of his heart, so, in 1900, renouncing a good salary and a comfortable life, he and his young bride, Esther Coletti, accepted a call to the Methodist Mission in Providence, Rhode Island. There he spent three years of hardships, work and study, since he was always striving to become better equipped for his life work. When Mr. Stokes asked him to go back to the work of the Y.M.C.A. in Rome, at twice the salary he had received formerly, he refused, although it was a real struggle with a family entirely dependent on him and with his expenses at Brown University, to exist on his tiny and uncertain salary.

While conducting the mission in Providence, Rhode Island, he received his A.B. from Brown University in 1903 and an M.A. in 1905. In the meantime he was called by the Rev. Nardi to the Presbyterian work, first in Vineland, New Jersey, and later in Philadelphia, Pa., where he managed to attend Temple University from which in 1905 he received a B.D., and the S.T.D. degree in 1906.

At the beginning of 1904, Mr. Nardi asked him to go to Philadelphia to preach in a tent, where he had started an Italian Mission under the auspices of the Presbyterian Church. Agide Pirazzini saw the possibilities for a larger field of service and accepted the call. Four years of work without rest, opening tents in various parts of the hot city during the summers, taking no time for vacation, brought great results. He organized the First Italian Presbyterian Church, and although the building was only a large tabernacle, it was always filled to capacity with people who were coming in large numbers from Italy. Here he encouraged and sent several young men into the ministry, and also established the work in West Philadelphia and in Germantown, where the Rev. J. Panetta, one of the young men he had inspired to enter the ministry, is still the faithful pastor.

Although he was blessed with unusual success in the preaching of the Word of God, yet teaching seemed to attract him more, and after some experience in teaching romance languages at Temple University, during the school year 1906-1907, he was induced by Dr. Nardi to organize the Italian Department at Biblical Seminary in New York, for the preparation of young men and young women for full-time Christian service. In 1915, he received a Ph.D. degree from Columbia University and published a thesis on the subject, "Influence of Italy on the literary career of Lamartine."

As founder and director of the Italian branch at the Biblical Seminary in New York, he had the opportunity of moulding the lives and preparing young men and women for the Lord's work among the Italians. Mr. Nardi was the moving spirit in

the enterprise because he alone seemed to have vision to see the
need and discover the men ready to fill these needs. Dr. Pirazzini consecrated the rest of his life to the Italian Branch of the
Biblical Seminary, and to the teaching of Semitic languages
for the entire student body.

He was able to mould the mind and hearts of eager young
people who had all the zeal of neophytes and who, fired by his
example, went out like crusaders to win their countrymen to
Christ and to the American way of life. Today, these men and
women are to be found in key positions from Maine to California, preaching the Gospel of Christ which is the power of
God unto salvation. The Italian congregations of all denominations have shared his evangelical spirit as expressed in his translation of some of the best old hymns.

Professor Pirazzini was a favorite with his students. They
admired him for his profound learning, they tried to emulate
his Christian humility and sincerity, and they loved him for his
warm heart and deep sympathies.

The writer met Dr. Pirazzini in the early part of 1918, while
he was giving the finishing touches, with the cooperation of
our evangelical poet, the Rev. Mr. Fragale, and of Miss Isa-
bella Fragale, now Mrs. Bisceglia, as musical advisor, to a
poetical translation of the Psalms for use by the United Italian
Presbyterian Missions, and was very much impressed by his
profound knowledge, his evangelical zeal and his quick wit
in every situation.

In an intimate note from the one who shared his joys and
his sorrows, his defeats and his triumphs, we transcribe the
following paragraph: "Regardless of the financial difficulties
in which the Seminary frequently found itself, and notwithstanding the many calls to positions of assured financial comfort, Agide Pirazzini, having set his hand to the plow, never
turned back. He struggled and suffered all of his life, counting
it all a joy, for the same Christ who had called him to be a
partner in His work, and has now called him to be a partaker
of His glory."

7

The Pioneer as a Waldensian Colonist
(Rev. Filippo Ghigo)

When one drives east from Montreat, the Mecca of Southern Presbyterianism, the first glimpse he receives of this Waldensian Community is a water tower with the inscription "Valdese, North Carolina's fastest growing town." In a few seconds one is on Main Street, where he sees the Church built by the pioneers, and, adjacent to it, the most recent addition, the educational building. A new bank building, a large bakery, high school and grade school, a community center, all kinds of stores, moving picture shows, gasoline stations, and streets busy with traffic, advertise at once the fact that this is a thriving, throbbing, fast-growing community.

It was our good fortune to meet some of the original ssettlers who had crossed the ocean in a Netherland ship the "Zaandam." The eleven original families comprising that first group proceeded by train on the Salisbury-Asheville line and on May 29, 1893, stopped in what was then a veritable wilderness, eight miles east of Morgantown, but now the flourishing town of Valdese.

On the night of their arrival, the families gathered around improvised tables and heard the reading of Psalm 103, followed by a meditation suited to the occasion. This first service of Thanksgiving and gratitude, including a solemn promise of faithfulness to the Lord, ended with a hymn and a prayer often broken with the tears of the brothers and the sisters. The foundation had thus been laid on the "Rock of Ages," so reads the memorable record.

The land was not as fertile as they had hoped it might have been, and so in 1894 they gave up some of the outlying acreage in order to draw closer together around the new settlement, and the Rev. C. A. Tron, pastor, paid $6,000.00 to retain for the colonists all the property that he could possibly save.

This in my humble opinion was a blessing in disguise, because had they been successful agriculturally they would have developed a farming community, whereas out of their misfortune they have made of Valdese a small industrial city with one of the finest bakeries in that entire region, branching in a number of surrounding towns, several hosiery mills, chief among which the Pilot full fashion mill, cotton mills, a lumber company, flour mill and fruit markets. Of course they have not forgotten their attachment to the land and vineyards and truck gardening flourish all around.

Contrary to current opinion on the sufferings and privations of these pioneers, we were surprised to learn from the lips of the grandfather of the community, called affectionately "Bobo" Garrou, that there were sufferings, of course, but that they had been part of the game.

When questioned if it was true that they had been fleeced, with a smile and a twinkle in his eye, which cannot be easily forgotten, he said: "We had brought nothing with us, how could we loose anything, and furthermore," he continued, "we have all prospered and we have forgotten the many hardships we had to endure. As I look back now I believe it was all worthwhile."

Besides the church and the educational building, Valdese now boasts a beautiful community center building with a gymnasium and swimming pool, which is known as the Francis Garrou Memorial Hall.

A weekly paper, known as the Valdese News, is published and the educational needs are served by up-to-date grade schools and a modern high school.

During our stay in Montreat last August we had the privilege of preaching in Valdese twice to a fine congregation of Christians who, though still clinging to their French hymns, since we had the pleasure of listening to the French choir, and they still have one service a month in French, yet the people are becoming more and more Americanized in their thinking and perspective and they are really proud of being Americans.

It would be difficult here to describe adequately the first pastors who served the community, therefore, I am going to present one who came to this country as a young man almost from seminary, ministered to the Church of Valdese, later served the Italian people in Pennsylvania and New Jersey and finally returned to Valdese to die among his people. His wife and daughter are still living there, while a son is teaching Romance languages at Hampton Sidney College and Duke University.

The Rev. Filippo Ghigo was born in Prali, Valle di San Martino, on December 16, 1869. After completing his college course at Torre Pellice, in the Waldensian valleys, he went to Florence for his Theological studies (since that time the seminary has been transferred to Rome) and after he received his diploma he went for two years to the University of Leipzig in Germany.

His first missionary assignment was in the Italian section of Switzerland where he worked among his countrymen, and in September, 1896, he was ordained by the Waldensian synod at Torre Pellice. His next assignment was in Argentine in the province of Santa Fe, where he started a Mission in Rios de il Chaco, and preached in three languages: Italian, French and German.

In 1903, he was sent to the United States by Dr. Prochet, then Moderator of the Waldensian Church in Italy, to conduct the work in Valdese, North Carolina. A year later his bride arrived from Italy and they were married in New York on September 22, 1904. In 1906, he was called to Scranton, Pa., where he labored for five years, and then he went to the Plane Street Italian Church of Newark, New Jersey, where he had a very fruitful ministry nothwithstanding the fact that he taught Italian as a parttime professor at the Bloomfield Theological

Seminary and frequently preached in French to the Waldensians in New York City.

When they arrived in Scranton, Pa., in November, 1906, they met at the station a man who upon reading on the boxes of books the name, "Rev. F. E. Ghigo," turned to the stranger abruptly and said, "Pardon me, are you a priest?" The tall, dark, bearded man, smiling graciously answered in the negative, but this man, who was later known to them as Vincenzo Testa, was a bit puzzled as he remarked, "How can this be then, if you are a Reverend, you certainly must be a priest." Mrs. Ghigo, who was always vivacious and ready with an answer, explained in simple but clear language that her husband was not a priest but an Evangelical minister. This explanation, however, did not clear the puzzled mind of the stranger, since he had never heard of a Protestant minister.

Vincenzo was invited to attend the adult education classes at the mission, where each evening a brief worship service preceeded the Italian and English classes. At first he failed to keep his promise, but later they discovered that he had tried to bring other Italian young men who refused to accompany him saying, "Why, don't you know that Protestants worship the head of a horse, and walk on the cross of Christ?" Mr. Testa's curiosity, however, had no bounds, he went to see for himself if it was just as they had told him, and, after he had ascertained that it was not true, he was instrumental in bringing to the mission the more intelligent members of his group.

Mr. Testa's marriage was the first performed at the mission, and when the first born arrived he named him Michael and dedicated him to God saying, "I pray and hope that some day my child may become a minister of the Gospel just like the Rev. Mr. Ghigo." God answered the prayer of a godly father for in the summer of 1941 the writer had the privilege of having with him in the pulpit of the Waldensian Church, Valdese, North Carolina, for the morning prayer, Michael Testa, a graduate of Princeton Seminary, then Pastor of the First Presbyterian Church at Bedford, Mass.

The missionary among the Italians more than any other owes much of his success to his wife and the Ghigos were no exception. The following incident reveals how alert and ready she was in every situation. Coming out of the Plane Street Italian Presbyterian Church in Newark, New Jersey, one beautiful spring Sunday afternoon, the Rev. Filippo Ghigo, tall, slender, erect, with a black beard showing here and there a silver thread, deep dark eyes, was walking with one of his students, while Mrs. Giulietta Ghigo, also tall, but well built, with beautiful auburn hair, a healthy complexion, acquired in the Wadensian mountains, was following with another student, attached by filial devotion to them, when a couple coming from the opposite direction remarked in French, "I did not know that there were Italian Protestants." Quick as lightning Mrs. Ghigo turned to her escort and in her beautiful, rich soprano voice said in French, *"Don't you know that the Italians were the first Protestants in the world? Why, have you not read of the Waldensians!"* The poor young man, who did not understand a word of French was dumbfounded, and, for a moment, he thought something was wrong with Mrs. Ghigo's mind, until later she was able to explain.

The home life of Professor Ghigo was a happy one. Many students of Italian extraction forgot their nostalgia around the fireside, when accompanied by a mandolin played by one of his nieces, they would all join in the touching Waldensian songs, or around a long table they devoured the excellent spaghetti prepared "con amore" by Mrs. Ghigo. Before and after dinner, Anita, three or four years of age, with beautiful black curls, or Bob, a real boy, made them feel more at home with their incessant questioning and childish games.

In 1912, he was appointed as full-time professor of Italian at the Bloomfield "Cosmopolitan" School, which was not only a veritable league of nations but students ranged all the way from grade school to Seminary graduates. Here he spent some of the happiest years of his mature life, instilling in the hearts of his students those qualities so eloquently expressed in his own life: *Franciscan* humility and Christian gentleness, coupled with thoroughness, for he often admonished, *"whatever is worth doing must be done well,"* and profound scholarship.

It is amid supreme happiness that we are often tried by the most severe tragedies, and it was in Bloomfield, that a heart-rending experience darkened the horizon of this man of God, for one day, while he was teaching at the Seminary, he received word that his first boy, Valdo, five years of age, had drowned in the creek running behind the house which had been their nest of love and happiness. At first they wept bitterly but later faith triumphed over their sorrow, for they knew that he had gone home to the Father, where he is in the company of angels, singing praises to our risen Lord.

In 1916, he was called back to his first love, the church in Valdese, North Carolina, but on December 16, 1917, he answered a higher call from his Heavenly Father, to the House of Many Mansions. We visited the cemetery in company with his widow, we bowed in gratitude for his life before his grave, and the words of the poet came tripling upon our tongue:

"For he has gone where His Redeemer is,
    In that far city on the other side,
And at the threshold of His palaces
    Has loosed his sandals ever to abide.
I know his Heavenly King did smiling wait
    To give him welcome as he touched the gate."

8

The Pioneer as God's Salesman
(Rev. Pasquale R. DeCarlo)

"How do you do, Dr. DeCarlo! Why, don't you remember me?"

"Just a moment, just a moment," and, thus saying, he assumed his well known pose of resting the forehead in the palm of his hand, to bring out from his rich gallery of pictures crowding the walls of his memory, the one fitting the well dressed man who had interrupted our conversation, following a much enjoyed dinner at the Lido in Chicago.

The interlocutor, a bit voluble, interrupted: "Don't you remember twenty-five years ago, you saved the life of my wife?"

The lucid mind of this octogenarian was a bit puzzled!

"You have not forgotten when my wife had to have an operation and I was broke," and, in a torrent of words, which betrayed his Neapolitan origin, "you came, made all arrangments, saved my wife's life, found me a job, and helped my brother Gennarino?"

His face was lighted with a contagious smile as he said, "O, yes, yes, and how is your wife, the children and your young brother?"

"They are all well but Gennarino is still a bachelor. He makes lots of money but he gambles all he earns."

Then turning to me, since I had already been introduced as a speaker from Kansas City, the Neapolitan went on: "This man was the most important person in Chicago." We all referred to Dr. DeCarlo's hospital (which Dr. DeCarlo hastened to correct, Presbyterian Hospital) "a card from Dr. DeCarlo would open for our people every office and every factory door in Chicago; it was his city; it was Dr. DeCarlo's church that they all spoke so highly of and Dr. DeCarlo's God."

Here the 79-year-old veteran, with his face radiating the joy of the true believer, turned to his interlocutor and said, "He wants to be your God, too, why don't you come this evening and tomorrow evening to hear this great preacher from Kansas City?"

And the other: "I do not know about this evening, but to-morrow evening I'll be there with my family. You know I live so far away now. I am in the fur business in the loop and my children are all engaged in the same business. Just as I was trying to approach your table I had a telephone call which enabled me to conclude a thousand-dollar business deal, you always bring good luck."

Chicago has been fortunate to have had a man like the Rev. Pasquale R. DeCarlo, who has been a mighty force for good in the "bloody nineteenth ward." Although he is no longer young in years, since he was born in Calitri, Avellino, Italy, on the twenty-second day of February, 1863, yet his spirit is young and he carries on with the zest and the vigor of a much younger person.

He came to this country when he was twenty-six years of age, he went in business but as soon as he was converted from Romanism, through the reading of the Bible given him by an ex-priest, he saw God's concern for other people, he gave up what was fast becoming a most profitable business and volun-teered his service, for he says:

> "I heard Him call,
> Come, follow—that was all.
> My gold grew dim,
> My heart went after him;
> I rose and followed—that was all.
> Who would not follow
> If he heard Him call?"

He plunged immediately into missionary work, first in

Providence, Rhode Island, then Springfield, Massachusetts, and later in Hartford, New Haven and Waterbury, Connecticut, Schenectady and Mount Vernon, New York. In 1906, he went to Detroit, Michigan, and since 1914 he has been in the "Windy City."

Thousands of people have felt the magnetism of Dr. De-Carlo's preaching, the name of those brought to Christ is legion, and he has been instrumental in leading a score of young people into full time Christian service. He is proud to number among those who have accepted Christ under his blessed ministry two priests: Marco Mazzucca and Pietro Vodola, who eventually entered the gospel ministry, and two members of his church have served long and well in the ministry: the Rev. C. Cerreta of Bridgeport, Connecticut, and the Rev. Pasquale Codella of Waterbury, Connecticut. Patriotic organizations, Masonic lodges and many American churches have been carried by his enthusiasm and his eloquence in patriotic and religious addresses.

During all these years of fruitful activities Dr. DeCarlo has been interested not only in the spiritual life of his countrymen but in their intellectual and moral elevation as well. He has conducted evening classes in order to teach the new immigrants our language, our customs and our laws. He encouraged many young people to strive for an education and to aspire for higher goals in life. More than any other home missionary among the Italians he has used the printed word as a suitable vehicle with which to inform and to elevate his people. He started with the newspaper "Il Cittadino," then "La Fiamma" and later the magazine "Vita Nuova." For his unusual achievements through "Vita Nuova" he was awarded the Diploma of Collaboration at the V Triennial International Exposition of Decorative, Industrial and Modern Arts, Milan, Italy, in 1933.

Like many of his brother pioneers, he felt the urge to unburden his heart and soul in simple but forceful writings. We find many fine articles in his native language and several important pamphlets in his adopted tongue, through which he attempted to interpret America to the Italians, and his countrymen to his new fatherland. The following quotations are taken from one of his printed addresses entitled, "His Majesty, the American Citizen":

"Forty years ago, at the Court of Common Pleas, County of Fairfield, in the city of Stamford, Connecticut, I received a Certificate of Naturalization, in which it was duly stated that the Court admitted and declared that Pasquale R. DeCarlo was to be recognized as a citizen of the United States of America.

"Among other things that I promised, I declared on oath to support the Constitution of the United States of America. The special piece of paper that has been and still is a very precious and valuable document indeed. But unless I had the power, the will, and the ability to assimilate the meaning of the entire Constitution of the United States of America, this paper presented to me by a duly authorized magistrate would be absolutely worthless and I should be ashamed to be called an American Citizen, and what is true for me is true for every single American citizen, by birth or by adoption.

"We have two kinds of American citizenship, that of the flesh and that of the spirit. I know a good many foreigners who are citizens only in the flesh, and I know a good many American-born who are citizens only in the flesh. They have no more the spirit of citizenship than this glass, and I am speaking to the foreigners and the native Americans when I say that, unless America recognizes the failures of the past, it will follow the history of other big and powerful countries that have died. By reading the history of the United States I found that our forefathers had four things that were very dear to them: the home, the red schoolhouse, the church, and the court. Those are the four institutions you will find emphasized at the very beginning of this country's history in New England and other places.

"I firmly believe that the fundamental principles of Americanization for both natives and foreigners are to live and uphold the Christian ideals and traditions upon which America was founded, to obey scrupulously the laws of the state and nation, to elevate the social and ethical prestige of all, to propagate the doctrine that every privilege enjoyed in America carried with it obligations.

"Can this be achieved? Yes, by an intensive and expansive work of evangelization, by an efficient evening school system to teach English, civics and American ideals of citizenship; by public lectures in Churches, halls, public school buildings, and theaters on American history and the makers of this country; by reading the Holy Bible in the public schools, regardless of creed, without animosity against other religions."

Dr. DeCarlo has demonstrated broad vision in the establishment of a community center, which has been a model for many institutions of its kind. Realizing that from slums we breed our own destruction, and that we can counteract such anti-social influences only by replacing them with moral and educational activities, he began at the beginning by starting a kindergarten, a boy scout troop, mothers' clubs and a bureau of information and employment, which is now ministering to a teeming population under the name of "Garibaldi Institute."

Very early in his ministry he organized the Italian Baptist Missionary Association which is still in existence and doing a splendid piece of work among our brethren of that denomination. At St. John Presbyterian Church, now under the able leadership of his successor the Rev. Saverio Scalera, he has a well organized Sunday School with a flourishing congregation, young people's societies, with classes in violin, piano and voice, and leagues for men and women.

All these and many other activities have been created, governed and have prospered under the splendid leadership of this wonderful man of God.

Dr. DeCarlo holds a unique place as God's salesman, not only among his brethren of Italian extraction but among ministers and missionaries of all backgrounds, since, during his stay in Chicago, he has been able to raise over one million dollars for the various organizations with which he has been connected.

Early in his ministry he realized that it is impossible to conduct God's work without money, and being a man of action, rather than a visionary, he took courses in salesmanship which, coupled with his innate ability, gave him such proficiency that he was eagerly sought by many secular and religious organizations to raise money for good and well deserving causes. Dr. DeCarlo might have made plenty of money in business because he has the proverbial ability of selling straw hats in the heart of winter, but he dedicated all his energies to the one single purpose, that of giving the gospel to his countrymen and contribute his best in ushering in the Kingdom of God.

The Presbyterian Extension Board of Chicago, recognizing his unusual abilities in this field, sought him for the position of field secretary, and for twenty-five years Dr. DeCarlo served his Presbytery with dignity and power. That this sphere of his endeavors was crowned with unusual success is attested by the fact that he raised more than $800,000.00 for the various causes, as well as by the following incident:

One day Dr. Henry S. Brown, superintendent of the Chicago Presbyterian Extension Board, had returned crestfallen to his office. He had approached a rich business man, positive that he would receive a generous contribution, but instead he had received a flat refusal. His assistant, the Rev. P. R. DeCarlo, saw his superior's disappointment and volunteered to go and see the man himself. The interview began with almost certain failure staring him in the face, but before long a check for $5,000 was written. Anyone else would have accepted the check and rushed back to report a whale of a success to his colleagues, but not Dr. DeCarlo. Simulating disappointment, he held the check in his hand, and looking at the figure, he exclaimed: "$5,000.00! What do you think I am, a beggar? I am here as an ambassador of God, who is the owner of the world and all the gold thereof." Before leaving the office he had placed in his portfolio a neatly written check for $10,000.00.

This gives you a glimpse of an important phase of the dynamic life of this comparatively small man, erect, notwithstanding his 79 years of age, with lady-like hands, well-chiseled features and long gray hair.

Being a man of such unusual abilities he was not without honor at home and abroad. Several years ago the National Inventors of the United States of America elected him national chaplain of the association. He is chaplain emeritus of the Central Civitan Club of Chicago, and in 1940 Dubuque University of Dubuque, Iowa, conferred upon him the honorary degree of Doctor of Divinity.

Had he been born in this country and had he served American Churches, he would have filled very important positions in the Church, and would have received the highest honors within the power of a denomination to confer upon one of her loyal sons. But, alas, he is only a pioneer, and his work must be by necessity to prepare the way and point to new horizons. His real reward must come from One who in the end will say, "Well done my good and faithful servant, thou hast been faithful in the small things, I will make thee ruler over many things: enter thou into the joy of thy Lord."

Any man would take a well deserved rest at 79, but not Dr. DeCarlo, who still dreams, hopes, plans and works for a greater future, since with Browning he can truly say:

"Grow old along with me!
The best is yet to be,
The last of life, for which the first was made;
Our times are in his hand
Who saith, "A whole I planned,
Youth shows but half; trust God: see all, nor be afraid."

Dr. DeCarlo passed away after this sketch had been published in the Messenger.

9

The Pioneer as God's Trail Blazer
(Cerchiara-Fresina)

The colporteur is the advanced guard of the Christian Army. He is the one who breaks the ground, removes the brush, destroys the weeds and bears all the brunt, as do all true pioneers who blaze new trails in a new country or across a newly discovered continent. His hands and feet bleed often, his face is scratched many times, his heart is on the verge of breaking, before seemingly insurmountable discouragements, therefore, he has to walk by faith oftener than by sight.

These humble soldiers of the cross very often had to face the blind rage of housewives, who chased them with their broomsticks, shouting after them that they were peddling devil's books. They had to listen to the vilest cursing words of people drunken either with wine or fanaticism, and many times were stoned by paid riffraffs of the community.

My hometown, perched upon a high mountain, boasts a famous and supposedly miraculous St. Michael, which is visited by 100,000 pilgrims each year. It is a modern Diana of the Ephesians, since it assures an income to most of the 25,000 inhabitants. My townspeople used to recount in low tones how one of these unhappy colporteurs was stoned and rushed out of town with abuses and vulgar invectives, until he reached the plains, where two policemen, who happened to pass by, saved his life.

Although their lot is hard, their compensation poor, their future dark, they never retreat, they never flinch, but with undaunted courage they go forward in their humble mission of preparing the ground and blazing the trail for those who are to follow.

Lorenzo Cerchiara was born in a small town, San Lorenzo Bellizzi, in the province of Cosenza in 1873. From his early childhood he was impressed by the fact that there is no salvation outside of the church, and it was the fear of hell which induced him to serve mass when he was barely nine years of age.

His father died when he was fourteen years old, and since his home town was full of sin and corruption, he followed the easier way and became a reproach to himself and a thorn in the flesh of his mother.

When he was twenty years of age he came to this country, and when he arrived in New York, five lire and an extra suit of clothes constituted all his worldly possessions. In Brooklyn he was met by an uncle who kept him in his home for a week. He decided to learn the barber's trade, and in his testimony he related that "Giorgio Volpitto, now a minister of the Gospel, came to look for work in that same shop and it was he who first spoke to me of the Gospel, secured a Bible for me, and left me with these words still resounding in my mind and heart: 'This is truly the book which makes over people.'"

His conversion took place at the Broome Street Tabernacle in August, 1897, under the dynamic preaching of the Rev. Mr. Arrighi, and after 45 years of Christian living and service for the Master, he can still sing:

Happy day, happy day, when Jesus washed my sins away;
He taught me how to watch and pray, and live rejoicing
    every day.

Under the guidance of the Rev. S. Testa he became a colporteur, and in his 40 years as an evangelist he has had the privilege of founding five missions, of which two are in Derby, Connecticut, another in Brooklyn, New York, and the last in Harrison, New York; he has distributed and sold thousands of Bibles; he has written several tracts and distributed and sold many thousands, and he has had the privilege of bringing many souls into a saving knowledge of Christ and Him crucified.

The testimonials of two of his converts will give us a better idea of the work of this humble servant of the Lord Jesus Christ.

From Darkness to the Marvelous Light of the Gospel

During the month of June 1914, while I was in my study, a man rang the door bell. I opened the door and there he was with a satchel in his hand, a wide smile on his face, as he inquired in a sonorous voice: "Is Prof. Arichiello in?" As soon as I told him that I was the man he was looking for, he came in and began to talk about his son's violin lessons, after which he spoke of God. As I was not interested in religion then, his words did not make a lasting impression on me at the moment.

The following week he came to see me again and gave me another testimony of his faith. I told him that I was disgusted with religion, but he did not lose faith. In departing he left with me a copy of the New Testament and some Christian literature, saying: "Read it and judge yourself whether I am telling you the truth or not." When he had left, I opened the New Testament and began to read it. For two weeks I was absorbed in its reading, after which I could not help but come to the conclusion that the religion revealed by that book was true. It did not take me long to accept Jesus as my personal Saviour, my refuge, my hope, my all.

Today I am a new man, a Christian in the real sense of the word, and I owe it all to this man of God, Mr. Lorenzo Cerchiara. May God continue to bless him in this wonderful work of ushering souls into His Kingdom.

JOHN S. ARICHIELLO
Lyncrock, L. I., N. Y.

Once a Priest, Now a Presbyterian Minister

From my early childhood, I experienced great pleasure in building altars and in imitating the priest in the celebration of the Mass. This attraction for the ceremonies of the Roman Church increased, as I became older, to the point that I resolved to become a priest myself. My parents welcomed my decision since in many Italian homes it is considered a great blessing to have a son in the priesthood.

In 1885 with profound joy in my heart I donned for the first time the garb of a priest. After spending several years in College and Seminary, where I learned what priests really are, I received my ordination and I became the spiritual leader of a small country parish.

My stay in the first charge was not very long for in 1903 I left Italy and came to America. My first residence was in Brooklyn, New York, where God in His infinite mercy brought me in contact with the Italian Missionary-Colporteur, Lorenzo Cerchiara, who was selling evangelical books and Bibles around my parish and preaching the gospel in various sections of the city.

I had many discussions with Mr. Cerchiara who, although a former barber, impressed me so deeply with his simplicity, knowledge of the Bible and Christian experience, that even I, a priest, inwardly many times felt utterly defeated in those encounters. As my interest in evangelical Christianity grew, I began to attend in the company of Mr. Cerchiara the services of several Italian Protestant churches where I saw the light which caused me to cast away my priestly garb, and, under the blessed ministry of the Rev. Mr. Arrighi, became first a member of the Broome Street Tabernacle, later a deacon, and still later a Presbyterian minister.

(Signed) Rev. A. M. Pizzi,
Cleveland, Ohio.

Mr. Cerchiara is now approaching his three score years and ten and, notwithstanding his trials and sufferings, he faces the future with the same joy experienced when he first accepted the Lord. His secret is found in the verses he often quotes: "Nevertheless, I am continually with thee; thou hast holden me by my right hand. Thou shalt guide me with thy counsel and afterward receive me to glory." Ps. 73:23-24.

Mr. Cerchiara belongs to that noble company whose name

is legion, who in all ages and under every sky has had one supreme desire, namely, to give this priceless gift, *the Word of God*, to all those who had not had the opportunity of acquiring it in any other way. The following poem is a beautiful tribute to these great souls.

The Vaudois Missionary

"O, lady fair, these silks of mine
Are beautiful and rare—
The richest web of the Indian loom,
Which beauty's self might wear.
And these pearls are pure and mild to behold,
And with radiant light they vie;
I have brought them with me a weary way:
Will my gentle lady buy?"

And the lady smiled on the worn old man
Through the dark and clustering curls
Which veiled her brow as she bent to view
His silk and glittering pearls:
As she placed their price in the old man's hand,
And lightly turned away:
But she paused at the wanderer's earnest call—
"My gentle lady, stay!"

"O, lady fair, I have yet a gem
Which a purer lustre flings
Than the diamond flash of the jewelled crown
On the lofty brow of Kings;
A wonderful pearl of exceeding price,
Whose virtue shall not decay;
Whose light shall be as a spell to thee,
And a blessing on thy way!"

The lady glanced at the mirroring steel,
Where her youthful form was seen,
Where her eyes shone clear and her dark locks waved
Their clasping pearls between;

"Bring forth thy pearl of exceeding worth,
Thou traveller gray and old;
And name the price of thy precious gem,
And my pages shall count thy gold."

The cloud went off from the pilgrim's brow,
As a small and meagre book
Unchased with gold or diamond gem,
From his folding robe he took:
"Here, lady fair, is the pearl of price—
May it prove as such to thee!
Nay, keep thy gold—I ask it not—
For the Word of God is free."

The hoary traveller went his way—
But the gift he left behind
Hath had its pure and perfect work
On that high-born maiden's mind;
And she hath turned from her pride of sin
To the lowliness of truth,
And given her human heart to God
In its beautiful hour of youth.

And she hath left the old gray walls
Where an evil faith hath power,
The courtly knights of her father's train,
And the maidens of her bower;
And she hath gone to the Vaudois vale,
By lordly feet untrod,
Where the poor and needy of earth are rich
In the perfect love of God!

—(From the *London Observer*)

Humanity accords its plaudits only to a few of our heroes
and benefactors. Millions, equally heroic and beneficial, perform their task with Franciscan humility and eventually go,
seemingly, into oblivion, unknown, and unsung, albeit not
forgotten by One who said, "Inasmuch as ye have done it

unto one of the least of these my brethren, ye have done it unto me."

Whereas most of these humble pioneers have been satisfied to remain in the front trenches and minister to the least, the last and the lost, on the highways and by-ways of our city slums, some have felt impelled to acquire more education and lift themselves with the straps of their boots. Suffice here to mention just a few: Gualtieri, Casanova, Patrono, Serafini, Pastore, Moccia and Frisina, who have done conspicuous work. We are going to describe the contribution of just one of these pioneers.

Phillip Frisina was born in Delianova, Reggio Calabria, May 24, 1875. He came to this country in 1900 and found employment at the Baldwin Locomotive Works in Philadelphia.

Like most immigrants he very soon discovered that, in order to improve his conditions, he had to learn English, therefore he enrolled in a night school conducted by the Rev. Michele Nardi. He was a bit upset when they announced a prayer meeting, after the lesson was over, since he had been admonished by his home town priest to be on guard against those accursed Protestants in America, because they worshipped the head of an animal. Notwithstanding the protests of his friends, he attended the Sunday Service, but what was his surprise when instead of the head of an animal, he saw a beautiful picture of Christ in Gethsemane, and from the singing of the hymns, the reading of the scriptures, the prayers and the sermon, he discovered that they worshipped God in Spirit and in truth. He was given a copy of the Bible, which he read at first with fear and trembling, since he had been taught that only priests could read it, but soon he found such enjoyment and spiritual delight that he had to read it from cover to cover.

It was not long before he felt the urge to go into some form of Christian service, and being a man of action, he gave up his job and became a colporteur for the American Tract

Society. He was assigned almost immediately to help Dr. Pirazzini in the establishment of the South Philadelphia Italian Mission, and later to West Philadelphia, where the first meeting was held under a pear tree in the back yard of Mr. Scott, a real Christian gentleman, and where now stands a beautiful church building. The Macedonian calls were many and insistent in those days, however, when ship loads of Italians were arriving constantly, hence, he was sent first to Bristol, Pa., and later to Wilmington, Delaware.

Eager to overcome his educational deficiencies, he entered a teachers training school in New York, but the need for workers was so urgent and wide spread, that he was called back to Philadelphia, thence to Auburn, New York, again to Philadelphia, and providentially once more to Auburn, where he entered Seminary and was graduated in 1908.

"He was able to build a flourishing church in Auburn, but not, however, without much persecution from the Roman Catholic Church. It was necessary to turn to the police for protection during a series of open-air meetings. It seemed that even with this protection trouble stirred, for the police department sent an Irish Catholic policeman who did exactly nothing to protect the Christians in their meeting. On one evening a young Catholic boy prepared a paper bag of sand mixed with broken pieces of glass to throw at Mr. Frisina as he preached. His aim was poor, for the bag did not strike Mr. Frisina, but the policeman who was on duty, and who consequently lost an eye. This grieved Mr. Frisina very much and so he went to the hospital to visit the unfortunate policeman, but the incident made him change his mind and heart toward the work of the Mission."

"Among the new Christians in the Auburn Mission there was a family of devout Catholics who had recently come from Italy. The mother, a fine elderly woman, was so devout that she scarcely let a day go by without saying her rosary. It was at such a time that Rev. Frisina called to see the family. He introduced himself a book-seller offering a book that God

Himself had given to the people. Of course, the woman was delighted to know of such a book, and as she could not read, she asked Mr. Frisina to read from the book. He did it gladly and as she often remarked in later years, "It was as though the darkness had turned to light." When she was informed by her neighbors that the man who called so often was a Protestant minister, she said that if this was the kind of religion the Protestants professed, then this was the religion for herself and her family, whereupon the whole family accepted Christ and Mr. Frisina married the youngest daughter, Stella."

In 1912 he was called to Norrisville, Pa., where his ministry lasted eleven years, bringing both joy and sorrow to his heart, for it was here that he saw a church building erected to the glory of God, it was here that he saw a goodly number of men and women accept Christ, it was while he lived here that the elder of his seven children, Samuel, at 11 years of age gave a concert in New York City and was acclaimed by the musical critics as a real prodigy, but it was here also that two years later the strings of his heart were stretched almost to the breaking point when his firstborn was drowned.

Meanwhile many of the Italians in Philadelphia had moved in the neighborhood of the Holland Memorial Church, and Mr. Frisina was called to begin the work among his countrymen. He worked diligently and assiduously for four years, organizing a number of activities, among which a Sunday School of about 100, a daily kindergarten and preaching services, he gave unstintingly of himself. One evening after prayer meeting, he was brought to a hospital suffering from a severe hemorrhage, and three days later after undergoing a major operation, he was called to join the invisible army of Christ, and hear from his blessed lips "Well done my good and faithful servant: thou hast been faithful over a few things, I will make thee ruler over many things: enter thou into the joy of thy Lord."

(Mrs. Passiglia, wife of the Rev. Walter B. Passiglia of Tampa, Florida, is a daughter of the late Mr. Frisina.)

10

The Pioneer as a Builder of Men
(Dr. Antonio Mangano)

Calabria, one of the least known sections of Italy, has enjoyed a most enviable history, for it has given the world, almost at stated intervals, great stars which have not been dimmed by the rolling shadows of time. It was the home of Pythagoras, of Telesi, of Companella, of Misasi, the last, who has revealed the country and its people to the rest of Italy, and of many other bright luminaries.

As soon as immigration to the United States assumed vast proportion, many of her children left those rugged mountains and deep valleys for the land of their dreams. Protestantism, in its work among the Italians, has attracted a goodly number of young people from that region who, being fired by the Gospel of Jesus Christ, have become torch bearers among their countrymen in America.

Antonio Mangano was born in Acri, Cosenza, on December 7th, 1869. He came to this country with his father at the age of six, became an orphan when only nine, and was brought up to manhood in an American family of Hempstead, Long Island. His real education, however, did not begin until he was 21, when he became an American citizen and enrolled at Colgate Academy in the same year, from which he graduated in 1894. The following lines from the pen of Markham apply in a peculiar way to our good friend:

> *"We are all blind until we see*
> *That in the human plan*
> *Nothing is worth the building*
> *That does not build the man.*

Why build these cities glorious,
If man unbuilded goes?
In vain we build the world unless
The builder also grows."

His thirst for knowledge knew no bounds, and to satisfy it he attended Colgate University 1894-95, Brown University 1896-99, where he received his Bachelor of Arts Degree, was awarded the Hicks prize in debating and was elected class orator, as well as commencement speaker. He received his theological training at Union Theological Seminary 1900-1903. He earned his Master of Arts at Columbia University, majoring in sociology, he received his degree of Doctor of Divinity from Colgate in 1919. He spent some time in Italy, studying the language and customs of his people, and in 1922-23 he studied at Oxford and Cambridge universities, residing at Westminster Theological Seminary.

In 1904 he became general missionary for the Baptist Home Mission Society, and although the Baptist work among the Italians in America had been started in 1893 by the Rev. Ariel B. Bellondi in Buffalo, New York, while he was still a student at Colgate Theological Seminary, Dr. Mangano was nevertheless one of the real pioneers in his denomination, since from the day he was converted in the Baptist Church of Hempstead, Long Island, New York, in 1888, he began to testify of the saving power of the Gospel of Jesus Christ. His first real love, however, was the first Italian Baptist Church of Brooklyn, New York, which he founded in 1904 and of which he has been the inspiring leader throughout the years. It is interesting to read how a simple act was crowned with so much success. A Bible was offered way back in 1897, by a colporteur of the Brooklyn City Mission Society, to a shoemaker who refused the gift unceremoniously, when a middle aged Italian, who was present, interjected the statement "I'm sorry that I can't read it, otherwise I would buy the book," but after a moment's reflection, he added, "Just a moment, my son

Dominick will read it to me." Dominick DiGiacomo read the book in his father's house to a group of neighbors, who listened almost in transfigured ecstasy to the reading of the Gospel's stories and the Acts of the Apostles.

This seemingly unimportant occurrence started a train of influence which continued to acquire momentum until a church came into being, and, in the words of Dr. Mangano, the Bible found its way into the hearts of many immigrants who read and treasured it, despite persecutions arrayed against those innocent seekers of the truth. "Conversions followed and the numbers that attended the meetings in the home outgrew its capacity." The work continued to make so much progress that in 1903 it was taken over by the Baptist Church Extension Society. In 1904 Dr. Mangano began his work there and under his blessed ministry, splendid cumulative Christian influences have emanated from this evangelizing center. Friends of the work point to the fact that one fortunate circumstance in 1905 was the coming of Miss Mary Godden, who had been a teacher in Salem (Mass.) Normal School for thirty-five years, and now began her ministry among the Italians of Brooklyn as a teacher in Daily Vacation Bible School. The immediate result of these consecrated energies and efforts was the Marie Louise Deitz Memorial Church, dedicated March 2nd, 1911, from which the gospel of Jesus Christ was preached for a generation to an increasing procession of men, women and children.

A very important event in the life of Dr. Mangano took place January 21st, 1907, when he married Miss Mabel Austin Farnham, a graduate of Vassar College. The couple sailed to Italy for their honeymoon, but even during this well deserved holiday in his native country, he took time to produce a study on *Causes and Effects of Italian Immigration* which was published in five articles in the Christian Magazine, now the Survey Graphic. I was present at the interdenominational meeting held in the Broome Street Tabernacle, New York City, in 1935, and at a popular meeting in the Fifth Avenue

Presbyterian Church, of which the speaker, the late Rev. Stasio, reminiscing on the work and the workers of pioneer days, related in a most cordial and genial mood how one day in his home in Italy, while he was taking his afternoon siesta, he heard a voice calling from below his balcony. Upon inquiring from above, he imitated Dr. Mangano as he must have sounded to him when he introduced himself, in a strange mixture of Italian, Calabrese and English, as a Baptist missionary who had returned to his native country to study the language in order to better equip himself for his life work. Dr. Mangano was the most amused person in the audience, showing that large congregation how he could take a joke.

Dr. Mangano will long be remembered as a progressive teacher, a stimulating and informative writer and a forceful preacher. The finest service of this versatile man to the Kingdom of God, in the humble judgment of the writer, was rendered from 1907 to 1931, as Dean of the Italian Department at the Colgate-Rochester Divinity School, which was created for the specific purpose of preparing young men for the Gospel ministry, and the subsequent arrangement to send these young men for a year of study and travel in Italy. He took the first group to Rome in 1924 and returned to America by way of Palestine.

Those who are familiar with the school recall how the students lived for three years in rented houses in Brooklyn. For a time they slept in Hope Chapel, were fed in a restaurant and attended classes in the eastern district Y.M.C.A. But as soon as the Dietz Memorial Building was completed, the Italian Theological students were given living quarters and class rooms within its walls. In 1928 the Department was moved to Hamilton, New York, and in 1929 to Rochester.

Even a superficial knowledge of Dr. Mangano's many activities will convince us of his marvelous energy and ability, for besides being the beloved Dean of the Italian Department, he taught church history, Old Testament, ethics, Italian and English, and was at all times "all things to all men in order to win some." A majority of the men in the Italian Baptist ministry were inspired by this man of God, and many of us in other denominations have been blessed by his gifted mind and warm sympathetic heart.

Dr. Mangano was one of the first wise interpreters of the Italians in America, with the publication of the Interdenominational Mission Study Book, *Sons of Italy*, which won him almost overnight national recognition as an author and student. In 1917 he prepared a comprehensive study of the religious work among the Italians in America, which was published in a pamphlet form with other studies of different foreign speaking groups by the American Home Mission Council. It is beyond the scope of the present work to give a complete list of all the articles and pamphlets published by Dr. Mangano, but suffice here to say that, in his long and blessed ministry, he has assimilated the finest production of the American and the Italian people, and presented in a sympathetic and understanding way the rich gifts of each to the other. With the permission of the American Baptist Home Mission Society we reproduce a short story, which reveals how our friend has used effectively the spoken as well as the printed word.

"The Brigand"

It is now more than forty years ago that Roberto was one of a gang of bandits roving over the Calabrian hills. He had wandered away from the company in search of a friend, and was walking leisurely along the provincial road. All at once he turned his head backward and became startled. He looked about him for some secluded spot where he could hide from view. He had just discovered that on the same road over which he had come there was a group of mounted carabinieri—soldier police—whom all brigands feared. Roberto crouched down in a hollow space and was protected by the friendly branches of a scrub pine tree. As the footsteps of the mounted police faded away in the distance he came out of his hiding place, looked about him to make sure that no one else was in sight, and hurried off to the secret meeting place in the woods, to inform his companions of their approaching danger.

"I hope I can reach my friends before they are taken unawares," Roberto was muttering to himself. "I have had a narrow escape myself, but I must save my friends."

But already the carabinieri had been informed of the whereabouts of the band, and before Roberto could give them warning they were surrounded and all were put under arrest. Roberto saw at a glance that the end had come. He could do nothing but lay down his arms or lose his life. Owing to the intercession of good friends, Roberto was freed and later given a place in the force of the State Police.

After several years of service Roberto surprised his friends by telling them he was going to America. He said nothing about the reason for his sudden decision, but his mind was made up that the rascal who had heaped shame and infamy upon one of his relatives must die. The Italian is proud of his clean blood, and woe to the one who pollutes it.

He landed at "Old Castle Garden." It was easy then for people to land on American soil. He found no difficulty satisfying the officials as to his qualifications, and in a few hours he was walking along "Mulberry Bend" looking on every hand for his victim. Two days later he saw the object of his hatred turn a corner just ahead of him. He hastened his step—almost caught up with the man and was about to grab and strangle him. But he restrained himself; he feared he would be caught and at once thrust in prison.

"I must end him, but I must also plan for my escape." He followed him to his home. He marked the spot well. "I'll wait now till my opportune time comes. It will come," he said to himself. Several days passed and his heart was being consumed with anger and delay. He said: "I cannot wait any longer; I must end his life."

But that night, while reading a book which someone had put into his hands, he chanced upon this expression:

"The Lord saith, the most perfect vengeance is an act of pardon." This came like a thunderbolt out of a clear sky. Almost in an instant Roberto's desire to shed the blood of his enemy lost its edge. He walked out into the street, and as he was aimlessly wandering along the sidewalk he came upon a group of Italian Salvation Army men and women, who were conducting a meeting in the open air. Instinctively he stopped to hear what the leader was talking about. Before he could hear very much a stone was thrown by someone, which struck one of the women in the eye. Roberto expected to hear the woman cry out, and possibly use some blasphemous expressions. But instead she simply pulled her handkerchief out of her pocket, wiped the blood from her eyes and, lifting her face heavenward, muttered something which was not audible to the crowd, but which impressed Roberto very much.

"How can this be," he said. "She says nothing. She must be praying. There is a mystery here. I want to know more about it. I have never seen anything like this." Roberto was disarmed. He wandered back to his room, but only to wait for next Sunday to see more of these people. During the week he could think of nothing except the woman and her gaze heavenward. Sunday came: Roberto was there on the spot where the Salvation Army group held their meeting.

The leader of that meeting, who had much experience, spied out Roberto, and sent a man to where he was standing, saying to him, "I am sure that man is seeking for God," pointing to Roberto. Five minutes later Roberto and his new friend were kneeling in the street engaged in prayer. God heard Roberto's prayer, and he rose from his knees a transfigured man. The hatred had departed from his heart. For twenty years he has been serving God and testifying to His wonderful grace and power to save a sinful man. There is scarcely a Sunday passes that Roberto does not in joy, and with effectiveness, testify publicly about his wonderful salvation.

In 1931 he returned to his first love, home mission work, as pastor of the first church he had helped to found, the Dietz

Memorial Church, where he remained until his retirement in
1942. It was during this part of his ministry in 1937, that the
building was condemned by the city in order to construct
a new boulevard leading to the World's Fair. Without giving
up in despair, Dr. Mangano set himself at once to raise additional funds with which to erect a new edifice on Devoe
Street near Graham Avenue, and a fine building location,
in the heart of an Italian Community of 35,000, was purchased
for $11,500. The award from the city had been $40,000, the
Italian congregation, under the enthusiastic challenge of their
veteran leader, subscribed about $15,000, his friends con-
tributed over $5,000, and the result was a beautiful chapel
completed in 1940 at a total cost of over $50,000. Dr. Car-
penter of the Brooklyn Church Federation says: "It is the
only Protestant project in Williamsburg (the name of the
division in which it is located) that is ministering to the people
of this community." For this reason Dr. Carpenter believes
this church, which is to a very great extent the result of Dr.
Mangano's work and one of the most important Italian projects, has a much brighter future than any of the other Protestant churches in this section.

We visited Dr. Mangano in August 1941, who with all the
energy of a younger man, the enthusiasm, the vision and the
zeal of the artist who has finally produced his dream on canvas,
or chiseled it on marble, a living thing of beauty, showed us
the attractive, commodious, up-to-date building, explaining
every department as we proceeded from the basement to the
sanctuary and then to the Sunday School rooms, and at the
same time sharing with us some of his hopes, dreams, and
aspirations for the future.

At the beginning of 1942, Dr. Mangano reached his retirement age, and as a good soldier of Jesus Christ relinquished
his post, handed the torch to a younger man, the Rev. A.
Vasquez, not to spend the days in idleness, however, but to
use his splendid gifts in the cause which with the passing years
has been growing dearer and nearer to his heart. Our prayer

from a distance is that God may preserve him for many and many years to come and that his mantle may truly fall upon the shoulders of his young successor.

Doctor and Mrs. Mangano are universally regarded among the Italian Baptist pastors and missionaries as their spiritual parents, since they have done more perhaps for the Italian work than any other couple in the field. They have earned for themselves such a tender spot in the hearts of the Baptist people in America that on Tuesday afternoon, May 26th, 1942, the delegates to the Northern Baptist Convention, meeting in Cleveland, Ohio, paid them a well deserved tribute when they stood and applauded as a token of their esteem and appreciation, after these veteran home missionaries had been introduced to them by Secretary G. Pitt Beers; but their greatest joy is derived from the contributions made to the Kingdom of God by the men and the women in the different parts of the country who were inspired or prepared by them for full time service, for they have long learned with Webster that:

> "If we work upon marble it will perish. If we work upon brass time will efface it. If we rear temples they will crumble to dust. But if we work upon men's immortal minds, if we imbue them with high principles, with the just fear of God and love of their fellowmen, we engrave upon those tablets something which no time can efface, and which will brighten and brighten to all eternity."

11

The Pioneer as a Faithful Servant of Jesus Christ
(Rev. Joseph Brunn)

The distinction which the Apostle Paul claimed for himself, of being a faithful servant of Jesus Christ, could be accorded easily to almost every one of our home missionaries among the Italians, since they have all labored long and well without regard to clock or pay check, refusing many times greener pastures and places of importance, in order to remain faithful to their first love or their sacred trust. Our choice for this sketch is the Rev. Mr. Brunn, because he embodies more clearly those qualities which are indispensable to a successful home missionary among our people.

Under the caption "America gave me a new Father," the Rev. Mr. Cherubini of Detroit, Michigan, related a short time ago in "Il Rinnovamento" how, when he was only nine years of age, his father had left a wife and eight children in Italy and had come to this new promised land. For three years he had completely forgotten his family, since they received no news from him, but finally through the work of the Rev. Mr. Brunn, then pastor of our Italian Presbyterian Church in Hazelton, Pennsylvania, his father accepted Christ as his personal Saviour, consecrated his life to God, and resumed his obligation to his family. For it was after his conversion that he wrote to his wife for the first time, enclosing twenty dollars in American currency. Mr. Cherubini adds that his father continued to remit from his meager earnings a goodly sum each month until he sent for his family. "These letters," he states, "were warm with affection, very enthusiastic of America, and revealed a clear transformation which God had been pleased to bring about in my father's heart."

The Rev. Mr. Brunn was born in Trieste on September the 5th, 1871. Since his mother had migrated from Andreis, Udine, it was their custom to spend their vacation with the grandmother. In June of 1883 they started from Trieste in the family coach, and as they approached Andreis they were greeted by considerable noise and then they saw a mob of women throwing stones, while boys were beating petroleum cans.

As they came closer they discovered that a man with a long beard was running for his life before that frenzied crowd. Fortunately for the man, two national policemen arrived just in time to stop that mob and with the arrest of about 50 women, the gentleman disappeared, and the coach was able to proceed to grandmother's house.

As soon as they reached the home which had been the object of their dreams during the long school year, Joseph, who was about 13, related in an excited and dramatic way to his grandmother what he had seen on the way home. Her answer was, "My boy, they told us last Sunday to drive that man out of town, because he is a minister of the devil. He holds his meetings in the house of Sebastiano Salvadore."

Afer a delicious and abundant evening meal, curiosity impelled the boy to go and see what was happening at the house of Salvadore. Since the windows were wide open, he was able to see without much trouble that same gray bearded man surrounded by a dozen people. The man had a book in his hand from which he was reading but, of course, the boy did not understand what it was all about. After the singing of a hymn, the man got down on his knees and, imitated by those present, he offered a prayer in his rich musical voice. But what was the surprise of the boy, when he heard the man pray for the people who had stoned him as well as for those present. Mr. Brunn says that "that prayer sank deeply into his heart," and it was that prayer that made him a follower of Jesus Christ, although he did not make a public confession until he came to America.

The story of how Joseph and his brother, James, came to America was at one time a most common one. Some of his town's people had returned from Pittsburgh, Pennsylvania, with stories that in this country they earned as much as $2.50 a day, that they had not to beg for jobs, and that they could earn that much every day in the year. The two brothers, James and Joseph, with good minds, strong bodies, and business ability said to each other "if they can earn two-fifty a day, we can certainly earn $5.00 a day." They decided to try their luck, they left their home town and traveled toward Glasgow, Scotland, selling their wares in every town and city they passed through, until they boarded the S.S. Ethiopia, and on the 25th day of August, 1890, they set foot on this strange land.

For seven years the two brothers lived and worked almost entirely in New Britain, Connecticut, experiencing all the ups and downs of the immigrants when they first came to America. In 1895 Joseph was baptized in the historical Hudson Memorial Church on Washington Square and did some Missionary work in Hartford, New Britain, Connecticut; Astoria, Long Island; and helped in the founding of the Italian Baptist Association of America. At the end of seven years the two brothers separated. James remained in Connecticut, while Joseph accepted a position in New York. He made his way to the Broome Street Tabernacle, met and fell in love at first sight with the dynamic Dr. Arrighi, who in turn was so attracted to the young man, that as soon as it was expedient, asked him to teach a Men's Bible Class, and as he became impressed with his leadership ability and keen interest, he persuaded him to prepare for the Gospel ministry. In due time Mr. Brunn graduated from the Parkesie Training School for Christian workers, which became Dr. White's Bible School of New York.

In those days the need for missionaries among the Italians who were flooding the highways and byways of America was great. The enthusiasm of the American Protestants knew no bounds, while the supply of workers properly trained or even superficially prepared was very meager. But where knowledge was lacking, love for lost souls seemed to abound. There was a call from Hazelton, Pennsylvania in 1898 and Dr. Arrighi, in his fatherly manner, presented the challenge to his new spiritual son. Hazelton was a mining town and the church was located in Hazel township, just outside the city limits. It had a population of 9,000 with just two graded streets and no sidewalks, no police or fire protection, and whereas the school was taught by inferior teachers, the community boasted 79 saloons, due to the fact that the cost for license in the city was $500.00 while in the township only $75.00. Political conditions were so appalling that as soon as the young minister arrived he decided that something had to be done at once.

Here is a typical illustration of what was happening among our poor immigrants. A man had come from Italy on borrowed money, with the promise that he would repay it in six or seven months. He had found a job in Hazelton through Mr. Brunn's help, and had been saving his money to pay off the debt. In those days the storekeeper was a banker of some sort, and this poor laborer entrusted him with his money, to be transmitted to his wife in Italy. The storekeeper-banker did not send the money and the poor woman in Italy saw all her belongings seized by the money lender. When the husband heard the news, he went immediately to the banker and demanded an account of the money. The storekeeper-banker threw him out, called a constable, had him cast in prison, and since the poor man was not able to pay a $25.00 fine imposed by the alderman, he was kept in jail to weep over his troubles. As soon as Mr. Brunn heard the story from a member of his church, he visited, first the prisoner, satisfied himself that he was telling the truth, went to the mayor's office to secure his release, and then went to see the alderman. The man of the law was surprised to see a minister interested in a "green horn" and advised him to attend to his business of preaching the gospel, while he would attend to his high calling of administering the law; to which Mr. Brunn retorted, "My dear sir, I preached the Gospel last Sunday, and right now I am practicing what I preached." In a short time the case was reopened, and the accused and the plaintiff appeared in court. After a receipt for the money was exhibited, the banker admitted his guilt, and offered to make restitution. The alderman was now convinced that he had been duped by this small time politician, and was going to send him to the penitentiary, but Mr. Brunn and his client, after a brief conference, decided that they would not prosecute if the man would be willing to return the money. The alderman having changed his judicial mind, thundered: "Very well, you may consider yourself fortunate to get off without a prison sentence. I order you to return this man his money immediately, plus court cost and a $50.00 fine."

Mr. Brunn had become such a friend of the people that he was prevailed upon to become a candidate for the city council, and improve conditions from within. Out of 502 votes cast in his district, he received 500. It was his privilege during his term to introduce a number of ordinances such as the grading of the streets, motorizing the fire department, putting electric lights in the streets, and the erection of a new city hall which was considered one of the best Italian Rennaissance buildings in Pennsylvania.

During his 15 years in Hazelton he received 274 members on confession of faith; in 1908 he was honored by being elected moderator of the Lehigh Presbytery, and in 1910 the General Assembly of the Presbyterian Church U. S. A. sent him as the official delegate to the Waldensian Synod.

In 1913 he received a letter from Dr. A. F. Shauffler, who was then president of the New York City Mission Society, saying briefly, "Mr. Brunn, please be kind enough to come to New York for a little conference with me. Wire me when you are coming." Mr. Brunn of course obeyed, and to his amazement he was informed that, since Dr. Arrighi had retired and Mr. Nardi, who had been supplying the pulpit, was also retiring because of ill health, the board had looked to him as the logical person to follow in the footsteps of his spiritual father. He received a formal call, and on May 1, 1913, he assumed his duties as pastor of the Broome Street Tabernacle and of the Charlton Street Memorial Church.

During all these years Dr. Brunn has held his sacred trust with distinction and honor, winning not only the admiration and love of his people, but of all those ministers and laymen who have had the privilege of knowing him. He has shared his energy and ability unstintingly in the many causes of the church, among which we must mention the Waldensian Aid Society, La Casa Materna in Italy, and the Italian Evangelical Society, which for the first time has produced a publication "Il Rinnovamento," largely supported by the Italian Protestants.

He was the first Italian to be elected moderator of the Presbytery of Lehigh. The General Assembly sent him again to Italy as a fraternal delegate to the Historical Waldensian Church Synod which meets every year at Torre Pillice. In 1928 he was accorded five months leave of absence to enjoy a richly deserved rest, in company of his faithful wife who had shared through the years his hopes and aspirations, his joys and sorrows, his defeats and victories. He served as representative of the Waldensian Church in America, for five years he taught Christian Doctrine in the New York City Missionary School and for several years he was chairman of the Child Crime Prevention Bureau of the New York Police Department.

When Mr. Brunn returned to Andreis (Udine) in 1922 he was received by the Mayor of the town and was presented with his family's coat of arms, accompanied by this motivation, "I am proud that a son of this little town is an Evangelical minister, honoring our town in America."

He has dedicated his best energies and his marvelous gifts to the Broome Street Tabernacle, which has become the center of Italian Protestantism in America and is affectionately known, at least by the Presbyterian missions, as the mother of Italian work in the United States. He has developed such a well-rounded program that the entire week is filled with a beehive of activities and he has continued to shepherd, with the aid of his assistant and co-workers, a very active congregation. The secret of his energy and success may be found in the words of the Apostle Paul, "I can do all things through Christ which strengtheneth me."

During the celebration of his 25th anniversary at the Broome Street Tabernacle, he received many testimonials of affection from members of his church and friends, far and near, all inspired by filial devotion for the man who had moulded their lives, shared their joys and sorrows, lifted them above the average level of our people and brought them to Christ.

On September 1, 1943, after thirty years as pastor of the Broome Street Tabernacle, Mr. Brunn tendered his resignation which the New York Missionary Society accepted reluctantly. We join our prayers with those of countless friends, that he may continue to bless our mutual cause with his contagious zeal, his undiminished faith and his fatherly wisdom.

12

The Pioneer as a Medical Missionary
(Rev. Joseph A. Villelli, M.D.)

A fine looking boy thirteen or fourteen years of age was walking with his father along the streets of Santo Stefano Di Camastra, when his attention was attracted by a song of which he could catch but two disconnected words. The melody, more than the words, aroused his curiosity and he inquired from a passerby, "Pardon me, but can you tell me who is singing?" The reply, rather abrupt and not too friendly, came from his father. "Never mind, it must be Don Rosario the Protestant priest." "A Protestant priest! Do Protestants have such beautiful tunes? But father, didn't you hear the word 'Christ' mentioned? I have always been told that Protestants don't believe in Christ, don't believe in the Virgin Mary, don't believe in saints, don't believe in anything!" The father somewhat exasperated commanded that they had better change the subject of their conversation. Joseph obeyed, but that song had set a trend of thought in motion, not so easily swept aside at such an inquisitive age.

One day he asked some students if they knew anything about Protestants, and, to his surprise one answered, "Why, I am one of them and I'll be glad to take you to the mission tonight." His first visit was disappointing due to the appearance of the place and a testimony given by a young man with very little conviction. He was entreated to return Sunday evening, but on hearing that Mary had given birth to a half dozen children after Jesus, he lost all sense of propriety and shouted "It is a lie." The minister in a most kindly spirit asked him to withhold judgment until the end of the service when he would be glad to answer all his questions. A conversation after the service helped him somewhat and he left with a copy of the New Testament and the injunction "Read this attentively and the Holy Spirit will enlighten your mind." After reading the first gospel, he felt that he knew it all and returned the book to the minister, but even from that casual reading, the last command of Jesus, "Go ye therefore and teach all nations" made such a profound impression on his mind that when he returned to school that fall, he determined to become a monk missionary to China. He expressed his desire to the Father Guardian, who replied that he would gladly interest Father Mendola who was to visit the convent in two weeks, and make the necessary arrangements.

In July, Joseph was graduated from the Ginnasio of Patti "summa cum laude" but nothing had been done to send him to the convent school for missionaries, and to his inquiries he was informed that he needed five hundred lire. There was no money available, and his brother, a jurist, who was already paying for the support of their two sisters who had taken the veil, advised him to abandon the idea for the time being and continue his classical studies.

He had completed his second year in college when he was literally hypnotized by the exaggerated descriptions of America given by a woman who had just returned from New York. He became infected with the fever of getting rich quick and on December 20th, 1899, he was treading the goldless street of the largest metropolis in the world. One can easily imagine the disappointment that he had to experience in America where, in order to support himself, he had to dig, carry coal and ice to the fourth and fifth floor, be a helper to a blacksmith, a painter, a tailor, or a plumber, wash dishes and what not. In 1903, having lost all hopes of going back to Italy, he married Miss Filomena Volpe, on a princely salary of $5.00 a week. He soon discovered that man cannot live on love, that two cannot live as cheap as one, and that bills become mercilessly due. He lost his faith in God and in his fellowmen, and would have committed suicide had it not been for his companion whose tears had the strength of washing away all evil thoughts. God works in a mysterious way and one Saturday morning, while he was at a desk preparing bills in the plumber's absence, a gentleman entered the shop, and when he saw him writing fast and well, he inquired "What schooling have you had?" Upon hearing, "Two years at college," he remarked, "It is a shame that with such an education you are a plumber's helper." "Do you attend Church?" asked the stranger, and having answered in the negative, he received an invitation to attend the Broome Street Tabernacle, with the promise of a job as an insurance agent at $15 per week.

The lure of a better job at a tripled salary and the opportunity for social expression brought him to a Bible class at the Tabernacle, conducted by the gentleman of the day before. Several weeks later the teacher was absent one Sunday and the rest of the scholars induced Mr. Villelli to take the class. While he was teaching, the Rev. Arrighi, then pastor of the church, stepped in and after listening to the new teacher, he placed his hands on his back and said prophetically, "Gentlemen, Joseph will soon become a missionary." It was not very long before Mr. Arrighi asked him to go to the Presbyterian Church of Sea and Land to have an interview with the American pastor who wanted to start some work among the Italians who were moving increasingly into the neighborhood. On October 27, 1904, he gave up his position with the insurance company and started a work which he had the privilege of continuing for thirty-eight years.

It all started like a dream. An elderly lady who had been working at the church for some time told him that they wanted to organize a sewing school, and for him to get some Italian girls. Like Moses he said to himself, "If they ask who I am and what I want, what shall I say?" But without losing courage, he entered a tenement house, took off his hat, offered a prayer to God, began to knock at every door, and within half an hour he had a group of twenty girls following him to the parish house. The following day he was told to organize the boys into a club and later to start English classes for adults. By Christmas he had a good sewing school, several clubs, a Sunday School of over one hundred children, and a good adult class in English. The Presbytery of New York became cognizant of the needs and in April 1905 received Mr. Villelli under its care, and had the work supported by the Church Extension Committee.

After a year and a half, the first harvest was gathered with thirteen persons received on confession of faith. Eager to equip himself for this task, Mr. Villelli attended the Wiona Bible School, later known as the Biblical Seminary of New York, from which he graduated in 1906. Two years later he received a master of arts degree from Columbia University, in July 1909, he became a full fledged citizen, and in 1910 he received the degree of Bachelor of Divinity from Union Seminary.

As soon as his work began to march forward, the Roman Church awoke from its lethargy, started a settlement house nearby, and dispatched nuns in every home to put fear in every heart. About the same time the Board of Education started classes for future citizens, and the bottom seemed to fall from his work. Fortunately, with an M.A. in education he was able to qualify as a teacher, and by insisting on an assignment near his church, he taught four nights a week for five scholastic years.

A new difficulty arose at this time when due to lack of funds, the Church of Sea and Land had to give up its nurse and first aid activities. This work had meant so much to the poor people of the neighborhood that it was almost a calamity. How to overcome this difficulty? After friendly advice from kind physicians and friends, Mr. Villelli decided to solve the problem by taking a medical course, and in 1922 he had completed his studies, and was licensed to practice his new profession. Later he spent over a year at the clinic of a post graduate hospital, including some time in the Bellevue Hospital. Since his services were free of charge, his office never lacked patients, and in his dual capacity of a pastor and a physician, he carried a staggering load. The suggestion for an American co-pastor with his residence in the parish house was readily accepted, but when the depression came the minister was permitted to go and Dr. Villelli had to carry on alone.

Luke, the loved physician, has been an inspiration to all those who have ministered in the name of the Great Physician to the mental and physical needs of suffering humanity. The work of the foreign medical missionary is better known because of the greater needs and larger numbers of volunteers, some of who have attracted worldwide attention, like Livingstone, Grenfell, Schweitzer and Kellersberger. Although in the home field, due to an adequate supply of physicians and superior medical facilities, the need has not been as great, yet a number of missionaries among the Italians have felt the urge of studying medicine. Some entered the profession for financial gain. After having received their preparation at the expense of churches, and having achieved their goal they forgot all about the church. Others obtained financial independence but remained faithful to the Gospel of Jesus Christ as volunteer workers, while a smaller number remained with the great Physician in the Home Mission trenches, and ministered to body and soul in His name and for His glory. Prominent in this last group is undoubtedly Dr. Joseph Villelli who for over thirty-five years blessed the New York Sea and Land Presbyterian Mission with the ministry of the word as well as with the ministry of healing.

From his rich experience Dr. Villelli has not taken time to relate how many children, mothers or fathers he has treated, how many bones he has mended or how many people he has pulled out of the valley of the shadows, but he wrote the following incident which started as he was visiting in the home of one of his parishioners.

Reverend, I want you to meet my brother Giuseppe, recently from Italy, said Mrs. D . . . . . , a faithful member of the Italian Congregation of Sea and Land.

I am so glad to know you, Giuseppe. I hope you will like this country and pay us a visit every now and then.

A visit? Where?

To our church.

My curate told me that I should go only to a Roman Catholic Church, since America is Prostestant and Protestants worship the head of an ass.

That's true: America is mainly Protestant but if I invite you to pay us a visit, it is only to give you an idea of our church. Your visit will not make you a Protestant.

Oh no, never. I am surprised how my sister has foolishly left the religion of her fathers to worship an ass. If mother knew about her change she would surely die.

Giuseppe, do you intend to go back to Italy?

Of course. I'll go back as soon as I have a few thousand lire.

Well, I am sure that when you go back to your small town in Basilicata you will be asked many questions about America, one of which will undoubtedly be about the Protestants and their object of worship. How embarrassing it would be if you could not answer those questions! If I were you, I would go to a Protestant church only to get a fair idea of the church building as well as the head of an ass against which your curate warned you so carefully. What do you say, Giuseppe? Am I right or wrong?

I might do that.

Well, suppose that you will do it next Sunday by coming with your sister?

I'll try.

Why don't you say: "I'll surely be there"? If you assure me that you will pay me a visit next Sunday, I shall endeavor to let you see everything in a very short time.

I'll be there with my sister.

Sunday as Mr. Villelli started the service, Mrs. D . . . entered, but not Giuseppe. What had happened? Had he changed his mind? Was he detained by fear? The minister went ahead with the service but somewhat disappointed. Time had come for the pastoral prayer, the door was slowly pushed in and a man appeared all frightened and uncertain as to whether he should step in or remain on the threshold. He crossed himself several times and then stepped in, remaining standing during the time the minister was praying; after which one of the group bade him to have a seat. What was going on in his deceived mind while the minister was praying? His eyes were restless, turning here and there in search probably of the famous head of an ass. The sermon was on the text: "Behold the Lamb of God that taketh away the sins of the world." Giuseppe was astounded—he was all ears and took in every word uttered by the preacher.

When at the end of the service the minister walked to the door to greet the congregation, Giuseppe like an automaton got up and walked to the door with his sister without saying a single word. The minister taking his hand—"Well, Giuseppe," he said, "I am so glad you have kept your promise. Did you see the ass's head?"

"No sir."

"Would you like to see it?"

"If you please."

"There it is"—pointing to the cross on the lectern—"you heard my prayer; you heard my sermon; do you think that civilized people such as the Americans are, would be so foolish as to worship what you were deceitfully told by the curate? We worship God in spirit and in truth; our symbol is the cross on which Jesus died for your salvation and mine."

"You are right. The curate was either ignorant or false. I like the way you preach. I'll come again."

There was not a meeting after that Sunday, which Giuseppe did not attend. He really was hungry and thirsty after the truth. After a few months he gave himself to Christ and joined the church of Sea and Land.

After a few years he went to his minister and said: "I want to go to Italy to get married and then come back to America for good. I don't know what to do about the ceremony. You know that the only church we have in my little town is Roman Catholic. Is it advisable for me to let the curate perform the marriage ceremony? If I don't go to church my folks will suffer and if I do go my conscience will bother me. I am afraid I might commit a sin."

"Giuseppe, there is no sin on your part. It makes no difference who performs the ceremony, as long as you remain faithful to the living Christ." Giuseppe is still a faithful disciple of Christ and so is his loving wife and their children.

Dr. Villelli at all times, but especially during the depression was all things to all men in order to win some. Many times he worked long into the night; he knew no boundary lines; he redoubled his energies in order to serve his fellowman on life's highway. It was during this period that he approached two other churches in the neighborhood doing practically the same type of work, and asked them to unite in a common effort, and he was happy to see that at least one responded favorably, so that in 1938 the Sea and Land Presbyterian and Mariners Temple Baptist, decided to combine their work under the name of the Henry Street United Church with each church maintaining its identity.

Under such continuous stress and strain, wear and tear, even the most robust constitutions give way in time, and in December 1939, he was taken to the hospital and then helped to go to Florida for rest and recuperation. After about three months, greatly benefited, he returned to his post and resumed his work as though nothing had been the matter with him. But after two more years, he had a relapse and for his own sake, as well as for the sake of the work he loved, he resigned, and with his faithful companion who had shared all the bitter and sweet of life, and sustained him whenever he faltered, retired to the milder climate of Florida.

We are sure, however, that Dr. Villelli will continue to bless those around about him in a most rich way in his double ministry of doctor of the soul as well as of the body.

13

The Pioneer as a Layman

If we were to trace the history of missions among the Italians in America, we would discover that many of them were started by humble laymen and women, who have gone to their graves unknown and unappreciated, but who must have heard from His blessed lips: "Well done, my good and faithful servant."

The contribution of these humble pioneers is not limited to the various communities in America, but extends to Italy, where one could find today at least a dozen churches started by poor laborers, who had been converted in America, and then returned to their native country at their own expense for the specific purpose of bringing their loved ones to Christ, and organized missions in their respective home towns. Their influence was so beneficial that the mayor of Pulsano said to Mr. Brunn at a reception in his honor during one of his visits to Italy: "You have revolutionized our town; you have done in America what no one could have done here. Men who were drunkards and immoral have returned models of soberness and morality; men who were ignorant and superstitious have returned bright and intelligent."

If it is difficult to evaluate the contribution made by the missionaries among the Italians in this country, it is much more difficult to try to measure the contribution made by our laymen to the work of the Kingdom, who often assumed heavy burdens when still children in the faith, and some of them even carried the entire support of the new mission. Our chief difficulty here is in trying to choose only two representative pioneer laymen from such a splendid company of men and women who have made such an excellent contribution, and then to find enough available details concerning any one of these to reconstruct an interesting readable story for our people.

THE DI DOMENICA BROTHERS

One of the outstanding illustrations of this type of work is furnished by Vincenzo Di Domenica, who was born and reared in Schiavi D'Abruzzo. From letters received by families of the first immigrants to America, the land of affluence and well being for all, he was so impressed that, notwithstanding the objections of his parents, he sailed for this modern wonderland, in order to earn enough money with which to provide an adequate dowry for his sister. After two years he was back in Italy, but it was not very long before he began to feel "homesick" for his adopted country, and returned to New York.

He had heard of Protestant missions helping the immigrants to find work and make adjustments in the new environment, but the very word Protestant horrified him. One day, however, passing by the Five Points Mission House, he heard the singing of the hymn "Safe in the Arms of Jesus" in his own native tongue, and although the building did not look like a church, upon the invitations of the janitor, who was at the door, he went in. The preacher was none other than the Rev. Arrighi, who spoke from the text "The wages of sin is death" (Romans 6:23), and among other things he dwelled on the ten commandments, with special emphasis on the fifth. The newcomer was so impressed that he decided to return on the following Sunday, and as he was coming out, after the service, he noticed a table with many books, and lacking the courage to ask for one, he decided "to steal one," read it and then return it without letting anybody know. When he returned home, he discovered that it was the New Testament, and like a hungry youth, he began actually to devour the book and did not stop until he had read it from cover to cover.

As soon as he was converted he decided to send for his younger brother Antonio, in order to bring him to Jesus

Christ. In due time he experienced the joy of bringing his younger brother to Christ, but now there was a mutual desire to share their newly found treasure with the family in Italy. They decided to send a New Testament on which the sister spent many happy winter evenings, reading the life of Jesus to the rest of the family. Very soon it was voiced throughout the town that they had received a Protestant book from America, and you can imagine the suffering of that poor mother who, being most scrupulous to do what is right, sent the book to be examined by a relative, priest and teacher in the grade school, who assured them it was all right to read it since they could not understand it all anyway! From the letters received, the two brothers in America became deeply concerned about their relatives in Italy; they were haunted by the verse: "Go to thy house, unto thy friends, and tell them how great things the Lord hath done for thee" (Mark 5:19). They felt as if it were pulling the very strings of their hearts, hence they decided to leave America and bring the good news to their loved ones in person.

As soon as they arrived home, they began to preach the gospel to all the people who assembled there to receive news of their loved ones abroad. When the priest heard of the preaching, he told the parents that this must stop, but, like those of the blind man, they answered: "They are of age, let them speak for themselves." They went to see the prelate who, in his arrogance, asked, "Who gave you permission to preach this poisonous religion in our town?" Their answer was clear and brief: Jesus, who said, "Go into all the world and preach the gospel." As the group grew in importance, persecutions were intensified, but gradually the mission work was well established not only in their town but in the surrounding country.

In due time the entire family was converted to the gospel of Jesus Christ, and a church was founded which has been a power for good in that entire district. The minister in charge is the Rev. Antonio Amicarelli, a native of Terra Bruna near

Schiavi, who had been converted at that same mission, where he had gone as a novice at the request of his father superior to find out about the Protestant movement. He had a definite Christian experience, he had been rejected by his parents, had left the monastery and had gone to South America, where he had helped in the organization of several Missions in Argentina. Upon his providential return to Italy, he established himself in Schiavi, where he married the sister of Di Domenica, and preached the gospel without remuneration for twelve long years, because he loved the Lord and he wanted to see the work go forward.

Out of such humble beginnings, God permitted not only the establishment of a Mission in Italy, but the organization of one of the finest pieces of work among the Italians in America, the First Italian Baptist Church and Community House of Philadelphia, by a younger brother Angelo Di Domenica, converted during that fruitful trip of the two brothers to Italy. Angelo was born in Schiavi on May 29, 1872. He came to this country in 1892. He prepared for the gospel ministry at the Yale University Divinity School from 1901 to 1910 when he received a Bachelor of Divinity degree and, after serving in Newark, New Jersey, and New Haven, Conn., he went to Philadelphia on June 1, 1914, to the settlement house, which was located at the corner of Federal Street and Passyunk Avenue. Four weeks later they started another mission in the chapel of the South Broad Street Baptist Church, three blocks from 15th and Tasker Streets, where the work is now located. On March 22nd, 1921, the Baptist Union of Philadelphia purchased the present property, and on March 13th, 1923, the community house work building was dedicated. This has been developed into a splendid institutional church, with a fine congregation, many children and young peoples activities, and a good social educational program which, like a veritable beehive, fills two substantial buildings.

During these twenty-nine years four young men have gone out from this mission into the Gospel ministry and a number of young women have gone into full time service. Families of three generations have been baptized and 515 people have been received into the Church. The active membership is now over 275 and contributions have surpassed the $4,000.00 mark. In celebration of his thirtieth anniversary in that field, his people paid the balance of the mortgage and became self-supporting. In recognition of his outstanding work, Mr. Di Domenica has been honored by his denomination repeatedly. In 1937 Dennison University, Granville, Ohio, conferred upon him a well deserved degree of Doctor of Divinity, and in 1938 Bucknell University, of Lewisburg, Pa., conferred another upon him. He is highly respected by his denomination and by his brethren in the ministry of all denominations.

Dr. Di Domenica has used the printed word most effectively. He edited the Baptist Italian Paper "L'Aurora," for many years, he published a large number of pamphlets of a controversial nature, chief among which: "Who are the Protestants?", "Between Light and Darkness," "The Religion of our Fathers," "The Rusellites," "The Pentecostal Movement," etc., most of them in the two languages. He has compiled a grammar for the study of English which has been used with profit by our immigrants, and a bilingual hymnal used by many missions of various denominations. His beneficial influence has been felt far and wide, all because his brother, a humble immigrant, received the light, and felt that it was his sacred duty and privilege to dispel the darkness in his own household in Italy.

Rosario Procopio

Mr. Rosario Procopio was born in Vincolise, Catanzaro, in 1866. He came to America about 1900 and settled in Chicago, Illinois, where he opened a printing shop for his countrymen. In 1901 he was converted in a Methodist mission where he had gone to learn English. The wise teacher, Miss Aphra Johnson, taught from a New Testament in Italian and English, thus killing two birds with one stone. She taught them the language and gave them a knowledge of salvation through

Jesus Christ our Lord. This mission, located on South Clark Street, became the refuge of many men away from home, and during the lean years of 1893, '94, it was the only place where they could get a meager meal consisting sometimes of plain boiled potatoes sprinkled with salt and other times of plain corn mush.

Procopio's conversion had been slow, but positive, he related how he found it difficult to drop some of the habits which had gripped him in this land of freedom and opportunity. The teacher came in the mission hall one day and found some of the men smoking. Everyone tried to dispose of their pipes as quickly as they could. Procopio put his in his coat pocket red hot, only to feel the fire spreading to his clothes. He was so embarrassed that when he reached the Clark Street bridge, spanning the Chicago river, he spoke to his pipe in this fashion: "You are not going to hold me a slave to this nasty habit; you go down into the river now, and only when I find you, I will smoke again." That settled one habit. The same was true of strong drink. When he made his decision to live for Christ, he remarked that as he had lived for the devil, he would now live for God faithfully, and he did. The first evening that Miss Johnson asked him to give his testimony, he invited all his "paesani" (home town people) most of whom had been his chums in drinking, playing cards, attending theaters, etc., on whom he made a profound impression, but they thought it would not last and that he would return to his old ways again. He prayed for courage, and the right message, and the Spirit led him to speak from Romans 8:31: "If God be for us, who can be against us."

About 1904 he moved to the North Side of Chicago and began venturing on his own, seeking men for Christ. He started a Bible study circle in his own home, then on Illinois Street near Orleans. In 1905 he united with the Moody Church, and as he became better known, the Sunday School Superintendent asked him to start a Bible class in Italian. Mr. Scorza was the only member of the class on that first Sunday, but gradually men came one by one, until the class grew to about thirty. The only woman in it was Mr. Procopio's own sister, who coming to Chicago with her husband and children began to see the light of the gospel. His interest in his own household is evidenced by the fact that he brought his sister, her family and his two brothers to the knowledge of Christ. He had a profound love for his fellow countrymen, and his shop soon became a meeting place for many of his fellow countrymen, who were strangers in a strange country. His zeal for the Gospel may be illustrated by the following testimony from the Pastor, A. F. Scorza: "My first contact with the gospel was in the early part of the year 1905, when unexpectedly I met Mr. Rosario Procopio right in the heart of Chicago's loop, State and Madison, which is known as the busiest corner in the world, with a million people going by each day. He was then unknown to me, but was acquainted with my father with whom he had worked in Italy, and whose image he said I was. He asked me to come and visit in his home because he had a gift for me. I kept my promise and I called on him in company of several young friends. His gift to me proved to be a New Testament, which, strange to say, was the very thing my spiritual leader in Italy denied me, when only 11 years of age. He treated us so well that we soon called again. This time he took us to a little mission hall located on Milton Avenue near Chicago Avenue. When we returned in the summer, however, the little group met in his home and continued there until 1910."

As we examined the meager records we were impressed with the fact that Procopio in his humble way started a chain of influence that will never end. His one ambition was to magnify Christ by life and lip. According to those who knew him, he lived and died poor in this world's goods, but rich in faith and full of good works. As to charity, suffice to say that he would part with the last dollar if he knew of someone in need. The widows, the orphans, the poor, were always with him. The proof of his liberality was found at his earthly end, when it was discovered that he was poorer than the poor he had helped. I wish it were known how many Bibles and New Testaments he had given away. He had a part in the two suitcases of Scriptures which Mr. Scorza had taken to Italy, after his conversion in 1906. He would say: "As formerly I served the devil with all my might, so must I serve the Lord now."

The Mission was located in a congested district known as the lower North Side, thickly populated with people who had come chiefly from Sicily and southern Italy. His work was primarily with the poorest among the poor. One day he met a young man in the gutter, spoke to him of Jesus, lifted him up to himself, brought him to his shop, fed his hungry body which had existed on refuse from garbage cans, and led him to Christ, whom to know aright is life eternal. Today this young man is preaching the Gospel of Jesus Christ, which is the power of God unto salvation, in a Methodist church. He once related his testimony under the caption: "From Garbage Can to Canaan Land."

An outstanding example of what God was pleased to accomplish through the work of this pioneer is the Rev. A. Scorza, who received the Gospel from this humble servant of Jesus Christ, returned to Italy, converted his family, led two of his brothers into full time service in Italy and in America, and returning to Chicago organized and served with marked success the Moody Italian Mission for over 25 years, and now is pleading the cause of the poor minority Protestant groups of Europe.

Like a good soldier of Jesus Christ, Procopio had learned to endure all sorts of persecutions. Rev. A. Scorza bears witness to the fact that he has seen his mentor display the most Christ-like spirit, during all his adventurous career. He related how a great big Italian approached him, called him some vile names and struck him on the face, in front of the mission. Procopio, though comparatively small in stature, could take care of himself and was not known to run away from trouble. But this time he actually turned the other cheek, whereupon the aggressor was so impressed and felt so ashamed that he changed his mind and came inside to hear the Gospel.

Up to the last moment Rosario Procopio continued to be concerned about the souls of lost men and women. During the last week of his earthly life, he wrestled with a young man about his soul and in departing he gave him a New Testament. Is it any wonder that when God called him to his heavenly reward in 1925, at only 59, friends and foes alike, people from all walks of life, repeated, as soon as the news spread throughout the neighborhood: "Truly he was a Christ-like man."

14

The Pioneer as a Minister's Wife
(Isabella Fragale Bisceglia)

No apologies are necessary, I am sure, if I do not "go out-side the sacred precincts" of my home to choose the pioneer as the queen of the manse. Born in a manse, of imported stock, she has exemplified, at all times, those qualities which are indispensable in the wife of a minister, and, especially, of a foreign-home missionary. In truth, she fits into her position "like perfect music into noble words."

Her parents had come from Italy to New York, were there converted—as we described in *The Pioneer as an Evangelical Poet*—and were among the earliest missionaries to the Italians. She was born in Hammonton, New Jersey, where her father was the head of the Presbyterian Mission, and, being the first girl after three boys, her arrival was the occasion for a real celebration.

When she was about four years old her father was called to the pastorate of the First Italian Presbyterian Church of East Liberty, Pennsylvania, where he remained until his retirement. Since church pianists were at a premium in those days, she began to play for Sunday School as soon as she could co-ordinate her fingers with the keyboard, her diminutive body with the piano and the bench, and her feet with the floor. When most girls would consider it a great honor to play for Junior Church, she was playing one of those very trying pump-organs for all church services. She received all her formal education in Pittsburgh, Pennsylvania, first in the local grade and high school, and later at the Pittsburgh Conservatory of Music, where she was a pupil of the late Dr. Charles Boyd, famous church musician and organist, who taught music-appreciation at Western Theological Seminary. Next to music, strange as it seems, she was proficient in mathematics, and she has always been able to extricate our children from some of their intricate problems in high school and college.

The training for her life's avocation began very early in life. Her father's house was a meeting place for lonely men whose families were still in Italy, for women who were slowly becoming acclimated to America, for children who were experiencing the usual difficulties with the English language, for missionaries visiting the smoky city, as well as for distinguished representatives of the Waldensian or other Protestant groups in Italy who made appeals in the industrial heart of America. Thus she became familiar with the tears and tragedies, the frustrations and disillusionments, the hopes and aspirations, the joys and victories of the workers among the Italians.

Because of these experiences, she had determined never to marry a minister. As far as I was concerned, at the time of our betrothal the ministry was most remote from my mind as my life work.

As soon as I felt a definite call to the ministry, however, I unburdened my soul to her, offering to release her from her promise. She assured me quickly and convincingly that she did not wish me to disobey my heavenly vision, and that she would gladly share my life and work. Bove was correct when he said: "Next to God we are indebted to woman, first for life itself, and then for making it worth while."

In June, 1918, upon graduating from Western Theological Seminary, I left for Kansas City, Missouri, and in March, 1919 —during my Easter vacation from William Jewell College, where I was taking special work in sociology—I left for Pittsburgh on a Monday evening. We were married Thursday evening, March 27, and started for Kansas City that same night. But let a daily paper, *The Pittsburgh Leader*, describe our wedding:

At 7:00 o'clock this evening Miss Isabelle Fragale, daughter of the Rev. and Mrs. Thomas Fragale, of Turrett Street, East End, will become the bride of the Rev. John B. Bisceglia, of Kansas City, Missouri, son of Mr. and Mrs. Frank Bisceglia, of Pittsburgh. The ceremony will be performed in the living-room of the home of the bride's parents before an improvised altar of palms, ferns and white roses. The bride's father, who is pastor of the First Italian Presbyterian Church, of the East End, will perform the ceremony.

Miss Fragale will appear in a gown of white charmeuse and georgette, the bodice studded with pearls, the tunic falling from the waistline also trimmed with pearls. The bridal veil will be Egyptian in design and sprays of orange blossoms will be used around the head. Her bouquet will be a shower of white roses, satin maline. The bride will wear a diamond and platinum necklace, a gift from the bridegroom.

Miss Italia Fragale, a sister of the bride, will be maid of honor and will wear a soft pink taffeta gown, draped, and trimmed with silver lace. She will carry a shower bouquet of Killarney roses.

Miss Lucy Coscia will play the wedding-march and the bridal couple will descend the steps in the reception hall preceded by Mary Bisceglia, small sister of the bridegroom, and Lena Galati, as flower girls. They will wear frocks of white silk and lace and will carry baskets of white roses. Charles Bisceglia, a brother of the bridegroom, will be best man, and Michael Bisceglia, another brother, and Frank Fragale, a brother of the bride, will serve as ushers.

Following the ceremony a buffet luncheon of thirty covers will be served, after which the Rev. and Mrs. Bisceglia will leave for Kansas City, where they will remain for at least three months, after which they will return to and make their home in this city.

Miss Fragale is a graduate of the Pittsburgh Conservatory of Music and is well known throughout the city in music circles. The Rev. Bisceglia is a graduate of the

Western Theological Seminary and of the University of Pittsburgh.

The guests interrupted the festivities, as we were about to leave, to sing, accompanied by the orchestra, *Till We Meet Again*. A blizzard struck us, which caused us to miss our connections in Chicago, Ill., for Kansas City. We greeted the delay as providential, and, notwithstanding a biting March wind in the windy city, we had an improvised honeymoon on Friday, and on Saturday morning we entered the heart of America. Externally, that was our only honeymoon, but our spirits have been on an uninterrupted honeymoon ever since.

Since our apartment at the mission was not quite ready, our castle was my one-room "apartment," attractively and understandingly re-arranged by Mrs. DeMaio, an excellent housewife with a real appreciation for the beautiful and fine things of life. On Sunday morning we were greeted from the pulpit of Central Presbyterian Church by Dr. Nisbet. During the day, my bride met first, the eager children of our little Sunday School and later our few but expectant and appreciative church members. Having never had a real home for our children, I have prayed often that I might not find myself in the circumstances of David Livingstone, who, after costly years of toil and suffering in Africa, when he buried his wife at Shupanga, cried: "O my Mary, my Mary, how often we have longed for a quiet home since you and I were cast adrift at Kolobeng."

In the intervening years, my wife has become the understanding mother of our four fine children, two girls and two boys; the sympathetic partner of an exacting husband; a capable and hospitable homemaker; the organist; the choir director; the Sunday-School pianist. In church gatherings and great conventions, competent observers have said repeatedly, "No one plays the hymns as she does." She has been the motivating power for our clinics; "mother" to many lonely expectant mothers; a wise counselor for their babies; the soul of our Daily Vacation Bible School; playing and teaching classes in knitting and embroidery; the life of our mothers' clubs. She has introduced hundreds of girls to the piano; she is captain of a most successful scout troop; and she still has plenty of energy left to play volley ball with a girls' team.

Truly, with an ancient writer, I can say: "Her price is far above rubies. The heart of her husband trusteth in her and he shall have no lack of gain. She doeth him good and not evil all the days of her life. She stretcheth her hand to the poor; she extendeth her arms to the needy. She is clothed with strength and dignity; and she shall rejoice in the days to come. She openeth her mouth in wisdom, and kindly counsel is on her tongue. She looketh well after her household and eateth not the bread of idleness. Her children rise up and bless her— her husband also—and praise her. Many women have done well, but you have excelled them all. Charms are deceptive and beauty is vain; but a woman who feareth the Lord, she shall be praised. Give her of the fruit of her hands and let her own works praise her in the gates."

Second to music, she has been vitally interested in the physical welfare of our women and children. The maternity clinic began right after our first child was born, and her physician, the late Dr. M. A. Hanna, started the work and remained chief of staff up to his untimely and tragic death. During the first years of the clinic, she had to plead with expectant mothers to go to a hospital for confinement—since in the small towns in Italy they entered a hospital only to die —and often by day or by night she was the friend and mother of new mothers through that first glorious experience.

This is how our babies' clinic was instituted: Several years ago my wife and I were called into a home where we saw something which we have never forgotten. It was not the poor living quarters, because that was not unusual; it was not the poor young parents, for they represented the average; it was not even the squalor. . . . It was a baby, about eighteen months old. Its head was large, out of all proportion; its eyes bulging out, pleading, accusing; the cheekbones protruding; hands and arms, only bones covered with skin; it tried to cry and we saw feverish lips opening a burning cavity. The baby was mercilessly starving, through poverty and ignorance. We went home; we could not sleep that night. In my wife's words: "A finger was pointing at me," and those eyes would not let us go until we resolved to appeal to Dr. John Aull, eminent pediatrician, who had taken care of our own children, to come and take care of this baby, and later to start a clinic to prevent the recurrence of such cases.

My wife has been the confidante of most of our women—young and old alike; she has been assigned first place in times of joy, as well as in sorrow; she has prepared our young people for special programs; she has been the favorite on missionary programs from small missionary societies to large gatherings at summer conferences; she has been my constant companion in home visitation. All of this, and much more which can neither be measured nor described, has been done for twenty-nine years as a volunteer worker.

As wife of a home missionary, she has never been burdened with a large salary, although our Father in Heaven has always supplied our needs, and, having constantly refused to become a paid worker or accept a position as organist in a large church, she has had to manage wisely. She has had to be on the alert for bargains in clothing and feeding her family, and that she has done an excellent job is attested to by the fact that we have been properly clad and our table judiciously supplied, and the many visitors—missionaries on furlough, church dignitaries from other countries, or humble last-minute arrivals from Park College and the Methodist National Training School—often as many as five and ten a Sunday, have all marveled at her culinary ability and capacity for work.

No sacrifice has ever been too great for her nor ever accepted grudgingly. When our children, due to the nature and location of our work, had to be sent away to school—the girls to Peace Junior College, Raleigh, North Carolina, and the boys to Chamberlain-Hunt, Port Gibson, Mississippi; later the first girl and the first boy to Park College, and the second girl to Agnes Scott, while the last still at the Academy, using over one-half of our income—it was she who had the heroic spirit to suggest that we borrow on our insurance, that we sell our little house, and move into a two-room apartment at the Northeast Community Center, thereby plunging ourselves into the vortex of a continuous program from early morning until night; this for the children's benefit and to give the work we love a good start.

Flowers and tears for the dead, yes, but praise and glory for the living, and these, in my humble opinion, belong to this pioneer of the manse, the queen of my heart, for whom I can truly appropriate the lines of the poet:

> Teacher, tender comrade, wife.
> A fellow-farer true through life,
> Heart whole and soul free,
> The august Father gave to me.

She has been my constant inspiration, be the horizon filled with light or with shadow. She has deflated my ego at the opportune moment and has often winged me away from the slough of despond. Never too strong physically, but with plenty of stamina, she has never missed church two Sundays in succession except at childbirth and, all told, not more than ten Sundays in twenty-nine years.

One Saturday evening I took her to Menorah Hospital, despite her protest, with a very low blood count, near the valley of the shadow. I almost carried her to the elevator, as she kept asking, "How are you going to manage with the children and the church services tomorrow?" Fortunately, the late Dr. Hanna, our friend and her physician for many years, recovering from a serious illness himself, had a room next to hers. In the morning he took charge of the case and, with his able associate, Dr. VanDel, they gave her immediately a blood transfusion, and administered the best-known remedies. That Sunday morning, as I began the service without my organist and without my choir, I told my congregation that I felt like a cripple from whom his crutches had suddenly been snatched away.

She has been my loyal companion. It having been my privilege to address many and sundry gatherings, she has always gone with me whenever possible. Bravely and patiently she has listened to some of the same addresses over and over again—one of them fully a hundred times—always attentively; and if at any time I was dejected at my "failure to put it across," she dispelled the clouds by saying, "Why, it was fine; the response was grand," and she would repeat the gracious remarks dropped from some kind soul.

We have always gone on our vacations together; we went for her father's funeral; later to her mother's; we were home when my father passed away, and made a trip together when my mother went home to God.

After twenty-nine years of ups and downs, triumphs and defeats, joys and sorrows, smiles and tears, both literally and figuratively, she still measures up in disposition to the name given to her by Mr. Baron, one of her wise old Sunday School teachers: *My Sunbeam.*

In appearance, as well as in her concern for others, she is truly worthy of the appellation *Madonna* (given to her by the most prominent philanthropist in Kansas City), while to me she is still what I wanted her to be, and would choose over and over again—the mother of my children and the constant companion of my life.

As we visit the home of an aged couple, an illiterate woman —but one who would put many of us to shame with her knowledge of the Bible; one who has suffered much in having borne twelve children and lost them all, the last and oldest tragically, but one who through it all has kept her faith in God unshaken, one who is endowed with an extra dose of good sense—as she sits admiring my companion, invariably exclaims, "God truly made you two for each other, and both for His work." I always blush inwardly, since I feel unworthy of such a compliment.

Is it any wonder that in retrospect I am profoundly grateful to God, the giver of every good and perfect gift, for such a constant, patient, long-suffering, kind, and self-effacing companion of my life; and that I am in perfect agreement with Tennyson when he says:

> The woman's cause is man's; they rise or sink
> Together, dwarf'd or godlike, bound or free.

15

The Pioneer as a Woman Missionary
(Lydia Tealdo)

Women have played a very important part in the life of Jesus and of the Church, from the moment He spoke to the Samaritan woman at the well of Jacob up to the present day. Where can we find greater loyalty than in the three Marys who followed Jesus to the very end or where can we find so much love as we find in Martha and Mary? The Church of Philippi was blessed by Euodias, Syntyche and Lydia. This last one was the first Christian woman in Europe; the Church of Cenchrea near Corinth by Phoebe, to whom Paul entrusted his letter to the Romans; the Corinthian Church by the charming Priscilla, wife of Aquila; Athens by Demaris and the Church at Rome by Julia, Claudia and Mary.

Many times women fostered His cause through their good works like Martha, Mary and Dorcas; often with their resources like Susanna and Joanna the wife of the governor of Herod, but more often they answered His call to assist ministers, to start missions, to prepare the ground, and some to carry on all alone for many years.

We would go too far afield if we were to list all those American women who, in the providence of God, felt impelled to work among our people, but we must mention at least two. My first recollection is of a cultured young woman, Miss Mauro of Washington, D. C., who had gone to Italy to learn the language, in order to conduct services in Italian for my countrymen, and was performing this work of love not only without compensation but paying herself for all the expenses. One of the noblest women in Pittsburgh, Pennsylvania, Miss Jennie Bryan, who descends from a long line of ministers and educators, whose brother made a splendid record as President of Indiana State University, gave practically all her time as a volunteer worker in the once crime-infested area in which the Italians had innocently drifted. The number of those who have served on boards and on missionary societies is legion, and to mention even the most prominent is of course beyond our present scope.

Many women of Italian extraction consecrated themselves to the work of the Lord among our people. If it is impossible to give a complete list of those who have labored faithfully and long, we must, however, point out to your admiration and gratitude at least the following: Miss Marietta Alfani, Miss Rosina Pesaturo, Miss Anetta Rau, Miss Helen Cairus, Miss Corbo, Miss Luciani, Mrs. Christopher Russo, Mrs. Rosina Allegri, and Miss Lydia L. Tealdo.

A beautiful baby girl had come to cheer the parsonage of the Tealdos in Milano, located not very far from the famous Duomo. Those were days when real giants graced the ministry of the free church of Italy, under the inspirational guidance of Padre Gavazzi. Ministers were few, the needs many, the challenges unprecedented, and Mr. Tealdo was a powerful speaker, who gave freely of himself in season and out of season. At the height of his career, he was stricken with pneumonia and went very soon to his heavenly reward. In saying goodbye to his lovely wife, he took their child in his feverish arms, dedicated her to God and entrusted her to His care. His action was prophetic, because only a year later his wife died of a broken heart, leaving the tender child without the loving care of her parents. When she grew into full womanhood, she served her God with faithfulness and loyalty for many years.

When her parents passed away, a tutor was appointed for little Lydia, and for her brother who became a brilliant preacher. As soon as the little girl was old enough she was sent to the Ferretti School of Florence, where she remained until she was 18 years of age. It was providential that one of her schoolmates should have been a young American girl, who afterward became Mrs. Luigi Angelini. She is still remembered by many of our churches as Madam Angelini, who visited this country many times in the interest of the Waldensian Church, and our people remember her last visit to the Italian Mission in 1919. It was through her that she decided to come to this country, where she dedicated her life completely to the service of the Master, as an angel of love and mercy to the people who had come from her home land. In New York she entered the Training School for Christian Workers, conducted by the New York City Missionary Society, and, as soon as her preparation was completed, she became a worker at the Broome Street Tabernacle, assisting the Rev. Antonio Arrighi in a densely populated Italian quarter of downtown New York.

Long before Theodore Roosevelt became police commissioner of New York City, while Jacob Riis was being moulded into an American, on the very place that the city has planned to build its civic center, and where the Palace of Justice now dominates the scene, there was an open spot called "Five Points," otherwise known as Paradise Park. The name was a strange irony, for the section at that time was exactly the opposite. On the north side, where the state building is now, stood the "Five Points House of Industry," and in its chapel, the Rev. Mr. Arrighi began his work of evangelizing the Italians in that section. In his mission of love, he had from the very beginning the efficient and consecrated cooperation of Miss Brewer, under whose direction the work prospered. But in its seventh year, she was suddenly taken away, and gloom and dismay fell all around those who were vitally concerned about the work.

It seemed impossible that anyone could fill her place. Mr. Arrighi felt that he had lost his right hand. Several friends had tried to fill the void in a spirit of love and helpfulness, when one Sunday morning, in September 1888, at the close of the Sunday School a slim, dark eyed young lady, graciously introduced herself to the members of the school. "I am Miss Tealdo," she said, "and am come to be a missionary here." Everyone remained very quiet, and all proceeded as usual, for no one imagined that on such a modest, unassuming person, had fallen the mantle of a great worker.

Miss Alfani, her co-worker for many years, has been very kind to preserve for us the first impression of Miss Tealdo in her work among the Italians. She saw for the first time such poverty, misery and squalor as she had never seen before, so much that she could not believe her own eyes. Since they were a conglomeration of people from every section of Italy, while her education had been received entirely in Florence, she could not understand their many dialects; their manners were strange to say the least, but young, unafraid, fully consecrated, she went forth into the by-ways and highways, which many times led into the vilest and filthiest dens on Mulberry, Baxter, Bayard and Park Streets, so notoriously remembered for their vice and poverty. Many times the young, refined missionary found herself groping through dark alleys or going up dangerous stairways, meeting some poor drunk derelict, sleeping off the cheap liquor he had imbibed. Sometimes she was frightened by the rough voices of boarding house men, who lived alone in this country, but wherever she went, she knelt to pray with and for the people. She became a friend to women and children. She struggled with herself, especially that first year, whether to stay or to go, for in despair, like Jonah, she wanted to flee to some unknown country, she poured her heart to her Christ in prayer and, with tears in her eyes, she placed her hand in His, and decided to go the whole way, and give herself entirely to that one great cause. God had called her and, like her Master, her heart went out in compassion to the people, her love for the salvation of their souls enabled her to conquer all her aversion, and she plunged headlong into her life work.

What intense activity filled the days of the young missionary! Sunday School classes, mothers' meetings, clubs for girls, sewing school, visiting early and late, bringing the sick to hospitals and clinics, acting as nurse at the bedside of the sick, watching during the night at the bedside of a dying widow, and mothering little orphans. These needs incidentally made her oblivious to the distressing and repulsive conditions surrounding her.

She was a good organizer and with her consecrated life, her intelligent teaching and her inspiring personality, through which radiated the spirit of the Christ, she brought together a remarkable group of women, and she was instrumental in bringing most of those women into a full knowledge of the Lord Jesus Christ and His saving grace. The results of her work are not only evident to this day, but seem to acquire momentum as the years roll into the bright light of eternity.

How many men and women, young and old, live to bless her memory, is impossible to enumerate, for she had the joy of seeing many of them rise to fill places of responsibility and honor in almost every walk of life, while several, because of her example and influence, have become bearers of the glad tidings among our people. It is to her that Miss Alfani, who furnished most of the information for this brief sketch, owes her entrance into a blessed and fruitful career at the Broome Street Tabernacle, and all the inspiration and help needed to carry on. This is what she writes after working with Miss Tealdo for thirty years: "It was my happy privilege to have her as a co-worker and friend in the truest sense of the word, and as I endeavor to pay my humble tribute to the memory of one who served our God and our people for forty-four years, in joys and sorrows, in triumphs and defeats, of this hand maid of the Lord, I would repeat with Daniel: 'They that be wise shall shine as bright as the firmament; and they that turn many to righteousness, as the stars forever and ever' for she surely had the wisdom, the power and the glorious privilege of turning many to God."

When Lydia L. Tealdo went home to God in July 1936, there must have been great rejoicing in heaven as her father and mother admired the many stars in her crown, as those led by her to Christ came singing her praises, and as our Master and Lord greeted her "Come ye blessed of the Father, inherit the Kingdom prepared for you from the foundation of the World."

16

The Pioneer as a Journalist
(Rev. Francis J. Panetta)

In all our search through the meager records of our Pioneers to find the best representatives of their respective groups, we have never experienced as much difficulty as in arriving at a satisfactory selection of "The Pioneer as a Journalist." All the denominations, in their initial missionary eagerness to evangelize the Italians who were flooding the ports of entry to this country, recognized immediately the value of "the fourth estate" and subsidized various and sundry publications in order to facilitate the work among our people. Our pioneer missionaries in their zeal for the cause, and with true missionary spirit, improvised themselves into publishers and journalists, and forgetting their limitations, used the printed word to good advantage both as a weapon of defense and offense. Looking back we discover that although these periodicals published material which was deficient from a literary standpoint, not always following the best rules of journalistic traditions, yet they revealed zeal, determination and vision and, what is more important, they satisfied the longings of those poor people detached from their homeland who were eager to hear and to read, in the language they understood, a message which satisfied the deep yearnings of their souls. All in all these publications served a good purpose, enriching the lives of their readers, and, although the best did not always survive, when judged from the standpoint of style and thought content, the well known law of natural selection worked here also, for only those publications which served the needs of their readers continued to live.

No statement on this subject, however brief, should omit

the contributions made by some of our brave men. We should not forget Dr. Angelo Di Domenica, founder and editor for many years of the Baptist Publication *L'Aurora*, as well as other members of that great denomination, among whom were the Rev. Giuseppe Boccaccio, Dr. P. L. Buffa, and the Rev. Louis Zibelli. From the Methodist Church we would recall the Rev. Filoteo Taglialatela, editor of *La Rivista Evangelica*, the Rev. Piero Petacci, editor of *La Fiaccola*, and the Rev. Edward Mascellaro, editor for many years of *La Voce*. The ablest Italian journalist of this denomination however was the Rev. Salvatore Musso who launched a new publication in Pittsburgh, Pa., called *Il Buon Combattimento*, and who contributed to many publications and translated some of the finest hymns of the church. The United Presbyterians were represented by the Rev. J. B. Fortunato, with *L'Ape Evangelica*, which years later was continued as a venture of Presbyterians and United Presbyterians, under the name of *Vita*, edited by the Rev. Migliore and Rev. DiStasi. Smaller denominations were represented as follows: Reformed Church by the Rev. Pietro Moncada with *L'Interpetre*, the United Church of Canada by the Rev. Domenica Gualtieri with *La Favilla*, the Moody Church by Rev. A. Scorza of the Italian Moody Mission with *La Fiamma* (1915 to 1923), the Italian Christian Church of America has its own publication *Vita* edited by V. Moscato, a continuation of *La Vedetta Cristiana* by Galassi of Italy, and the Pentecostal Churches have been publishing *Il Faro*. Two definite attempts have been made by our own denomination, the Presbyterian Church in the U. S. with *La Rivista Italo-Americana* (1919-1920) and since 1928 with *Il Messaggero* semi-weekly for many years, but more recently a monthly periodical in magazine form. These publications have been edited by the writer and have been confined chiefly to the people of Kansas City. The Presbyterians of the United States have made their contributions through the Rev. Amedeo Santini editor of *La Fiamma*, Detroit, Michigan, Dr. Pasquale R. DeCarlo, who edited several publications at different times, his latest being *Il Cittadino di Chicago*, and *Vita Nuova*, the Rev. Giuseppe Buggello, the Rev. Louis Ordile, the Rev. Pietro Di Nardo, the Rev. Arturo Di Pietro, who under the auspices of the Presbyterian Board of Publication, edited from 1908 to 1915 one of the finest Italian Protestant papers in America, *L'Araldo*, which in 1915 passed under the editorship of the Rev. Francis J. Panetta, who had the name changed to *L'Era Nuova* (The New Era).

After examining the contributions made by all these fine brethren, dead or alive, we have chosen for this brief sketch, the Rev. Francis J. Panetta, since, in our humble opinion, he embodies all those qualities essential to a competent editor of an Italo-American religious publication.

The Editor of *Il Rinnovamento* is so modest and self-effacing, however, that we have been unable to secure much help from him in the preparation of this sketch. With all due respect to the feelings of our good friend, we must remind him that the life of a man exposed to the public does not belong to him alone, and that at a distance we can see his contribution in its proper perspective and evaluate it better perhaps than those who are too close to him, or the protagonist himself. Jack London used to say, "Go to any man's door, and open it and shout 'All is discovered' and you will find a story." For every man's life is full of interest not only for the family circle but for many far and near. For it is always intriguing to discover how others face life with its gay and grave moments, sharp contrasts, lights and shadows.

Francis J. Panetta was born in Agnana, Italy, on October 1, 1874. He received his initial education in his home town and later was sent to the Gymnasium Lyceum of Reggio, Calabria, from which he was graduated in 1897. He emigrated to America in April 1904, was brought to Christ by his brother, the Rev. Joseph Panetta of Germantown, Pennsylvania, and in 1905 joined the first Italian Presbyterian Church of Philadelphia. In his eagerness to evangelize his people in Italy, and with youthful nostalgia for his native country and his loved ones, he went back to Italy for a brief visit.

While returning to the United States on the *Critic*, of the White Star Line, he was surprised to find himself sharing a cabin with a young friar of the Franciscan Order. We prefer to have the ex-monk, who is now the Rev. Raphael Fenili, Ph.D., pastor of the Italian Methodist Church of our Saviour in Reading, Pennsylvania, relate the events of the voyage.

"The journey lasted eleven days, days of continued calm, religious discussions without a shadow of controversy or any sense of distrust. On the contrary, our conversations became more interesting with each passing day, we drew closer to each other and we felt a sense of affinity. Panetta was then young, quick, energetic, the most important person among the immigrants on the ship, since he spoke English and was always ready to interpret for us. He was returning from Agnana, his native town, after a visit to his family. I was his own age, and since I was dressed as a monk, I was reverently surrounded by the immigrants, who, kissing my hand every morning, expressed the hope of welcoming me to the Church of the Madonna of Pompeii in New York.

"In such an atmosphere our conversations assumed a serious character, since we were discussing the dogmas of the Roman Catholic Church. I was surprised to observe that an Italian young man was so interested in religious matters, and that he was able to discuss them with so much confidence. He, on the other side, was surprised that I, a friar, would not approve in a general way the teachings of the church nor its government and organization.

"During the last day of the journey, our conversation began with a question from Mr. Panetta: 'Father, if it is permissible, may I ask you a question?' 'Go right ahead,' I said. 'Father,' he continued, 'where are you going?' It was here that I became confused but I had an inspiration; hence I told him: 'Mr. Panetta, during this journey I have learned to know you as a serious and honest young man; I want to tell you the truth; I have abandoned the monastery without the knowledge of my superiors. I am going to New York, but I have no definite goal. I wrote a letter to one of my cousins, but since I did not wait for a reply I hope that he will meet me at the dock, because if I don't find him I shall be greatly embarrassed.' At this point Panetta arose, offered me his hand, and said: 'I'll be with you. I am so happy to know that you have left the monastery.' 'And why are you so happy that I have left the cloister?' I asked. His answer was no less surprising to me, when he said: 'I am a Protestant missionary from Bristol, Pennsylvania. Our conversations have created an increasing desire in my mind to have you become acquainted with the simplicity of the Gospel, since you could be of great help to our missionary work among the Italians.' In that moment I did not understand the full meaning of those words, but I had so much confidence in him, that, from that day on, we have been like brothers. I told him the story of my spiritual agitations and the reasons which prompted me to take such a step, which I have always considered providential.

"A year before I left the monastery, as a private secretary of the papal delegate, Father Anselmo Sansoni, later Archbishop of Cefalu Palermo, I aided in an investigation of the moral conditions of the Diocese of Calabria, and it was this apostolic visit which caused me to repudiate Romanism.

"In the meantime Mr. Panetta, after returning to Bristol, had an opportunity to interest in my behalf Dr. Agide Pirazzini, who in turn wrote to Mr. Michele Nardi, his intimate friend, and he wrote to the Rev. Antonio Mangano who came to see me and help me to find the Truth. When Dr. Pirazzini organized the Italian Department in the Biblical Seminary in New York, Mr. Panetta and I found ourselves enrolled as theological students in the same seminary, and there we had greater occasion to strengthen the bonds of our friendship."

After receiving his theological training at the New York Biblical Seminary, under the inspirational guidance of the late Dr. Pirazzini, the Rev. Mr. Panetta was graduated in 1910, and was ordained in November of the same year by the Presbytery of Philadelphia. Between 1905 and 1907, he gave all his energy and zeal to the Board of Publication and Sabbath School in and around Philadelphia, and made a fine contribution to the work of the Kingdom of God.

In 1908 the Presbyterian Board of Publication, in order to reach the large number of immigrants coming from Italy, to keep in contact with the various missions scattered from New York to California, and to furnish some spiritual food not only to the missionaries but to the newly born Christians, sponsored a paper entirely in Italian called *L'Araldo* (The Herald), with the late Rev. Arturo Di Pietro as its editor. Mr. Di Pietro did excellent work not only as an editor, but as a distributor of books and a publisher of tracts. He was also very popular as a speaker in the various Italian Protestant churches. He was tall, rather handsome, and possessed a facility of speech equalled by very few in our ministry, and although he was never profound, he was more or less brilliant. He was always pleasing, therefore he had succeeded in capturing the interest and support of his brethren in the ministry as well as of their growing congregations. In 1915 he resigned his post and the Rev. Francis J. Panetta was called to edit the paper which came out under a new name, *L'Era Nuova*. He remained at this task until 1927, giving to it his fire and his enthusiasm, and making of the paper not only the voice of the editorial staff but that of the church at large. It is said that all good things must come to an end, and, giving as a pretext the fact that immigration from Italy was greatly reduced through the new restrictive laws, and that the newly-organized missions were not supporting the paper as had been expected, a myopic Board of Publication caused the demise of this valuable medium of evangelism and missionary propaganda.

Several years ago a group of ministers, under the leadership of the Revs. Brunn, Di Nardo, and Ordile, formed an organization for the purpose of giving the Italian churches a publication of their own, to be supported largely by their respective membership, and in part by the American Tract Society, and the New York City Mission Board. The result was *Il Rinnovamento* (The Renewal) which appeared in 1934 edited by Rev. Di Nardo and the Rev. Ordile with the cooperation of several others. Soon it was discovered that a pastor, with many calls upon his time and energy, cannot and should not be burdened with the editorial work of a newspaper, therefore after the publication was soundly established Mr. Di Nardo resigned from his work of love and the Reverend Panetta was called to become its editor. That *Il Rinnovamento* is appreciated by the various churches and Missions among the Italians, is indicated by the fact that from 1934 to 1942, our people contributed over $12,000.00 thus making the publication almost 75 per cent self-supporting.

Mr. Panetta brought to his editorial work rare ability as a writer and fine tact and succeeded admirably in keeping together the old and the new, the Italian speaking and the English elements of the Presbyterian Church, as well as of other denominations. He discovered the secret of being clear and forceful in order to convince, and, at the same time, agreeable in order to please, and how to keep the machine running as smoothly as possible. He has performed a superb piece of work and deserves the appreciation of the entire church.

He pours out all the gentleness of his Latin soul in truly inspired religious lyrics, and conversely, all the fire of his southern Italian heart, in his cry for social justice and in patriotic writings, but he reaches his full stature when he translates his spiritual experiences into clear, forceful, convincing articles, controversial at times, but more often positive affirmations of his faith and belief, revealing always the sterling qualities of a Christian gentleman and the rich mind of a trained scholar.

The Rev. Mr. Panetta has advocated one good independent publication for all the Italian Protestants in America. Since the Methodist Episcopal Church discontinued its publication and the United Presbyterians did likewise, there are only two monthlies left of a denominational scope and circulation;

L'Aurora (Baptist), and *La Vita* (Christian), while *The Renewal* (Presbyterian), is published twice a month. How much better it would be if we could combine these scattered energies, arouse all the others from their lethargy, and produce a strong, aggressive weekly publication, which would be acceptable to all our churches and in every Italian Protestant home. Such a publication should contain worthwhile articles molding public opinion, special features of particular interest to our group, and a rich harvest of news from all our fields. For, lest we forget, the newspaper came into existence in 1622 after Richelieu granted a patent to publish the Paris *Gazette* to a French physician who had found his "news" or "gossip" welcomed as he visited the homes of his patients. People will devour news when they will not read doctrinal and controversial articles. As for the preacher, he can find his inspiration and help in the professional and denominational papers and magazines.

The work of the Rev. Mr. Panetta has not been confined to the editing of a newspaper, for he has remained primarily a missionary at heart. His zeal for the cause of Christ among his people has been ably expressed in the founding of the Italian Presbyterian Church of Bristol, Pa., in 1906; the Presbyterian Mission of Germantown, Pa., in 1907-09, the Bleeker Street Memorial and Bethlehem Chapel, New York City, 1909-15, and through his fruitful service to the Italian Branch of the East Harlem Presbyterian Church from 1915 to 1923. He is a favorite speaker in all our churches, and during the years when Dr. Solla, the pastor of the Bristol, Pa., Church, was serving as a chaplain, with the rank of Major in the armed forces of our country, Mr. Panetta was the much-appreciated supply pastor.

Mr. Panetta's kind and generous heart has responded to appeals coming from everywhere, but especially to those coming from our people in this country or from our native land. Just now he is taking an active part in raising funds and collecting clothing for the unfortunate minority Protestant groups in Italy. He has actually felt the pangs of hunger, the suffering of the sick and of the wounded, the shivering cold of the poor betrayed people of Italy, and he has been pleading their cause with the spoken and the written word in such a superb way as to melt the hearts of his Protestant countrymen for those of our household of faith.

17

The Pioneer as a Writer
(Genaro Gustavo D'Anchise)

In a comedy by Moliere, there is a personage named Jourdain who shows great surprise when he is informed that he has used prose for forty years without knowing it. Most of our pioneers would be equally surprised if I were to tell them that they also could claim the title of writers, since all of us, more or less, have composed poetry in our youth; have written prose all of our life; and have published articles, sermons, letters and pamphlets.

It was with real prophetic vision that the wise man of old wrote that in the making of books, there was no end. This is especially true in our generation and in the country in which we live. Everyone seems to take seriously the advice of the old Greek philosopher, that in order to be a man one must build a home, plant a tree, have a boy of his own, and write a book, since the ambition of every educated American is more or less four-fold.

However, our pioneers were not prepared by training or inclination to write books, since they lacked the necessary means and the indispensable facility in the new language, and even for their mother tongue, their reading public would have been very limited. This would have made publication financially prohibitive. Yet they published studies on immigration, grammars for the study of English, hymnals, controversial booklets, manuals for the worship service and tracts for propaganda purposes. For Bibles and New Testaments, they depended on the excellent translations by Diodati and the more recent and more up-to-date, by Luzzi.

To give a complete list of the writers and a bibliography of all the children of their brains would be an impossibility, aside from the fact that it is not within our scope to compile a list of so comparatively vast a production. We must mention, however, several of the pioneers and their respective productions: Dr. Arrighi, who published a very readable story of his life's experiences under the title, *Tony, the Galley Slave;* Rev. Prof. Fragale, D.P., with a text book on *Didactics*, a number of pamphlets and a collection of poems; Dr. Mangano, whose volume, *Sons of Italy*, was the first missionary study book prepared by an Italian—a book which attracted the attention of many missionary societies in America; Dr. Pirazzini left a volume on *The Influence of LaMartain on Italy*, and a translation of many Psalms in poetical Italian; Rev. Giuseppe Panetta published a collection of sermons in Italian; Rev. E. Sartorio published a volume on *Italians Today;* Rev. Mr. Conti a volume on the Italians in this country; Rev. Mr. Pecorini, a book on the Italians in America and a grammar for the teaching of English to the Italians; Dr. Di Domenica published among other things a bi-lingual hymnal, a volume for the teaching of Italian to American Christian workers—and many pamphlets; Rev. Fenili has published, among other things, a brief sketch of his conversion from a monk to a minister of the Gospel; Dr. DeCarlo published many useful pamphlets among which was *My Americanization*, and the writer, among other things, published a volume on *Italy's Contribution to the Reformation.*

So far as we know, a volume from the pen of one of our pioneers that made a general appeal at a propitious time in the history of our immigration was *The Soul of An Immigrant*, by Pannunzio, in which he relates his ups and downs as an immigrant, his call to the ministry, and his work with the Y.M.C.A. in Italy during the first World War. But Pannunzio turned his interest to sociologic studies in relation to the family. The first novel written in English by one of our pioneers is *Westward Leading* by Rev. Prof John Tron. This book has been described as a lively novel, spirited in its short narratives, vigorous in the descriptions of every-day occurrences, over-flowing with genuine human interest. It relates the life of a young minister in the Waldensian Church, his dealings with the Roman Catholics, his converts, among whom is his future wife, their coming to America, and their work among the immigrants in this country. We could go on indefinitely if we had the time and were not afraid to abuse the patience of the reader, but we must present our representative Pioneer as a Writer, Genaro Gustavo D'Anchise, Ph.D., who combines in a most admirable way the old and the new, the Italian and the English, a gentle poetical note with rich harmonious prose.

Most writers begin their career very young, since they feel impelled to express themselves to a not always expectant public. D'Anchise was only sixteen when he plunged into his first journalistic venture. His uncle was a well-known book-seller and publisher, and among other friends who used to gather in the book shop in the evening, there was an eccentric, wealthy old lawyer whose hobby was printing. D'Anchise obtained from this gentleman permission to use his equipment, and secured the aid of a few friends and a retired printer who acted as pressman and was legally responsible for the publica-tion. They issued a four-page weekly paper, under the name of *Il Vero* (The Truth). This strange enterprise was a great success. The boys began to make fun of everyone and every-thing. D'Anchise wrote sonnets on Nero and the city mayor, on Martin Luther and the President of the College. In a few months, however, the publication, having become dangerously true to its name, had to be suspended voluntarily on the advice of the parents, teachers, friends, and the police.

When D'Anchise was eighteen years old, he wrote, at the request of a local publisher, a novel in verse, *Myriam*, which was sold in a few weeks, and became very popular among fellow students. The novel was greatly appreciated by the foremost poets of Italy, who sent very encouraging messages to the young poet, among others, Giosue Carducci, Mario Rapisardi, Matilde Serao, and Raffaele De Rensis. A critic of

Roma's daily paper *Il Giornale D'Italia* wrote: "Your poetry has a remarkable and timely social content—don't give up and you will surely succeed."

In 1903 when he was not quite twenty, he accepted an invitation from a friend, who was preparing himself for the gospel ministry, to come to New York. Though very young, he already had a good literary preparation and some experience in journalism. The night he arrived in the new world he slept at Union Seminary in the old building in lower Manhattan. He had not yet decided to study for the ministry. His heart was divided between preaching and writing for the cause of religious freedom, which he had always considered to be the most important of modern liberties. At that time the Reverend Filoteo Taglialatela, founder of the Jefferson Methodist Episcopal Church of New York, was publishing *La-Rivista Evangelica*, the first Italian Protestant paper in the United States. He also became co-editor of *Il Risveglio*, a fortnightly publication of New York. He recognized in D'Anchise a promising young man and employed him as Assistant Editor. All the assignments and more were fulfilled very satisfactorily, for D'Anchise wrote articles and poems which were often reproduced by publications in the old country. In Cleveland, Ohio, there are people who remember how teachers in the public schools of Campobasso read, on patriotic occasions, two poems written by D'Anchise on Garibaldi and Mazzini, which had been reprinted by some Italian papers from the New World publications.

He studied theology at Drew Seminary and in September, 1906, the Presbyterian Board of Home Missions placed him in charge of the Italian work at the historic Church of Sea and Land in lower Manhattan. In February 1907, he was sent to take charge of a group of Waldensians (from the Churches of Schiavi and Garunchio, Italy), who had settled in the Melrose section of the Bronx. This resulted in the First Italian Presbyterian Church of Holy Trinity, under the Presbytery of New York. He was the first Italian to be ordained to the ministry by the Presbytery of New York (June 1908), and with funds from the Kennedy Bequest, the Church Extension Committee of that Presbytery erected for his congregation a building costing about $200,000. At the dedication service the sermon was preached by Dr. Henry Van Dyke, with D'Anchise as interpreter. The great poet and preacher wrote from Princeton, a letter of appreciation to the young Italian minister, in which he said, among other things, that his sermon translated into Italian was very beautiful.

During the first World War he accepted a call as Port Chaplain for the Episcopal City Mission at Ellis Island. In 1917, he became Director of the Bureau of Immigrants for the American Waldensian Aid Society, and in that capacity he organized the Patronato Degli Emigranti, a committee for the protection of the immigrants.

In 1920 he returned to Italy where he became very active in social, religious and cultural enterprises first in Palermo, then in Genoa and finally in Rome. In 1925, at the request of a progressive publishing house of Genoa, he prepared a collection of historical books and a history of early movements toward Humanism and Democracy. This volume was confiscated by the Fascist Government, but not before 9,000 of the 10,000 copies of the first edition had been already sold in Italy and in North and South America.

During the Fascist domination in Italy, freedom of speech was a thing of the past. D'Anchise had his ups and downs with the law. It was in Genoa, I believe, that he was once conducting a meeting with his usual poise and dignity, notwithstanding the tempest raging in his heart, since he had been admonished by the Government not to speak in public. As he looked over his audience, he noticed his old friend, an officer of the secret police, who had saved him once before but had assured him that he would not save him again. This time he was accompanied by two guards. Poets, however, go where angels fear to tread; and his gentle soul was inflamed by his burning heart, for he preached a most fiery sermon. "You have done it again," was the first remark of his friend. "You better get out through this back door and leave immediately! Otherwise you jeopardize your life and compromise my career." This closed another chapter in the life of our pioneer for very soon through the intervention of some of his influential friends he was permitted to return to America.

His heart and soul were always in America, where his character, as a citizen based on Democratic principles and as a religious leader based on a spiritual, liberal background, had been formed. In May 1929, when he could leave without detriment to this work, he came back to the United States and settled in Cleveland as Minister-in-residence of St. John's Beckwith Memorial Church, under the supervision of the Session of the Church of the Covenant. This work was started as a Sunday School in 1888, by two ladies of the Euclid Avenue Congregational Church. Soon a Mission was organized under the leadership of an Italian minister, and from 1905 to 1921 the work was in charge of the Reverend Professor Peter Monnet from the Waldensian Valleys in Italy. In 1906 the Congregational Church turned over the Mission to the Presbyterians who organized it into a Church and built a brick Chapel in Romanesque style, with a tower and bell, which was dedicated in February 1907. The Presbytery of Cleveland placed the work under the care of the session of the Church of the Covenant and both the Congregation and the Minister are part of the parish of that church, which is one of the prominent religious achievements in Christian America. St. John's, with a constituency of about 400 and a separate club house built for its boys' activities in 1938, has marked the 35th Anniversary of its organization as a Church, by dedicating a system of electric chimes in its tower on Sunday before Christmas, 1941.

In 1931, D'Anchise completed a course at Western Reserve University leading to the degree of Master of Arts, which he had begun at Columbia University in 1917. The degree of Doctor of Philosophy was conferred upon him by the same

University in 1933. His field of research was Efforts for Freedom of Knowledge in Medieval Literature. In 1934, he was appointed Fellow by courtesy of that University and has been a teacher of Romance Languages.

The cares and worries of a ministerial life with its thousand and one problems experienced when one serves a minority religious group within a minority cultural group did not reduce his literary activities.

D'Anchise's literary career may be divided into three periods.

To the first period belongs his first poem, *Myriam, a Novel of Zion*, published in Italy when he was seventeen years old, and inspired by the racial and spiritual conflicts in modern Jerusalem. Raffaello DeRensis, critic of the *Giornale d'Italia* of Rome, whote that the young poet had something new, characterizing his poetry as deeply human and social. "It is the poetry for the masses," he wrote. "Go ahead, D'Anchise. Your poetry is what we need today!" To this first period belongs also his production after coming to this country, an Italian hymnal for his church (1910), a poem on the Waldenses, *Holy Remembrances* (Sante Rimembrance), *Brooklyn* (1912), a popular story of Savonarola (1912), and many articles and poems in religious and secular papers.

The young poet wavered between pessimism, tempered by a great faith in the final victory of justice, and a renewed religious experience substituting for the old symbols learned at his mother's knee. A virile spiritual struggle, and a sense of the all-conquering power of God, for his soul and for the world, are reflected in his poems.

He sang, "When I hear in my soul the voice of my torment as I see wrong surrounding me, I cannot listen to the dearest voice of those who love me—and I become a poet-pilgrim, who seeks the sanctuaries of martyrs for the cause of justice. Then my voice rises toward a smiling sky and though it tortures me and other children of sorrow, yet I cry loud for revenge because social wrongs cannot go unpunished forever ..."

His second poem, *Sante Rimembrance*, was a poetic summary of the history of the Waldenses of Piedmont. Some of the most romantic and valiant episodes of the history of the Israel of the Alps were brought out with lyric vivacity and dramatized to lead the soul of the reader to this conclusion: "Oh, Italy! thou canst be justly proud of thy Waldensians—more proud of these lowly, valiant people than of thy costly monuments carved in stone and marble. May their spiritual monument be an inspiration to thy people for higher and nobler living."

The second period of his literary activities began upon his return to Italy, where he was pastor and teacher from 1920 to 1929, first in Palermo, then in Genoa and finally in Rome. The Libreria Moderna Publishing House of Genoa published his *Legami Spirtuali*, a collection of critical essays.

La Speranza publishing house of Rome issued his *Motivi Antichi* (Ancient Motifs), a collection of poems (1929).

To this second period belongs also a series of poems: *Gethsemane, Easter Morning*, two poems on Mazzini and Garibaldi and translations of English hymns for Italian hymn books. Pietro Chiminelli, former editor of *Coscienza* and a brilliant critic, wrote a brief biographic sketch of D'Anchise, entitled *Genaro G. D'Anchise and his work in Italy*, and as a sub-title *Poesia d'Anima* (Poetry of the Soul). He wrote that D'Anchise will occupy a well-deserved place among those poets who have been able to include in their songs the most exquisite emotions of the human heart and the aspirations of a faith filled with a breath of the infinite. In order to appreciate this new poet, one must have tasted first in its intimate essence that poetry of many souls of mother Italy which gives to his sad song a pattern of nostalgic beauty, lightly veiled in romanticism.

The late Dr. Eduardo Taglialetela, well-known author and teacher of literature in various Italian Universities, wrote in his preface to the last book published by D'Anchise in Rome, *Motivi Antichi* (Ancient Motifs) La Speranza, 1929: "To the reader who will enjoy these poems, so gently engraved and so vibrant with white visions, I wish to confess a sincere impression of mine, in case he does not know the poet intimately. Since the style reveals the man—G. G. D'Anchise is a soul always open to the pure and high visions which are a prerequisite to fervent faith. He makes of his life, poetry; and of poetry, his life! . . . In a few weeks he will sail the Atlantic toward the United States, after a fruitful decade of honorable efforts in Italy. The many and faithful friends he leaves in Italy, asked him to collect in a book, as a tangible token of the communion of ideals and love, at least some of his lyrics, in order that we may point to others and say "Behold the pure, beautiful visions that our beloved D'Anchise contemplates, sings and lives!"

There is a short poem *Vestal* of classic structure and of pagan-Christian delineations. In the Flavi Colosseum, he revived all the emotions of its stormy life, a contrast between a brute whose name can be seen radiating on the base of the monument of the house of the bestals at the Palatino across from Telemaco, and the Saint of the Colosseum, a martyr of the Christian Easter of the year 300, who struck a death blow to the bloody encounters of the gladiators. It is a contrast between two eras which we live here; a contrast between pagans, drunk for the games of the circus and Telemaco, the martyr and the vestal of the Christian song.

And again beyond Rome pagan-Christian, the contrast between heaven and earth, between the surrounding pagan sadness and the Christian peace which sings in his heart, takes hold of him while on the island of fire, in Alcamo, Sicily, among the ruins of its pagan temple.

The pioneer writer is sixty years of age now, but his Muse is still young and fruitful, as can be seen from recent publications, both in English and in Italian. Like all true poets, he lives in a creation of his own. In solitude, he communes with the sources of light, life, love and beauty. He has discovered what Coleridge said: "Poetry has soothed my afflictions, it has endeared my solitude, and it has given me the habit of wishing to discover the good and beautiful in all that surrounds me." In this mood and with this holy aspiration, a third period is taking shape to crown the literary career of our pioneer as a writer. To this period belong his volumes, *The Struggle for Freedom of Knowledge in Medieval Literature* (1933), *The Flower and Poetry*, didactic and allegoric (1931), *Italy and World Affairs* (1933), *La Canzone dell'Olivo* (The Song of the Olive Tree), which is being widely read in the Italo-American communities. The Reverend D. A. Porfirio, of Rochester, New York, said: "The poet becomes a mirror in which the future projects its gigantic shadow on the present . . . His poem renews Faith and gives Serenity." He writes truly (as Dante said, long long ago) as his heart dictates. To the insistence of his friends to write more and oftener, D'Anchise answers, "I am not afraid to be unpopular. I can only write what my soul desires and not what I should write to please others."

"D'Anchise, with his breviary of his poetry, reflecting the antinomies of the Italian spirit of today, still half pagan and half Christian, has raised a song of Hosanna to the Christ and has woven a golden crown around the immortal head of Orpheus of the centuries, who attracts souls to himself and makes them victorious with the magic sound of his enchanted lyre."

The reason why D'Anchise has not been able to take his place among those Italian poets, universally known and read, is that he belongs to a religious minority group, not well known, and unable to back the efforts of its promising leaders. Sometime, when poetry shall not be subjected to the will of the majorities which rule the material and commercial interests in the diffusion of books, he will probably have his day. Conscious of this handicap which makes him at the same time happy and proud, he proceeds quietly in his work, writing as if he prayed, not caring very much how many people read his poems, since above everything else, he is anxious that God hears him.

And thus victory will greet this spirit who upset all the cannons of satanic-humanistic art in which Carducci, D'Annunzio, and Stecchetti had imprisoned our poetry.

18

The Pioneer as a Friend of the Friendless
(Charles Fama, M.D.)

It was after midnight when, tired and worn to a frazzle, not so much from overwork, as emotionally, induced by all he had seen and heard that day from his poverty-stricken and tragedy-ridden patients, that the good doctor had finished reading his Bible, turned out the light, and had just gone to bed, when the door bell rang. He looked out the window; it was still sleeting. The bell rang incessantly. Duty and love pulled him downstairs before he realized it. Opening the door he saw a boy of twelve or thirteen years of age, mumbling some excuses and crying: "My Daddy is dying and Mother asked me to call you. She was sure you would come. Please, please, you must, you must!"

"All right, sonny, wait a moment," he said. In a short time, with the boy sitting next to him, the physician's car was rolling cautiously into the hazardous night toward the home where a WPA worker was delirious, sick with double pneumonia. He followed the boy into the tenement house and up one, two, three flights of steps. At the top he met a woman in her late forties, a talkative Neapolitan, crying aloud: "For St. Janarius' sake, for the soul of your mother, you must save my husband."

The physician administered the latest scientific remedies, prescribed what to do during the night, and with reassuring words departed into the unfriendly night.

The next day the patient was resting comfortably. As the doctor began his routine examination, the man opened his eyes. Was he dreaming or still delirious? He cried, "Why you, Doctor!" "Now calm yourself," said the doctor. "I am your physician. I am here to help you."

Doctor and patient knew of a fight to the death when the WPA worker, as a well-to-do member of the community, and like many others had swallowed the teachings of Fascism "lock, stock and barrel," had become one of its ardent advocates, and had fought the good doctor, tooth and nail, trying to injure his reputation, and whispering his elimination. But the depression had caught him in its merciless whirl and had reduced him to abject poverty.

Medicines, food, coal and clothing poured into that house, paid for by the doctor or secured from his friends, until the Spring sunshine returned and the man was well enough to go back to work.

Dr. Fama was born in Italy in 1887. He was the son of a police officer who had attained fame in Sicily by capturing the dangerous brigand, Mauro, who had been terrorizing with impunity the country side around Messina and Mistretta. The child inherited the strong character of his father, the tenderness and love of his mother, and the fire of his beloved Sicily.

Like millions of other honest, ambitious, liberty-loving Italians, who turned their backs on the homes of their fathers, most of them never to return, in 1897 they came to America, "the land of the free and the home of the brave," to improve their economic condition and to give their child those opportunities which only a young, rich and powerful country can offer.

Charles had already manifested a quick mind, a precocious thirst for learning, and an ambition to lift himself above the seemingly amorphous but precious human cargo which poured over our national shores from every country in the world, in the greatest immigration wave in the history of the world.

He was reared in the strict observance of the precepts of the Roman Catholic Church, and he writes in his valuable booklet, *From Darkness to Light*, that his earliest mentor in philosophy had been a learned old priest of more or less liberal views. As early as 1907 we find him studying philosophy at the St. Joseph Salesian College, Troy Hill, New York, while at the same time he was teaching in the same college. But God works in a mysterious way. The young instructor, thirsty for knowledge, happened to be the only one to possess a copy of the Holy Bible, which he began to devour and compare with the doctrines of his church and with the teachings he was imparting. The light began to shine through the darkness, and during the school year, 1907-08 he was tormented by his conscience which shouted repeatedly, "Hypocrite!" He arose to his full stature, resigned his teaching position, and rushed alone into the dawn to seek more light.

The booklet is an excellent synthesis of his adventure from Romanism to evangelical Christianity with a clear, concise and forceful statement of his beliefs. The table of contents is as follows: The Story of My Conversion, Romanism and Paganism, Saints Are Not Mediators, The Auricular Confession, Was St. Peter the First Pope?, Purgatory, and, What Are the Religious Conditions of the Italians Today?

As soon as the young professor was converted to evangelical Christianity, he was made the object of numerous and open attacks, base insinuations and physical threats; but among the many other attestations of his sterling qualities, we wish to reproduce the following letter:

St. Joseph's Salesian College
40 8th Street
Troy, New York

March 14, 1905

This is to certify that Mr. Carlo Fama has been an able and praiseworthy professor in our college for one year, and I recommend him for his integrity, honorability and excellence of character.

Augustine Burle, S.T.D.
Professor of Theology.

Like many other ambitious young men, he felt he could do more for the cause of Christ by practicing medicine, but unlike some who were trained by the Church and have forgotten Her in their mad scramble for gold, he remained faithful to the Italian Church at 204th Street and Villa Avenue in the Bronx, which he served while taking some courses at Dr. White's Bible School (1908-10). In this church he and his wife are to be found every Sunday morning in their accustomed pew, worshipping God in spirit and in truth.

He graduated from the New York Homeopathic Medical College and Flower Hospital in 1914. He was united in the holy bonds of marriage to Miss Henrietta Bedard of Canada in 1911. Although his practice grew by leaps and bounds, his scientific interest was kept alive and has been his guiding light through the years. Dr. Fama's attainments in his profession are attested by the fact that he served as captain in the United States Medical Corps during the first world war; he received a second medical degree from the old renowned University of Palermo; he filled many important positions in the largest city in the world, and, during the last twelve years of Mr. LaGuardia's tenure of office, he was chairman of the Medical Board of the Board of Estimate of that great metropolis, which position he relinquished as soon as Tammany returned to power. For two consecutive terms he was elected President of the New York State Homeopathic Medical Association and a member of the Medical Society of the State of New York, the City of New York, and the Association of Military Surgeons of the United States Army, a Thirty-second Degree Mason and a member of numerous other societies.

But his greatest asset is his human approach to all things in life. Friends or enemies, turning to him for help, find in Dr. Fama the Christian gentleman, ready to forget and to forgive, and let bygones be bygones; and if the request is at all reasonable, Dr. Fama will always lend a kind, helping hand.

As soon as Fascism came to power in Italy and began to spread its tentacles in America, Dr. Fama, with prophetic vision, saw the threat to our liberal institutions. With the fire of an apostle he began to fight almost single-handed with his fiery oratory and his forceful writings, from the pulpit and in the press, until he saw the complete debacle of the party that had hoodwinked millions, including some of the foremost business and professional men in America who were shouting "What we need in America is another Mussolini."

For his militant attitude he had to pay a big price. His wife was threatened, and as vengeance against his exposition, Fascism forced the University of Palermo to revoke his Medical Diploma, which had been conferred upon him in 1922. But the new government of Italy has already done justice to Dr. Fama by restoring in full force his Italian Medical Degree, and apologizing for the act of Mussolini.

Although his medical practice keeps him very busy from morning to evening, attending not only to his many patients who go to his office; but making home calls, covering a radius of about twenty miles, and half a dozen hospitals, he yet finds time to use the pen and his voice for those things which are near and dear to his heart.

Dr. Fama's oratorical abilities are used to great advantage not only as a speaker on civic matters; but as a preacher of righteousness and spiritual truths. His interest in religion has been displayed by the forceful sermons he preaches in Italian and in English; and the campaign he has waged as president of the American Committee for Religious Freedom in Italy. It is worthy of notice that the "Text of Drafts for the Italian Treaty," which was presented at the Paris Conference, contained the following section:

Part II Political Clauses

Section I General Clauses

Article XIV

Italy shall take all measures necessary to secure to all persons under Italian jurisdiction, without distinction as to race, sex, language, or religion, the enjoyment of human rights and of the fundamental freedoms, including the freedom of expression, of the press and publication, of *religious worship*, of political opinion and of *public meeting*.

Such a provision, if adopted, will bring to Italy that religious freedom which is the inalienable right of every human being, and which would never have been included without the efforts and leadership of Dr. Fama.

Dr. Fama has always been the defender of the oppressed and the downtrodden. His fight for tolerance, both religious and social, and against discrimination toward racial minorities, has made him a nationally known figure commanding the respect of the Federal authorities of Washington, who, especially in Italian matters, have often sought his counsel and advice.

Dr. Fama has been, and continues to be the friend of all in time of need; but especially the friend of the "under dog". His professional services are always free to the poor, his generous purse supplies the needs of his indigent brothers, and his heart pulls him always where the fighting is hardest for the freedom of shackled minds and spirits of his fellow pilgrims.

To a large group of Italian ministers and their wives, assembled at his summer home on City Island near Pelham Bay, New York, Dr. Fama greeted his brethren with these words: "Brethren, sisters, and friends. I welcome you to this beautiful place which does not belong to me but to God our Father. He has entrusted it to me to use it to His glory and for the welfare of others. At the end of my earthly existence, this place will continue to be used for the good of my brethren in the faith. I am very happy that the Lord has given me a very good companion who shares completely my ideals and my aspirations. Each morning before I go to my medical office, I kneel down before God and ask Him to direct my ways and to use me for His honor and glory."

These words reveal the man who has consecrated himself completely to God and who has given his best to his Master and his fellow men.

19

The Pioneer as a Chaplain
(Andrew G. Solla)

One of Uncle Sam's mighty fortresses of the sky was rising above the proverbial fog of England when an SOS was received to start immediately for an emergency landing field, opposite Holland, and pick up a crew just forced down. The plane had been over Berlin and, in the parlance of the boys, "the jerries had made it hot for them." A co-pilot had been shot in the foot, the radio operator had had his parachute shot from under him, and the entire crew was fairly well "broken up". Chaplain Solla was on the rescue plane, and as soon as they landed he ran to the crew. He got busy aiding, encouraging and comforting every man; and as soon as everything was under control every member of the crew from the pilot to the last man expressed his gratitude saying, "Sir, we want to thank you for your wonderful help." Major Solla writes modestly, "I had done nothing for them, but I was the representative of God, and those young lads looked up to me as the one who had interceded for them. If I did those boys any good, to God be all the honor and the praise." This incident reveals the spirit of humility of our pioneer Chaplain.

The Chaplains have done a superb piece of work of which the boys themselves, the country at large, and the Church in particular are very proud and for which we are indebted to them. A recent report states that in World War II we had 8,171 chaplains, that 1,682 army chaplains received a total of 2,243 decorations (as of November 30, 1946), that battle casualties among army chaplains have been exceeded on a comparative basis by losses among officers in only two other branches of the service—the air forces and the infantry—and that the outstanding episode in the history of the Chaplain Corps is that of the four army chaplains who gave their life jackets to other men aboard the torpedoed and the sinking troop-transport steamship, Dorchester, and in so doing sacrificed their own lives. This is a record that would do honor to any class or group of men anywhere and in any age.

During the first World War, Italian missionaries spoke predominantly their native language; therefore, they were not prepared to serve as chaplains, even if by natural inclination they had been attracted to such a career in time of emergency. So far as we know, we had only one chaplain of Italian extraction in the U. S. Army, the late Rev. Bartholomew Tron, a graduate of Western Theological Seminary, Pittsburgh, Pa., who proved very valuable because of his knowledge of French; but we had several Y.M.C.A. workers, especially after the disastrous retreat on the Italian front, and we recall two outstanding names: Dr. Pannunzio and Dr. Gigliotti. Gradually some of our young men found their way into the Chaplaincy and, among others, we would like to remember the Rev. Amedeo Santini, who left his pastorate in Detroit to go into active service during peace time with the rank of Captain, and died from an operation. During World War II, so far as we have been able to ascertain, we have had the Rev. James Salango, Presbyterian U. S., the Rev. Corrado Riggio, the Rev. Thomas Caliandro, and the Rev. Sam Morreale, Methodist, the Rev. M. Testa and the Rev. Andrew G. Solla, Presbyterian, U. S. A. The latter served as Major on the western front, and because of his rank and his excellent work, we have chosen him as the Pioneer in this important field of service.

Andrew Solla was born May 1, 1894 in the town of Marconi province of Benevento, not very far from Naples. His early schooling was rather meager. His first teacher was an old priest who taught him the fundamentals of reading, writing and arithmetic. One day he asked the boy how much was fifty plus fifty, and when he answered "one hundred" he informed the boy "You know enough now; don't bother-coming to school anymore." His next teacher was his sister-in-law; and later, his cousin, a retired prison warden who instructed him up to the seventh grade. He was encouraged by the boy's progress and advised him to go to high school. But his father was convinced of the impossibility of sending him to a school in a different town and, as a compromise, advised him to enter the Franciscan monastery and become a monk. This had no appeal for the boy and so, after two years of continuous arguments, at sixteen years of age he obtained his father's consent to seek his fortune in America.

Young Andrew landed in Philadelphia in March, 1911, and, after two or three days, his older brother who had preceded him there, advised him to go to night school in order to learn English. The classes were held in a little church by a fine Christian woman who took a real interest in the poor boys who were coming in large numbers from Italy. She was assisted by a young student from the University of Pennsylvania, Mr. Michele Frasca, who later prepared for the gospel ministry and has recently become the pastor of the First Italian Presbyterian Church of Philadelphia. He encouraged the boys to return Sunday morning for an hour of English followed by divine worship. The boy could not quite understand what he meant, since the only thing he had been acquainted with was the mass. But, young and curious, he attended; and there he heard for the first time a simple gospel message. During the Lenten season the boys learned to sing some of the beautiful hymns on the crucifixion, and one especially, about Calvary, made such an impression on his mind that he felt impelled to surrender his life to Christ. For about three years he continued to attend the evening classes; and in the summer of 1914 he confided to his Christian teacher, Miss Sallie H. Greene, that he might return to Italy and serve in the army. She answered, "Yes, and then what?" Her advice was to go to school and prepare for a profession. After sleepless nights he decided to remain in America and entered the Mt. Herman School for boys, founded by Mr. Moody. However, the United States entered the World War in 1917 and in September of that year young Solla found himself wearing the U. S. Army uniform at Ft. Devens, Mass.

Later he was transferred to the newly organized air corps; in two weeks he proceeded to Kelly Field, San Antonio and from there to Waco, Virginia, Long Island and finally aboard the Alpinor bound for England. He was on guard duty one night, just before landing. The fog was so thick that he could not even see the other guard and much less lurking submarines; therefore, he had plenty of time to pray, and this is what he said, "Dear Lord, if you permit me to get back to the States in two years, I'll continue to study for the ministry." The Lord was more generous than he had dared to ask—for in eight months he was back. After several weeks of idleness, he entered the Bloomfield College and Seminary, from there he went to Princeton where he received his Master's degree in Theology, and through extension courses he received a Doctor's degree in 1933.

In 1925 a fellow clergyman advised him to take a commission in the Chaplain Reserve Corps. After debating for a while, he made application and was commissioned a first Lieutenant. In 1926 he was again in uniform at Ft. Eustis, Virginia, with the 34th infantry regiment, and each summer he was transferred to a different outfit. In 1930 he was promoted to the rank of Captain, and when the depression came with the organization of the Civilian Conservation Corps the war department invited him to help in this service. However, he preferred to remain with his small congregation of working people in Bristol, Pa., sacrificing thousands of dollars, since he felt that this was his work.

When the clouds of war gathered in January, 1941, he was called into active service for one year with the rank of Captain, and that same year he was promoted to the rank of Major. But instead of one year he remained in the service for five years and two months, during which time he served in many parts of the United States, and then in Great Britain, where he served in the hospitals of the ordnance depot of the Eighth Air force. This was followed by a limited service in France and Italy.

During the time he was in the army it was his privilege to preach to thousands of men and to visit tens of thousands of them in hospitals. As he looks back to those years of great activity, in his Christian humility, Major Solla says "The seed I was permitted to sow, by God's grace I feel sure, will bear much fruit, since I never preached anything else but the saving Gospel of grace, and that there is no other name by which men can be saved but by the name of Jesus Christ, the son of God."

From his rich experience he has received many testimonials from men who have been helped to find God in the storm of life, but space permits us only two typical illustrations. One day, Dr. Solla relates, he was at Camp Blantford, England, and as he was going to get some food at the counter (for the officers' mess had burned down), he confronted a young soldier with a carving knife and fork slicing roast beef. When his turn to be served arrived, the soldier looked at him for a moment and said, "Sir, I remember a sermon you preached to us, and I want to tell you how much good it did to me." He continued quoting parts of the sermon, which the preacher had almost completely forgotten. This sermon had been preached four years before, at the reception center, Ft. Custer, Michigan; but the spirit of God had been at work and had gripped the heart of this young man during the very first part of his military experience. Only God knows the good that this fine Chaplain and others like him had done to the cause of Christ and His Kingdom, as they ministered to the boys, and during those tense years of the most terrible war in the memory of man.

One Sunday in August, 1945 the Chaplain was standing in front of a Chapel in Winborn, England, when a young Sergeant came and inquired, "Sir, when is the next mass?" He answered by saying that he was sorry that there was only one mass, and that was already over. "However," he said, "we have a Protestant service in about ten minutes, and you are welcome." He was so pleased and so blessed with the word of God that after the service he went to see Dr. Solla at his home to thank him for the benefit he had received.

Dr. Solla served well not only Protestant soldiers but Catholic and Jewish soldiers as well. We have read a very complimentary communication from Bernard J. Statman, Major M. C., in which he relates how Major Solla during their voyage to England as senior Chaplain, arranged for and conducted Jewish services on board ship for members of the Jewish faith; and while stationed with the hospital near Derby for almost one year, he continually stimulated interest in Jews, making it possible for patients and hospital personnel to attend services in the local community. He also made very frequent trips with a group on Friday nights and prayed together with the men in the synagogue.

Although Dr. Solla served so well as Chaplain as to reach the rank of Major, yet like most chaplains he is a pastor at heart. He began his evangelistic work first as an assistant to one of our pioneers, the late Rev. Francesco Pesaturo; and later, as a Seminary student, he was employed by the Sunday School Board of the Presbyterian Church, U. S. A., among the coal miners of West Virginia and around Rochester, Newport and Oswego. Upon graduation from Seminary in 1923 he was called to lead the Italian Mission of Bristol, Pennsylvania, started by the Rev. F. J. Panetta, now the able editor of Il Rinnovamento. It is not a large church; it has a membership of only one hundred honest hard-working people. His salary is less than one-third of what it was in the service. Although he was asked to remain in the service and received four calls to larger churches, he preferred to return to his people; which shows once more how much Home Missionaries are willing to sacrifice for Christ and His Church, even though their work is unappreciated by their prominent American brethren. They could do much better financially in organized churches or in other lines of work; but for the love of Christ which constrains them, their interest in the Kingdom of God, and their affection for their people, who like sheep have gone astray, they are faithful to their Home Missionary work.

REPORT OF THE COMMITTEE ON AMERICANIZATION OF THE ITALIAN BAPTIST MISSIONARY ASSOCIATION

Report adopted by the Association at its Annual Meeting in Brooklyn, N. Y. September 13th, 1918.

Reported by

The Americanization Committee for Circulation among Italians

AMERICANIZATION COMMITTEE
CHARLES A. BROOKS, Chairman
23 East 26th Street, New York City

INTRODUCTION

The Americanization of the people who have come to America to make their homes is a simple matter of adjustment and sincere determination to achieve complete and full union with the life of America.

They are admitted to the privileges and enjoy the rights freely offered them. They must also recognize that with rights go duties and with privileges go responsibilities. Hence there is the obligation to understand America, to learn to use her language, to take parte in all her undertakings, to uphold her Government and institutions.

America does not ask an Italian to forget Italy or to banish from his heart love for and interest in her welfare.. We only ask that America shall come first and in any conflict of interest his first loyalty and devotion should be for America. That is the supreme test which has come to thousands of German born men and women and thousands from Austria. The vast majority have been true to their new allegiance to both in the letter and the spirit.

Americanization cannot be achieved in a day or a year. It is a growth, a process. We can resolutely establish and maintain our contacts with all that is best and truest in American life and not accept as typical those things which the real Americans condemn.

I am glad to have heard the report which was entirely original and made without any hint or aid from anyone outside our Italian Association. I am proud of the 875 service stars which represent our Italian Baptist Missions and Churches: I rejoice in the true manhood and genuine Americanism of these Italians whom I know and love.

CHARLES A. BROOKS.

REPORT OF THE COMMITTEE
ON AMERICANIZATION

To the Italian Baptist Convention: (1)

Since the war broke out in Europe, it has been natural for the people in America, both Aliens and native born, to side with one or the other of the belligerent parties. Though the people were urged by our beloved President "to be neutral even in thought", they found that it was a psychological impossibility to be passive in such a colossal struggle as it was and is threatening the very existence of the people engaged in it, and the civilization of the world. Every living soul had and has his aspiration and hope for the defeat of one and the victory of the other; it cannot be otherwise.

As long as official America remained neutral, the pacifists and pro-German propagandists were left unmolested; but as soon as America severed her diplomatic relations with the German Imperial government, any one siding with the central Powers was considered and taken as an "alien enemy". From that time on American statesmen, patriots, educators, military men, public speakers and others seeing such a lack of real Americanism in these Aliens have apprehensively and rightly deprecated their attitude toward America.

These Americans reason th s way: Have not these Aliens been long enough in this Country to appreciate the laws and customs of America? Do they not make their livelihood in this fair land? Are not their children educated here? Do they not expect to remain, die and be buried in America? Why, then, have they not absorbed the American spirit and become thoroughly americanized? So strong and keen has been this feeling among the Americans that Secretary of the Interior, Franklin K. Lane, issued invitations to Governors of all the States of the Union, to the

---

(1) In the course of this report it is natural for us to speak mainly concerning the Italians; but on the whole the same can be said of all other foreigners in America.

Presidents of about three hundred corporations and to the representatives of State Councils of Defence, to hold a conference at Washington, D. C. This council was held on April 3, ult., to lay out plans for an effective and powerful drive to Americanize America.

As a result of this Conference, the Bureau of Education, through Dr. Wheaton, has drawn up two bills and introduced them in Congress for the appropriation of a large sum of money to be used in the Americanization of the Aliens. One is for the appropriation of $250.000 to be used in helping the different organizations which are already promoting Americanization. The other bill calls for another appropriation of $2.500.000 for the first year, which sum is to be increased proportionately every year thereafter until the sum reaches the total of $5.000.000!

This undertaking by the Government and the expenditure of such a large sum of money clearly demonstrates the magnitude of this great movement and the necessity to prosecute the same in this educational program on Americanization.

AMERICA THE MELTING POT

America has been properly or improperly called "the melting pot" of the various elements which come to her. Every immigration has proved, whether in America or elsewhere, that immigrants are bound to be assimilated in some direction of their life, with the people with whom they live. Their traits and customs and even their physiognomy are changed. But history proves that assimilation is easier in the outward appearance than in the inward part of man. The people of Israel had been for 300 years in Egypt, but all the Egyptian culture and civilization were not able to merge this people into the people of that country. Moses had never seen Canaan; he was born, bred and educated in Egypt, but when the test came he was found to be "an Israelite indeed". His people had been influenced to a certain degree by the environment there, but at heart they were the offspring of Abraham, Isaac and Jacob.

In the opening address of the aforesaid conference at Washington, secretary Lane, among many beautiful things, said: "We are trying a great experiment in the United States. Can we gather together from all ends of the earth peoples of different races, creeds, conditions and aspirations who can be merged into one? If we cannot do this, we will fail. If we can do this, we will produce the greatest of all nations and a new race that will hold a compelling place in the world."

Evidently Secretary Lane is aware of the extremely difficult task which is before America in merging into one people men of different races, creeds, conditions and aspirations. The success or the failure of this merging process depends entirely upon the means which America will use for the melting of these heterogeneous elements that a homogeneous unit may come out of it.

WHAT IS AMERICANISM?

The term "Americanization" has been pitifully misinterpreted and misused by many well-intentioned people in America. For some it means nothing else but to live "A l'Americana" by having a well furnished house with bath, screened doors and windows and with the rest of the paraphernalia with which an American house is adorned. The people in the house must eat American food, and must dress as the Americans, polish their finger nails, clean their teeth, etc. and above all they must not wrap their baby in swaddling clothes. As to their inability to speak English, it does not matter. As long as the foreigners talk softly and without the foreign gestures of hands and legs, they are americanized!

For others, Americanism is a matter of intellectual education. When one has acquired a fair knowledge of the English language and American history, has read the Constitution of the United States and is naturalized he is americanized in the strict sense of the world! Miss Frances A. Kellor, in her timely and incomparable little book "Straight America", says: "Every immigrant should be required to become literate in the English language within five years after arrival, provided facilites are offered to him. Deportation should be the penalty for failure to do this." She further says: "Every alien over school age and under 45 will be required to learn English," etc. This, at first, seems to be the only course to take to safeguard the Americanism of tomorrow, but evidently Miss Kellor does not take into consideration the difficulties which the majority of these "Aliens" meet in learning a new language. Only those who go through this experience can really appreciate the situation.

First of all, the greater number of the immigrants have

had very little education in their native country and they speak its language very incorrectly. If they have passed the thirties and have a family to support, it 's almost hopeless to expect them to learn English in a satisfactory way. These things have come under our personal observation during the past 18 years in which we have endeavored to teach English to the Italians with whom we have come in contact in connection with our work.

This, however, cannot be said of the younger and unmarried element. These have acquired more education and have not the burden of family laying heavily upon them. This younger element of immigrants can master the English language within a comparatively short time, will get acquainted with the history and Constitution of America, and if it is "convenient", will be naturalized. These younger men and women will also live "A l'Americana"; but do all these things constitute real Americanism?

Long before Christ came into the world, the Hellenic language had become so universal as to induce the thinkers of the Hebrew world to translate the Old Testament (The Septuagint) into that language for the benefit of the younger Jews who had forgotten the language of their fathers. Did the Greek language Hellenize the Hebrews? It is not the language which keeps the Aliens unamericanized but their spirit. It is their spirit that must change. By this we do not minimize and underestimate the value and importance of teaching them English, but this alone cannot do the work of Americanization.

There is still another class of people in America who believe that if we do not succeed in americanizing the old folks, we will surely succeed in assimilating their children through our public schools. We have every reason to be proud and thankful for the public school system we have in America, but experience and facts show us the fallacy of this hope.

The children will undoubtedly learn English and forget the language of their parents. For them English is their "mother tongue" and America their native Country. But will this make them Americans? In their industrial, commercial, social and professional life they will speak the English language, but unless something is done to americanize their soul, their knowledge of English would simply be a weapon in their hands to destroy every noble ideal for which americanism stands. These "Americans", born and educated in America, seem to give up all the good

traits which their parents imported from their country
and retain the bad ones, and on top of these they absorb
the worst customs of the American life. The combination
of these two evils is not an easy matter with which to
deal. In our estimation this element may know the English
language and may be willing to fight and die for America,
but measuring them by their ideals and aspirations and
the tenor of their moral life, they are far more unamericanized than their parents, in spite of the fact that these may
not be able to speak English. The life of the parents of
these "Americanized" youths is embittered every day by
the experience they have with their children who seem to
lose all respect of God and humanity. They cannot account
for their failure in raising their young ones in America as
they may have raised older children on the other side of
the ocean. They lay the whole trouble at the feet of the
American life!

THE TERM "AMERICANIZATION"

The term "Americanizing the Aliens" is very unfortunate indeed! Instead of being captivating, it is decidedly
repulsive to many foreigners

The best method of approaching this subject is by way
of analogy. Suppose an American should go to Italy and
hear from all directions that to enjoy every privilege there
he must be Italianized! No matter what hardships he may
have endured in America, the term "Italianize" would be
repulsive to him. The same peculiar feeling is b ng experienced by the man who comes to America when he begins to hear that he is to be "americanized". When he first
hears this term he begins to reason this way: Must I renounce every idea of my nationality, abandon every sentiment of love toward the land of my fathers, and destroy
its glorious traditions in order that room may be made
for Americanism? Must I seek the elevation of America
and the Americans at the expense of Italy and the Italians? He may not believe in the form of government they
have in Italy; he may not have sympathy for the Royal
family; but the thought of forswearing allegiance to the
country of his birth, at first, is repulsive to him; it is
almost treason in his estimation! He says that an adopted
mother may be kind and unselfish, and may do all she can
for her adopted child, but this should not be any reason
to forswear his sonhood to his natural mother. Any one
who was not born in a fore gn country can never appreciate

this feeling. Jacob and Joseph enjoyed all the privileges which the Egyptian Royal family offered them, but when the sun of their earthly career began to set on the horizon, their desire was that their bones should be buried in the land of their fathers!

In the mind of a new comer the term "Amer canization" carries with it other implications which are distasteful to him. He says: What do the Americans mean when they say that they want to Americanize us? Do they intend to say that we are socially, civilly, intellectually and morally inferior to them? Do they not know that Italy has been the mistress of the world in every line of human knowledge and civilization? This is the way we reasoned when we first came to America. The same may be said of all other nationalities which come to America. They may have suffered troubles and hardships in their native land, but after a while they would forget them!

A few weeks ago an American girl of Italian parentage asked us if it was proper for a girl, from the Italian standpoint, to let a young man pay her carfare, and added: "Of course I do not know how far the young man I have in m nd is Americanized... If I were sure that he was thoroughly Americanized I would not mind his paying my carfare." Of course we knew the spirit with which this girl uttered those words, but in sp te of our 26 years of American life and our profound interest in spreading Americanism, we cannot but confess that we felt a resentment within us, because the tone of voice in which the girl sa d those words would give anyone to understand that the American traits and customs are better and above those of all the nations of the earth. This sentiment is unfair to our friends of other countries. We must avoid these things because there is nothing more repulsive to human beings than to tell them that they are inferior to a certain class or people!

While it is too late now to change the term "Americanization", as it is in vogue among all classes in our days, yet if it could be substituted by the word "nationalization" or "assimilation", or some other analogous word, it would be a far more acceptable term to the foreigner than "Americanization". However, the feeling which has been described here does not last long. It disappears gradually in proportion that the new comer understands the spirit in back of it.

OBSTACLES AND REMEDIES
FOR AMERICANIZATION

Foreign Language Press

While there are always exceptions to the rule, the foreign language press in America tends to retard the work of Americanization by encouraging the Aliens to stand fast to the traditions of their fathers and the country of their birth. In almost all cases the Editors have received their education in the country from which they came. They are absolutely untouched by the American life and spirit. When they speak of America they seldom call it our adopted country but invariably "This Hospitable Land". These foreign newspapers always exalt their country's past history and feed their readers with its past glories and achievements. Before America entered the war these newspapers very seldom pointed out the good qualities of America and its people, but rather ridiculed many of their traits and customs.

There are certain Italian papers containing quack doctors and immoral advertisements which would cause even satan to blush! Such advertisements are so vile and low as to render the papers unfit to be put in the hands of any decent man or woman. Many men, both young and old, become victims of vice and sin because of such advertisements which promise to cure within a few dayse any disease, no matter how serious it may be! When men and women with a high moral sense see these advertisements, they shake their heads and, in a lamentable tone of voice, say: "This is America; anything can be done here!"

Oftentimes the owners of these papers are almost illiterate. To edit their publication they are compelled to engage men who are able to write. It pays them to engage "Professors" recently emigrated from the old world, because they will work for a meagre salary as they are unable or unwilling to do any manual work by which they could earn more money! What Americanism can the writings of these raw pens inspire?

The owners of these papers are generally considered the Kings of the Italian Colonies by both Italians and Americans. The American politician elevates them to the sky because they need them at election times. These and other Italian "Prominents" can obtain any favor from the officials of the city. Often even people arrested for crimes are released through the "Pull" of these men! What conception can the foreigners form in their minds of American law and order?

A leading Italian newspaper in America which is published in New York, some time ago had a Department in its columns under the title **Americanate** which cannot be properly rendered in English. The nearest translation of this word is: **Things of America,** but it conveys a scornful and derisive meaning. In this department people and things were derided, criticized and caricatured.

This paper has a question box through which its readers ask information on various questions. In most cases the answers are considered as oracles of God! Two years ago a man asked information concerning the difference between the Catholic version of the Bible and the Protestant. Here is the literal translation of the answer given: **"The Catholic text of the Old and New Testament is one throughout the whole world. For the Protestants it varies according to the denomination to which they belong, transforming it for one's own consumption. Hence it is untrue."** Invain Protestant Clergymen and laymen wrote to the Editor of the paper to rectify such an unpardonable and misleading statement. No rectification was ever published!

A Catholic Italian paper, writing on the "Italian Protestants", said: **"If you should ask the reason for their becoming Protestants, you would hear of two: A licentious way of living; second, their financial interest. Everybody knows the morals of Protestants, particularly of Italian Protestants. For them there is an eleventh Commandment which says: Do anything, but try to escape judgement. For them the Lutheran formula 'Crede firmetur, pecca fortifer (sic) is not a dead letter!"**

Since America entered the war the secular Italian Press has changed its attitude toward America. How long will this attitude last after the war, no one is able to predict.

But some one might say that since the foreign language Press retards the course of Americanization, the best thing for America would be to suppress it entirely! By doing this the cure would be worse than the disease. Let the foreign language newspapers continue their publication for the education of the masses which cannot read English. They could render a great service to America if they would publish the right things. However the Government ought to inform all the editors of the foreign language newspapers that if they publish anything detrimental to America and its Institutions, and retard the work of Americanization of their countryman their papers will be suppressed at once. It is not for us to enter into details of how this campaign ought to be carried on.

The American Press

The American Press has not done its full share toward the Americanization of the foreigner, but unintentionally and unconsciously has rather alienated them. If an Italian has been naturalized he has ceased to be an Italian; but if this same man should commit a crime, the American Press would invariably have a big head-line, reporting that an Italian has committed that crime! But if he has forsworn allegiance to Italy and has become an American citizen, why do they insist on calilng him Italian? Is this not a contradiction in terms? Do we not often read in the American newspapers: "The Italian Republican Club", — "The Italian Democratic Head-quarters" — "The Italian vote" etc. — Can there be any such things in Amer ca?

Since the war broke out, many American newspapers in different American metropolis saw great business possibilit es in publishing the war news in foreign languages. In Philadelphia. Pa., there are two evening papers and both publish war-news in Italian. Two years ago the editor of one of these papers told us that at that time they were selling 10.000 copies a day to the Ital ans in Philadelphia and vicinity, and he expressed his conviction that within a short time they would dispose of 25.000 cop es a day among them. If the American newspapers, beside seeing the business opportunity, had discovered the possibility of helping Amer canization among the foreigners, what attainments could have been achieved!

If this work has not been done in the past it must be done from now on for the various foreign elements we have in America. Each daily paper ought to undertake to work among a specif c nationality, so that the various newspapers could cover the whole ground in reaching all the nationalities in the city and other communities. If necessary, the Government ought to be willing to back up th s work by appropriating some money for the prosecution of the same. This work, if properly done, would be one of the most potent factors in the Americanization of the Aliens. By th s means even English lessons could be given, and gradually the foreigners would have Amer can ideas and would use the English language. The big American newspapers could very easily dispose of two pages for this work. The foreigners would much rather have a big American paper in their hands than a tiny one, such as a foreign language paper generally is. Gradually the American newspapers would supplant the foreign language dailies and weeklies entirely.

The most difficult problem would be in the selection of the various writers morally, intellectually and spiritually qualified for the task. No "political pull" should be allowed for the employment of these editors. Only men of high repute, morally and spiritually americanized should be employed.

"Little Italys", "Ghettos", Etc.

When a foreigner lands in America he generally goes where his people are. Everything he sees is not entirely new to him. He sees his old friends who have preceded him to America, and whom he considers "Americanized" simply because they dress a little differently than he does and speak words in English which he does not comprehend. He looks up to them and learns from them "all tricks" of how to "get on" in America. This is all he sees of America! Socially, civilly, ethically and spiritually he finds himself almost in the same atmosphere in which he lived in his native village.

If a family of another nationality has remained in the neighborhood, it is considered by all to be an American family. Whether American or of any other nationality, this family is not the one by which these Aliens may be best inspired, directed and Americanized, for they are not the best specimen of Americans. Very often these "Americans" are people of a certain nationality who think that they own America and the rest of the world. These are the people who generally call the Italians "dirty dagos" and the Jews "rotten sheenys" and other nationalities by other names. The language they use, the life they live, the deportment of their children and the whole tenor of their home, are anything but inspiring! The Aliens would invariably say: If these are the Americans, let us endeavor to have nothing to do with them. Not seldom Alien parents would consider it a great misfortune befalling their boys if they should marry American girls!

We often hear people speak contemptuously of the "Little Italys", "Ghettos", etc., but who has created these various places? The Americans themselves by moving away as soon as a foreigner has moved in the neighborhood. In certain localities these American separatists have bought tracts of land to build American homes. The Deeds have been drawn in such a way that no foreigner can ever buy a home in that particular locality, even if he is naturalized. Is this an endeavor to assimilate and americanize the Aliens? If America wishes to americanize the foreigners, let the better element of the American families remain where they are, and let them welcome the Aliens among them. This, however, should always be accompanied by a constant and immediate contact with them, both in and out the house, and by showing them a friendly attitude in their joys and sorrows. This is the surest road toward assimilation.

Festivals and Celebrations

Though the Italians are less devoted to the Roman Church than any other nationality, they are bound to implant and perpetuate their beathen celebration wherever they colonize by themselves. It is to the interest of the priests and saloon keepers to keep the Italians in this pitiable low state. They are told that they should never depart from the traditions and religious practices of their fathers. Very often the officials of the city, for political reasons, permit these people to have brass bands and processions in the streets on Sundays, thus disregarding the Sabbath laws for the sake of the vote. How can such officials expect the foreigner to respect and obey the American laws when they themselves who ought to be the custodians of them are the breakers of the same? Anything which tends to perpetuate certain things which alienate the foreigner from being americanized ought to be eliminated. Let no one say that this would mean interference with religious matters. This is not religion but simply perpetuation of mediaeval superstitions.

The American Employer

It is a well established fact that some of the American employers, both with or without the hyphen, study day and night to see what they can get out of the Alien while he is under their claws. These employers' sole ambition is to get-rich-quick, no matter what means they employ to reach that end. It is not the Alien employee who has established two standards of living, but the employer, no matter what branch of industrial or commercial line in which he may be engaged. Often we hear Americans say that the home of the foreigner is not an American home.

But whose fault is it? Have we not heard Americans say that certain wages or salary "ought to be enough for an Italian family, because an Italian can live cheaper than an American?" Does this double standard of living draw the Italians nearer to the Americans, or does it separate them farther and farther apart? Once an Italian Protestant Missionary was asked by a wealthy business man how much salary he was getting. When he was told the amount, he said: "This sum would not be enough to buy candies for my children!" Unless the American employer does not change his attitude toward h s foreign employee by showing him with words and deeds that there should be one standard of living in America and enable him to live accordingly, the foreigner will always look upon him as a selfish exploiter, opportunist and oppressor, and will study how to overthrow him from the place he occupies.

Let the American employer be less selfish and more altruistic toward his foreign employee. If he wishes to Americanize him, he must elevate him to the same social level on which Americans live.

Avoiding Causes For Frictions

The Allies and the world at large acknowledge the strength of America and the important part she is playing in this world struggle. Without the aid of America probably the Allies would have been defeated. However, let the Americans beware of uttering statements which would underestimate the sacrifices the Allies have made and are making in this war. It would be unfair and decidedly unkind on our part and would hurt the feeling of our Allies and those who sympathize with them.

After the second victory of the Marne, a group of men of various nationalities were talking about the victory. An American who was present, said: "They needed the Americans to force the Germans back... The Yankees will lick the Huns... Uncle Sam will cut the Kaiser's head.' While this American was talking this way, nobody said a word in disapproval of his boasting; but when he went away, some one remarked: "This is a real American bluff! The way in wh'ch th's man spoke would make any one understand that the Allies are good for nothing as they are incapable of defeating the Huns; but the Americans are all and in all in winning this war! Could the Americans alone, without the Allies, win the war?" Others in that group passed similar remarks and deplored this unwarranted boastfulness.

Whatever part we shall have in winning this war, let us beware of minimizing or underestimating the sacrifices that the Allies have made and will make in this struggle. This, beside being unamerican, would be unfair to the living and an insult to the dead of the Allies. And above all it would redound to the alienation of the foreigners from the American spirit.

Whether the war will stop soon or not, America will never be called upon to make the ascrifices that the Allies have made in this war. Therefore let the American press, public speakers, and every individual refrain from making remarks such as that American man made before those foreigners, because it would hurt and retard the cause of Americanization.

Accelerated Naturalization

There are two contradicting tendencies in America in regard to the time which ought to be given to the foreigner for becoming naturalized. One party says that a period of five years, such as we have now, is too long, while the other says that it is too short. According to our point of view it is not a matter of time as it is a question of fitness. A man may live for 25 years in America, learn English, live "A l'Americana" and yet be unfit for naturalization. On the other hand, a man may come from an English speaking country, or any other country, and stay in America 25 days, but intellectually, morally and spiritually he is well quaified to become an American citizen at once. Why should this man be put on the same level with the man who would be eternally unfit for naturalization? Many people in America think that as soon as a man is naturalized he has become an American. But has he really become an American? Another analogy here would not go amiss.

In the Old Book we read that according to St. Paul there were two kinds of Circuncisions: one according to the flesh; the other according to the spirit. Paul cared very little about the Circumcision of the flesh, but advocated incessantly that of the spirit. Likewise there are two kinds of Americanization: one according to the flesh; the other, according to the spirit. Those who become americanized only in citizenship and politics, belong to the former category; while those who become americanized in their soul belong to the latter. Alienism is not an old suit from which the foreigner must be divested; neither is Americanism a mantle with which he can be invested. Americanism is a life which must be born in the soul of the individual and must develope gradually in proportion as he grows into it. If a foreigner has not reached the stage in which he considers it a privilege rather than an advantage to become a citizen of our beloved country, he would much better remain forever an alien, than to clothe him with a mantle which he neither deserves nor is qualified to wear. His naturalization papers would simply be a weapon in his hands to lower and destroy all American ideals and aspirations.

When the Christian Church in its infancy began to receive into its bosom unregenerated heathen with the expectation that they might become fully Christianized afterward, she made the greatest mistake of her life. By a gradual and unconscious process, the Church, to satisfy the taste of the heathen, began to adapt herself to the tenor of their life, creeds and practices. But what was the result? In course of time the Church, instead of transforming the heathen into Christians, experienced the reverse of it. The influence of the heathen was so strong that they heathenized the Church! Why did Christianity need Reformation? Was not the Reformation of the 16th Century a sure evidence that the Church had been dragged from its primitive purity into a state of chaos and shame? If the founders of the Christian Church had come back to life, they would never have recognized the Church they had left in the world!

Now America has experienced the same thing. By admitting into its citizenship unamericanized citizens, men with low ideals, having the sole purpose of acquiring political power to get-rich-quick, she has been dragged into a state of reproach. Many laws and customs have been changed by the influence of unscrupulous politicians. Any law which did not satisfy the taste of those who put them in power was called "obsolete". So monstrous, persistent and virulent has been their work, that they have not rested until such laws have been repealed. The America of today is not the America of its founders. If the fathers of this Country could return to earth, how would they find the Country they established and which they sealed with their blood? Would they be proud of their successors, or would they call them unworthy of their heritage?

WHAT BEARING WILL THIS WAR HAVE ON AMERICANIZATION?

There are four outstanding features in this war which will be beneficiary to the cause of americanization, if properly understood and carried on.

In the first place we have already seen an awakening consciousness on the part of the Americans in regard to responsibility they have toward their foreign neighbors living within their gates. We have seen that they are realizing how neglectful they have been in the past in not rendering them any service which might have led them to understand America and accept its fundamental principles. They are seeing the mistake made in creating the various colonies of foreigners in our cities and towns thus leaving them at the mercy of unscrupulous exploiters, bosses and opportunists, both native and of their own nationality. This awakening has led the Federal authorities, as we have pointed out, to start a nation wide campaign on Americanization. The same can be said of the authorities of the different states and also of some cities and various social, educational and religious organizations. Hundreds of American women have already begun a new kind of work in going from house to house to teach English and show their interest and sympathy to foreign women.

In the second place the foreigners in America, seeing the altruistic motives for which this country entered the war, and the interest the Americans are taking in their welfare, will have a more receptive attitude toward the American way of thinking. There is nothing in the world more potent than the power of human interest and love. It was His invincible love toward humanity which enabled Jesus to conquer the most obdurate heart in the world. The foreigners will appreciate the kindness of the Americans, and when they convince themselves that no sinister motive is in back of it, they will gradually be brought into an atmosphere where the spirit of true Americanism can have free course.

In the third place the expedition of our American boys to Europe will have a tremendous bearing on the work which has to be done here on their return. First of all they will learn by bitter experience what it is to be away from home and be a stranger in a strange land, without understanding the language spoken therein, such as some of their foreign comrades and their parents experienced when they came to America. This experience will render them more sympathetic toward their immigrant neighbors. Those with keen insight will see the needs of the young men with whom they come in contact and will undoubtedly endeavor to help them out when peace and order shall be reestablished.

But this opportunity on the part of our American soldiers is not without danger and apprehension. We are afraid that at the end of the war a great number of these American boys may come back to us with an erroneous view of what constitutes true Americanism. They have seen their alien comrades at their side, fighting with courage, strength, enthusiasm and heroism for the American flag, and some of them have even won admiration and honor from their commanders. Taking all these things into consideration they will undoubtedly say: If these boys were willing to fight and die for the flag of this country, who can doubt of their sincere patriotism? Are they not more deeply American than many yankee slackers who have succeeded in finding some way or means to evade the draft? When they are so loyal to the American flag, could anyone be more patriotic? If they fail to distinguish between military heroism and American idealism, their comradership with their alien friends will produce more harm than good.

In the fourth place the mingling of our Alien boys with the American soldiers will be one of the greatest factors in the process of assimilation.

By their constant contact with the Americans they will get acquainted with their mode of living and with their traits and customs. Here, as never before, they will be compelled to use the English language in their daily conversation. Even their palatal taste will be trained to enjoy the American food.

But without minimizing the importance of this fourth point in the process of Americanization, let us not magnify its intrinsic value. These Alien boys will be more americanized in their social life, which has great value in its place, but will this constitute real Americanism? If Americanism is an ideal, is a life to live, it must be begotten in the inside and not in the outside of man. If the work of the outer Amercanization has been done, that of the inner part must be done on their return to the country for which they fought and bled and shall live to render it ever more amiable, loveable and habitable for those who shall enjoy its privileges and share in its obligations.

THE BASE OF TRUE AMERICANISM

Though this new continent was discovered by three Italians -- Columbus, Cabot and Verrazzanno —, named after another Italian — Amerigo Vespucci — and taken possession of by the true European Powers under whose flags these Italians had crossed the ocean successively, not one of these nations was destined to remain in possession of the new world. God in His infinite wisdom had planned that a band of despised and persecuted people of one of these nations, who lived and died for their ideals, should be the germ of a new generation and possessors of this promising continent. When the Pilgrim fathers established themselves here, their aims, endeavors and purposes were centered toward one direction: To found this Country on the immovable principles of Christianity, according to the teachings of theScriptures. It was this fact which has made America the greatest, strongest, wealthiest and most distinguished nation of the world. Many more beautiful things will be said about America at the close of this war when she will undoubtedly be called the defender of the week, the liberator of the oppressed, the emancipator of the slave and the saviour of civilization.

The primitive American ideals then were based upon Christian principles and later on found expression in the Declaration of Independence. It was the power of these Christian principles which molded the life of the fathers of this Country and directed them to shape its destiny.

The Gospel of Christ has not lost its power. It is the only means by which the life of the Aliens may be molded after the manner of those who are the real and worthy successors of the founders of this country. All other means of which we have spoken are necessary for the work of Americanization, and must be used; but they must be subordinated to this **main** one. If we fail in this one, all others will become "sounding brass or clanging cymball", If we make the tree good, the fruit will be good, but a corrupt tree cannot bear good fruit. The founders of other republics in the American continent, lacking the fundamental principles of Christianity, such as our fathers had, failed to establish their respective countries on solid foundations. They directed them toward other destinies which are not to be compared with the destiny of our Country.

As our army is composed of men of various classes, races and creeds, there will be a tendency in America to relax the work of Evangelization. Books have already been written in which the authors express their hope that as in this war we have no class distinction, no race prejudice and no difference in religion, so it ought to be in time of peace, when men should live in the same attitude of spirit one toward the other, not interfering with others' private ways of thinking, believing and living! But if this should be the attitude of America, why, then, should we endeavor to do a work of Americanization? At first this spirit of liberalism and broad-mindedness seems to be in keeping with the present American frame of mind; but will it be beneficial or harmful to America and especially to the America of tomorrow?

Either in time of war or peace men of all standards of morality have a military courage. But do all have a moral and spiritual courage? Peter showed great military courage when, at Gethsemane, he wanted to defend his master with the sword. At this moment he would have been "ready to go with him, both into prison, and to death"; but when the real test came, when he should have had moral and spiritual courage to confess that he was His desciple, then courage failed him!

It took us but a very few months to organize, train and equip in military science a powerful army which will be the main factor for our final victory; but could we organize the same number of men, train and equip them so efficiently for Christian service? If our powerful army returning to America would fight sin and unrighteousness with the same spirit, force, enthusiasm and determination with which it is fighting autocracy, then we would have no need of doing a work of evangelization among the people in America. But since this cannot be expected from a military army, it must be done by an army of Christian men and women whose belief is that there is no Americanization without Evangelization. This is the Universal concensus of opinion of all the Missionaries who are doing evangelization work among the various foreign nationalities in America, from whom we have gathered several testimonials on this important question. When these "Alien" heroes of the Cross of Christ and the cause of America say that there is no Americanization without Evangelization, they are often accused of being narrow-minded, bigotted and sectarian, adding that nothing else can be expected from "professional ministers and missionaries". These accusers little realize the sacrificers which such men are making for the passion they have in their heart to serve God, save their kinsmen according to the flesh and uphold American ideals and aspirations. Of all the means which are being used for the work of Americanization that of Evangelization is the cheapest for its prosecution, the quickest for its results and the most fruitful for its achievements. The native American soul needed a war to wake it up so it would see the necessity of americanizing the masses of Aliens in America since it failed to realize that the Missionaries of the Gospel have been doing this work incessantly. It is the missionary who, being socially, ethically and spiritually americanized, is doing the most effective and lasting work of American education among his people. It is he who defends American ideals and aspirations, and who presents to his people the best side of America. He may not be a native born American, but he is a true custodian of an undeluted Americanism.

Not long ago a certain sectarian institution of New Haven, Conn., for two consecutive times asked the State for an appropriation of $20.000 to be paid annually for the support of the same. Invain three Italian Protestant Clergymen appealed to the Ministerial Association of New Haven and vicinity to go to Hartford and oppose the passing of the bill. When they could induce none of the native born pastors to go, these three hyphenated missionaries went to the Capitol and fearlessly opposed the bill before the Board of appropriations, and succeeded both times in killing it. They had a stiff struggle to fight as the friends of that sectarian institution had gathered all the big guns of the State to favor the passing of the bill, but their efforts were invain! The three hyphenated missionaries defeated them all, thus upholding one of the greatest American principles — the Separation of Church and State. If missionary efforts among our foreigners could be multiplied one hundred fold, there would be no room for despair in the Americanization of the Aliens. The Honorablie Bird S. Coler once said: "Make a man a good citizen and you have brought him half way to the Church." But we say: Make a man a good Christian and he can be nothing else but a good citizen.

FUNDAMENTAL PRINCIPLES
OF AMERICANIZATION

To live and uphold the ideals and traditions upon which America was founded.

Scrupulous obedience to the laws of State and Nation.

Complete separation of Church and State.

Liberty of conscience, press and speech.

Compulsory education for all.

Abolition of racial prejudices and Class distinction, and elimination of segregation of immigrants.

The use of a common language for all.

Elimination of all causes which create a double standard of living.

A single standard of morals.

Protection of women and children.

Elevation of the social and ethical prestige of all.

Propagation of the doctrine that every privilege enjoyed in America carries with it its obligations.

MEANS FOR SPREADING AMERICANISM

Intensive and expansive work of Evangelization.
Efficient Evening School system to teach English, civics and American citizenship.

Presentation of popular Dramas (which are to be produced) bearing on American ideals and aspirations.

Moving and Stereopticon pictures on any educational line pertaining to this subject.

Public lectures in churches, public school buildings, theaters, etc. on American history and the makers of this country.

Appliance of all the means which have been suggested in the course of this Report.

Respectfully submitted

A. DI DOMENICA, Chairman

V. CORDO'

F. RUGGIERO

The Italian American Experience

An Arno Press Collection

Angelo, Valenti. **Golden Gate.** 1939

Assimilation of the Italian Immigrant. 1975

Bohme, Frederick G. **A History of the Italians in New Mexico.** (Doctoral Dissertation, The University of New Mexico, 1958). 1975

Boissevain, Jeremy. **The Italians of Montreal:** Social Adjustment in a Plural Society. 1971

Churchill, Charles W. **The Italians of Newark:** A Community Study. (Doctoral Thesis, New York University, 1942). 1975

Clark, Francis E. **Our Italian Fellow Citizens in Their Old Homes and Their New.** 1919

D'Agostino, Guido. **Olives on the Apple Tree.** 1940

D'Angelo, Pascal. **Son of Italy.** 1924

Fenton, Edwin. **Immigrants and Unions,** A Case Study: Italians and American Labor, 1870-1920. (Doctoral Thesis, Harvard University, 1957). 1975

Forgione, Louis. **The River Between.** 1928

Fucilla, Joseph G. **The Teaching of Italian in the United States:** A Documentary History. 1967

Garlick, Richard C., Jr. et al. **Italy and Italians in Washington's Time.** 1933

Giovannitti, Arturo. **The Collected Poems of Arturo Giovannitti.** 1962

Istituto di Studi Americani, Università degli Studi di Firenze (Institute of American Studies, University of Florence). **Gli Italiani negli Stati Uniti** (Italians in the United States). 1972

Italians in the City: Health and Related Social Needs. 1975

Italians in the United States: A Repository of Rare Tracts and Miscellanea. 1975

Lapolla, Garibaldi M. **The Fire in the Flesh.** 1931

Lapolla, Garibaldi M. **The Grand Gennaro.** 1935

Mariano, John Horace. **The Italian Contribution to American Democracy.** 1922

Mariano, John H[orace]. **The Italian Immigrant and Our Courts.** 1925

Pagano, Jo. **Golden Wedding.** 1943

Parenti, Michael John. **Ethnic and Political Attitudes:** A Depth Study of Italian Americans. (Doctoral Dissertation, Yale University, 1962). 1975

Protestant Evangelism Among Italians in America. 1975

Radin, Paul. **The Italians of San Francisco:** Their Adjustment and Acculturation. Parts I and II. 1935

Rose, Philip M. **The Italians in America.** 1922

Ruddy, Anna C. (Christian McLeod, pseud.). **The Heart .of the Stranger:** A Story of Little Italy. 1908

Schiavo, Giovanni Ermenegildo. **Italian-American History:** Volume I. 1947

Schiavo, Giovanni [Ermenegildo]. **Italian-American History:** The Italian Contribution to the Catholic Church in America. Volume II. 1949

Schiavo, Giovanni [Ermenegildo]. **The Italians in America Before the Civil War.** 1934

Schiavo, Giovanni E[rmenegildo]. **The Italians in Chicago:** A Study in Americanization. 1928

Schiavo, Giovanni [Ermenegildo]. **The Italians in Missouri.** 1929

Schiro, George. **Americans by Choice:** History of the Italians in Utica. 1940

La Società Italiana di Fronte Alle Prime Migrazioni di Massa. (Italian Society at the Beginnings of the Mass Migrations). New Foreword (in English) by Francesco Cordasco. 1968

Speranza, Gino. **Race or Nation:** A Conflict of Divided Loyalties. 1925

Stella, Antonio. **Some Aspects of Italian Immigration to the United States:** Statistical Data and General Considerations Based Chiefly Upon the United States Censuses and Other Official Publications. 1924

Ulin, Richard Otis. **The Italo-American Student in the American Public School:** A Description and Analysis of Differential Behavior. (Doctoral Thesis, Harvard University, 1958). 1975

Valletta, Clement Lawrence. **A Study of Americanization in Carneta:** Italian-American Identity Through Three Generations. (Doctoral Dissertation, University of Pennsylvania, 1968). 1975

Villari, Luigi. **Gli Stati Uniti d'America e l'Emigrazione Italiana.** (The United States and Italian Immigration). 1912

Workers of the Writers' Program. Work Projects Administration in the State of Nebraska. **The Italians of Omaha.** 1941